Recapturing the Spirit

RECAPTURING THE SPIRIT

Essays on the Bill of Rights at 200

ERIC NEISSER

MADISON HOUSE

Madison 1991

LIBRARY OF CONGRESS CATALOGING-IN-PUBLICATION DATA

Neisser, Eric, 1947–
    Recapturing the spirit : essays on the Bill of Rights at 200 /
    Eric Neisser. — 1st ed.
      p. cm.
    Includes bibliographical references and index.
    ISBN 0-945612-22-2. — ISBN 0-945612-23-0 (pbk.)
    1. Civil rights—United States. 2. United States—Constitutional law—
  Amendments—1st-10th. I. Title.
KF4749.N43 1991
342.73′085—dc20
[347.30285]   91-3594
                                           CIP

Printed on acid-free paper by Edwards Brothers, Inc.
Designed by William Kasdorf
Typeset and produced for Madison House
by Impressions, Madison, Wisconsin

Published by Madison House Publishers, Inc.
P.O. Box 3100, Madison, Wisconsin 53704-0100

FIRST EDITION

To
the memory of my parents and brother
and to
Joan, Michelle, and Yvette
who have made my life so rich

Contents

Foreword *xi*

Preface *xv*

Acknowledgments *xvii*

I

CONSTITUTIONAL RIGHTS TODAY—AN OVERVIEW

1

On Coming to America, Ivan Is Reminded of Home *3*

Embodying the Spirit—Justice William Brennan *8*

Constitutional Rights Are for Everyone, Every Day *11*

When Will the Government Ever Learn? *14*

Can We Risk a Constitutional Convention? *19*

A Civil Liberties Lawyer on Jury Duty 25

A Civil Liberties Agenda for the 1990's 32

II

FREE EXPRESSION

39

Mother England's Not-So-Free Press *41*

Flagging the Burning Issues: Disrespect and Offense *46*

Writing Letters May Be Hazardous to Your Rights *50*

Charging for Free Speech 55

Talking Politics Door-to-Door *59*

It's Scandalous What Some Think Is Slanderous *62*

Racial Slurs: Free Speech or Discrimination? *65*

CONTENTS

How Can You Petition When the Doors Are Closed? 70

Students Learn from Free Expression and Due Process 75

III
PRIVACY
79

Legal Roadblocks to Traffic Roadblocks *81*

Going Too Far: Police Strip Searches *88*

Do We Expect Our Garbage to Be Inspected by Police? *91*

Should We Tolerate "Zero Tolerance?" *95*

Job Tests, Not Urine Tests *98*

What Ever Happened to Probable Cause? *104*

Constitutional Rights Should Apply at Work *110*

The Abortion Debate Is Unresolvable and Avoidable *114*

The Right to Die: New Laws Are Needed *118*

IV
CIVIL RIGHTS AND DISCRIMINATION
121

Fight AIDS, Not the People We Fear Have AIDS *123*

Men-Only Clubs: Illegal Discrimination
or Protected Association? *127*

Anti-Gay Prejudice Should Not Be Public Policy *131*

Civil Rights Law: If It Ain't Broke, Don't Fix It *135*

Being Sterile Is Not a Job Qualification *143*

We Still Need Affirmative Action *146*

V
POVERTY AND THE RIGHT TO A HOME
151

Homeless Orators: Begging as Free Speech *154*

Why Homelessness Is a Civil Liberties Concern *158*

Mount Laurel: Government Action for Affordable Homes *165*

CONTENTS

VI
THE CRIMINAL PROCESS
175

Preventive Detention: Which Country Is This Anyway? *178*
Racism at the Gallows *182*
Advocates' Zeal Is Threatened by Court Contempt Power *187*
Overloaded Public Defenders: The Right to Counsel at Risk *191*
Law v. Justice: A Twisted Case *195*

VII
FREEDOM OF RELIGION
207

Of Carols, Creches, and Menorahs *209*
Do Children Need a Moment of Silence in School? *214*
The Free Exercise of Religion: When and How Far? *219*

VIII
OF WAR, SCHOOLS, YOUTH, AND LOVE
225

Declaring War on Undeclared Wars *227*
It's Time to Invest in School Finance Equity *234*
Rethinking Juvenile Curfews: Whom Are We Protecting? *241*
Why Can't Love and Justice Coexist? *246*

Conclusion *251*
The Bill of Rights *253*
Notes *255*
Glossary *269*
Index *273*

Foreword

During my forty years in Congress, I was afforded the unique opportunity of working daily with the Constitution. It was a rare privilege which carried with it a profound obligation. The magnitude of that responsibility was made clear to me in those dramatic months when the House Judiciary Committee, which I was privileged to chair, was asked to consider whether to impeach the President of the United States. The impeachment inquiry—the question whether sufficient grounds existed to remove the President from office—was the most agonizing experience of my congressional career. There were other grave issues with constitutional implications—civil rights, voting rights, the death penalty, and freedom of speech. But the Constitution was a consideration even as we debated other important, but less earthshaking matters—for example, how to formulate an equitable food stamp program or how to reform our immigration policy (a subject of special interest to me as a son of an immigrant). At bottom, the question on each matter was how can we improve the lot of the people in a fair, equitable, efficient and just manner.

There are two parts of the Constitution that were particularly helpful and important to me in that inquiry. First was the Preamble, which reminds us both that the people created the Constitution to direct the government and that our long-term goals include establishing justice (significantly the first of the listed purposes of this country), promoting the general welfare, and securing the blessings of liberty for both our generation and posterity. To help me figure out how we could best establish justice and secure the blessings of liberty, I regularly turned, of course, to the Bill of Rights.

The Bill of Rights, whose bicentennial Professor Neisser appropriately celebrates in this book on its current applications, is a fascinating and remarkable mixture of specific commands and lofty aspirations. It tells us specifically that the district from which a criminal

xi

jury is called must be defined in advance by law and that a homeowner cannot be forced to give a soldier room and board. At the next level up it describes basic protections without specific detail, such as that freedom of speech cannot be abridged, private property cannot be taken for public use without just compensation, nor cruel and unusual punishments inflicted. The Fourth Amendment is a classic mixture of both. It starts with the resounding broad affirmation that "the right of the people to be secure in their persons, houses, papers, and effects, against unreasonable searches and seizures shall not be violated," and then specifies that warrants must be supported by "oath or affirmation" and must "particularly describ[e] the place to be searched, and the persons or things to be seized."

There is a third level as well, of even greater generality. The Fifth Amendment, echoed years later in the Fourteenth Amendment, assures us that, whatever the reach of the other provisions, we cannot be deprived of life, liberty and property without due process of law, without defining either liberty or due process. Even more significantly, the Ninth Amendment states that "the enumeration in the Constitution of certain rights shall not be construed to deny or disparage others retained by the people." The Founders wisely inserted that warning lest anyone, whether a congressman or a Supreme Court justice, think that the first eight amendments were merely a shopping list, which once literally satisfied could be ignored or discarded. Certainly the many married men among the Founders who frequently travelled among the colonies would have been surprised if the right to marry and the right to travel, though not specifically listed in the Bill of Rights, were not considered fundamental rights.

Professor Neisser's wide-ranging essays remind us that the task of protecting the people's rights, both specific and general, is neither an easy nor a one-time job. Each generation must learn for itself the meaning of everything from free exercise of religion to cruel and unusual punishment. Just as the Founders worried about redcoats arbitrarily selecting warehouses to search for customs violations, today we must consider whether supervisors may randomly pick employees to test for drug violations. The Framers pondered the acceptability of what they called seditious libel, but they left open the question of whether burning a flag is a call to sedition, a libel of government, or just angry free speech.

But the Preamble, the Due Process Clause and the Ninth Amendment mean that we must also look beyond the rights expressly articulated in the Bill of Rights. How can we say that we are promoting the general welfare, establishing justice, and securing the blessings of liberty for our generation and the next, if we allow millions of our citizens to go homeless or to get a lesser education because they happen to live in a poor residential area? Whether you ground the right to decent shelter and an adequate education in the equal protection guarantee, as Professor Neisser does in his probing discussions of these pressing current problems, or in the Ninth Amendment, as I have previously suggested, it is clear that you cannot dismiss the question simply because the Bill of Rights does not specifically enumerate shelter and education.

Professor Neisser not only does not dismiss these questions, he explores them carefully. He has worked in the trenches of civil liberties and has dealt with real people. He protests the injustices he sees and then challenges us both to ask the hard questions and to search for new and better answers. He vividly compels us to recapture the extraordinary spirit and vision of that unusual group that worked so hard in the hot Philadelphia summer of 1787 to give us a legacy that would work for all and last forever.

Peter W. Rodino, Jr.
Chair, House Judiciary Committee,
1973–1989

Preface

The principles of the Bill of Rights, which is now 200 years old, are immutable. But they must be rediscovered by each generation and applied to the realities of each age. The Framers of our Constitution thought hard about privacy, free expression, and fair play. But they did not know about metal detectors or wiretaps; indeed, there were no airports or telephones. Mechanical respirators and intravenous feeding tubes were unknown; hence, no one agonized about disconnecting them. School suspension procedures and school finance schemes were not public issues, because there were so few public schools. Even their classic censorship debates had to be reconsidered once we were faced with deciding who could broadcast over limited airwaves.

If we literally heeded those who advocate adherence to the Framers' original intent, we would not apply the Bill of Rights at all to wiretaps, respirators, and television, because the Framers obviously did not think about such problems. Such an approach, however, would render the Bill of Rights a dead letter—a quaint eighteenth-century monograph. But the Framers were not just drafting a campaign platform; they were writing for the indefinite future. We live in that future, so we must work with the document, and the principles, that they left us.

Technological advances are not the only challenge to the Bill of Rights. Periodically, public hysteria, triggered by fear of economic, political, or social dislocation, results in retreats from those principles. For example, the entertainment industry, prosecutors, the Congress and, unfortunately, even the Supreme Court of the 1940's and 1950's abandoned the First Amendment when Cold War fears of communism led to the blacklisting of many conscientious Americans. In the last two decades, in response to public fears of growing drug use and crime and calls for "law and order," the Court has scuttled many of the established protections of the Fourth Amendment against over-zealous police efforts. What the Court and much of the public appear to have forgotten is that part of the law and the basis for our order is the Constitution.

New technologies and fearful overreaction are not the only threats to constitutional fidelity. Sometimes civil liberties are lost through distaste for those asserting them, inattention, public or official ignorance, or even worse, political grandstanding. For all these reasons, we regularly need a refresher course to help us recapture the spirit that inspired the Bill of Rights.

The goal of these essays is not to resolve the many complex issues we confront. Indeed they can never be fully resolved, because new challenges regularly require the same battles to be re-fought on new fields. But I do hope to remind the reader of our constitutional roots, and frame the current issues for thought and discussion, which are the very goals of the First Amendment.

I have strong views on how to apply the principles of the Bill of Rights. They have led me to write, teach, speak out, and litigate about civil liberties issues, and to work first as a volunteer attorney and then from 1986 to 1989 as the Legal Director of the New Jersey affiliate of the American Civil Liberties Union. The ACLU is a very special American institution. A private, nonprofit, nonpartisan, national organization with 300,000 members and affiliates in every state, the ACLU is dedicated to the enforcement of constitutional rights for all, regardless of background or viewpoint, through litigation, legislation, and public education. Although many of my views are shared by the ACLU and other civil libertarians, I speak here for myself only.

One need not agree with all, or indeed with any, of my positions to get something from this book. I hope only that by raising the topics and presenting my views and some of the countervailing concerns, I can help people re-think the work of James Madison and his colleagues and determine its meaning for today. These rights are, after all, *everyone's* rights.

Acknowledgments

It is impossible to have been involved in the law for over twenty-three years and to have written a book of this length without owing debts—both intellectual and personal—to a great many people. I could not thank all of them here without imposing on the patience of both my publisher and my readers. Some have done too much, however, to go without specific acknowledgment.

Bruce Rosen and Bob Seidenstein, successive editors-in-chief of the *New Jersey Law Journal*, have strongly encouraged and supported me over the four and a half years that I have written a monthly column called "Civil Liberties Today" in the *Law Journal*, the weekly publication for lawyers in the state. Many of the essays presented here were first published in a different and shorter form in that column; it was there that I first thrashed out many of the ideas I set forth here. I thank all the *Law Journal* editors for their support and advice.

My outstanding colleague and good friend Louis Raveson read and commented upon all of the essays in this book. I hesitated to give him each ensuing chapter, knowing of the heavy workload that he already carried. But his analysis was so incisive, his suggestions so worthwhile, and his editing so helpful that I just kept on imposing. His contribution is enormous.

Many other colleagues and friends read and gave me valuable comments on one or more columns or essays: Ben Buglio, Carol Buglio, Deb Ellis, Toni Johnson, Ed Martone, Neil Mullin, John Payne, Janice Robinson, Peter Shavitz, Nancy Smith, Nadine Taub, George Thomas, and Paul Tractenberg. Andrea Brizzi, Gil Carrasco, Wendy Gordon, Jonathan Hart, John Kaminski, and Laura Kramer assisted me with other aspects of the book. Michelle Filippone, S. Felecia Haywood, and John Mills provided helpful research assistance. Gwen Ausby patiently and graciously typed all the final editing corrections. Michael Jones, my editor at Madison House, was extremely constructive and supportive, deftly fine-tuning the language without changing my message. I am indebted to all of them. I am also grateful to Rutgers Law School for providing me with a sabbatical leave in the spring of 1990 during which I began the work on this book.

Last but far from least, I benefited immeasurably from the personal and professional support of three very special women. My wife, Joan Neisser, graciously read and incisively commented upon each of my columns before they were published. My daughters, Michelle and Yvette Neisser, each edited half of the essays in this book. Their editing insights were remarkable. The warm encouragement offered by all three was a constant comfort during the arduous process of writing and editing. My gratitude is only partially expressed by my dedicating this book to them.

Newark   E.N.
March, 1991

I

CONSTITUTIONAL RIGHTS TODAY— AN OVERVIEW

On Coming to America, Ivan Is Reminded of Home

Recently liberated, during a spasm of glasnost, from the chilling effects* of ten years of hard labor in a Siberian work camp for excessive Ukrainian nationalism, Ivan Chupenko† comes to America, the promised land of freedom. When he gets off the plane at the airport in New York, the customs officers ask for his passport, go through all his belongings very carefully, and ask him to walk through an open doorway that beeps. One officer picks up a machine and moves it all over Ivan's body. But he doesn't mind, he's so happy just to be here.‡

His first trip is a visit to relatives in New Jersey. As Ivan crosses the big bridge over the river named for the explorer Henry Hudson, he notices that all the cars are stopping. A police officer approaches his car and asks Ivan for his driver's license, registration, and insurance card. The similarity to police in Kiev ends, however, when the officer asks him if he has recently been drinking. After Ivan cheerfully

---

*In First Amendment law, courts often refer to the "chilling effect," by which they mean the deterrent impact of broad, vague or intrusive laws on citizens' willingness to express their views openly.

†The character is fictional. Any resemblance to an actual person is accidental.

‡In U.S. v. Ramsey, 431 U.S. 606 (1977), the United States Supreme Court held that a search at the border of the belongings of an incoming traveler, even a citizen with an American passport, is constitutional even though the authorities do not have a search warrant, the traveler's consent, or any reason to suspect him or her of violating the customs laws. Courts have also upheld the use of metal detectors at airports when used to check passengers boarding planes. See, e.g., United States v. Slocum, 464 F.2d 1180 (3rd Cir. 1972).

admits to a few quick vodkas, the police officer asks him to step out of the car, touch his toes, walk up and down a painted line, say the alphabet backwards (in English!), and blow into a little balloon. Once the officer and his colleagues are convinced Ivan can hold his vodka, they let him go on his way.*

Soon Ivan realizes that he's lost and stops at a small luncheonette in a big city to call his cousins. He hears funny clicks on the telephone while scribbling down directions, but ignores them, thinking that little stores probably can't afford very good telephones.†

Finally Ivan arrives at his relatives' home. As he unloads his suitcase from the car, he is approached by a police officer who asks if he has a permit. Confused, Ivan stammers: "But I was checked and cleared at the airport and the bridge." The officer explains that no one can move into town without a permit. He says that the office is not open today, because it's Sunday, and anyway you can't move on Sundays even with a permit. Ivan assures the officer that he is only visiting his cousins and will get a permit if he decides to stay.‡

The next day Ivan decides to learn more about this strange land where you must blow into balloons to cross bridges and need a permit to visit relatives. He goes to the library. He asks for books about America's history, its bridges and airports, and how the police operate.

---

*After three years of litigation by the ACLU, an appellate court ruled that road-blocks set up at the George Washington Bridge in September 1986 were unconstitutional. Although they were allegedly designed to catch drunk or drugged drivers, the county prosecutor admitted that they were also trying to catch persons who had bought drugs in Washington Heights and were returning to New Jersey. The primary reason for striking down the roadblocks was that they needlessly interfered with the travel of some one million travelers in the metropolitan area. State v. Barcia, 235 N.J. Super. 311, 562 A.2d 246 (App. Div. 1989). (See "Legal Roadblocks to Traffic Roadblocks," page 81.)

†During a prosecution of twenty-two alleged mobsters in Newark, New Jersey, the federal government revealed that it had conducted electronic surveillance, with court approval, for a long time at a small luncheonette in Newark called the Hole in the Wall where several of the defendants regularly ate. United States v. Accetturo, 623 F. Supp. 746, 756 (D.N.J. 1985). After a twenty-one-month trial, from fall 1986 to summer 1988, the jury acquitted all defendants.

‡In response to an ACLU challenge, East Orange, New Jersey dropped charges against a woman cited for moving out of town without a permit. East Orange v. Palmer, No. 12458 (E. Orange Mun. Ct. 1988). The town also promised to repeal the ordinance that requires a permit for moving in or out of town and prohibits moving on Sundays. (See "When Will The Government Ever Learn?" page 14.)

The books are politely provided, but only after the librarian carefully writes down his name, address, country of origin, and the titles of all the books he borrows, and asks him why he's interested in these subjects. Thinking that she's a very efficient librarian, Ivan goes off to read his books, not noticing that the librarian quickly goes off to make a phone call.*

From his readings and discussions with relatives, Ivan learns that one place with lots of jobs is Atlantic City. On his way down the highway, he is pulled over by a police officer who says it is illegal to have a cross hanging from his rear-view mirror. Ivan is surprised that this land of religious freedom has such a rule and wonders how the officer could see his little Ukrainian cross as he was driving at ninety kilometers an hour. Nevertheless, Ivan politely produces all the usual papers and explains where he is going. When the police officer asks if he may look at the ashtray and under the passenger seat, Ivan agrees, although he can't figure out what the ashtray and the seat have to do with the cross hanging from the mirror. He also doesn't understand why the officer lets him go without giving him a ticket or taking down the cross if it's illegal to have the cross hanging there.†

---

*At congressional hearings in 1988, it was revealed that, under the FBI's Library Awareness program, librarians were asked to inform the FBI of the reading requests of persons with Eastern European names. "FBI Counterintelligence Visits to Libraries," Statement of James H. Geer, Assistant FBI Director, before the House Judiciary Subcommittee on Civil and Constitutional Rights, July 13, 1988.

†For several years in the late 1980's, the ACLU, the NAACP, and the public defender's office in New Jersey received many complaints about state troopers stopping cars based on technical violations, such as items hanging from rear view mirrors. Many people complained that they were asked irrelevant questions, such as where they were going and whether the officer could examine the ashtray, glove compartment, seat, or trunk, presumably for drugs. In many instances no ticket was issued for the conduct they were told prompted the stop.

The organizations complained that the state troopers were targeting minority drivers with out-of-state license plates as possible drug couriers. A statistical study commissioned by the public defender found that although only 7 percent of the drivers on one crucial central stretch of the New Jersey Turnpike were African American, 70 percent of those stopped by state troopers were African American.

The complaints dropped dramatically after May 1990 as a result of two major changes. First, the new state police superintendent issued strict guidelines prohibiting use of racial and geographic "profiles" and limiting car searches based on the driver's consent. Second, the state supreme court held that police observation of a "furtive gesture," such as throwing something on the backseat of the car while being stopped, is not sufficient basis under the Fourth Amendment for the police to search the interior of a car. State v. Lund, 119 N.J. 35, 573 A.2d 1376 (1990).

When Ivan gets to the casino, he is first asked to urinate in a bottle. Then he has to fill out a ten-page application that asks whether he has ever been arrested; to whom and for how long he's been married; to what unions and other organizations he belongs; and what diseases he's had since he was five. He finds it hard to understand why all this is needed to sweep the floors or clear the tables, but figures it must be the American way.*

After his first exciting weeks in America, Ivan gets a package from home. It seems odd that the brown paper wrapping is torn and sloppily taped together, because Mama is always so neat and careful. And the envelope inside with family pictures seems to have been ripped—again not like Mama. But not to worry, the letter says everyone is fine.

The next morning, a nice man in a gray suit comes to the door.

"Can I help you?" says Ivan in his best new English.

"Yes sir. I'm with the FBI and I want to talk with you about the packages you're getting from Russia."†

Ivan does not know what the FBI is and he's surprised that anyone but the mailman knows he got a package from home, which is in Ukraine, not Russia. He explains that his mother sent him brownies, a letter, her recipe for borscht, and some family pictures, and pro-

---

*In a case called In re Martin, 90 N.J. 295 (1982), the New Jersey Supreme Court approved Casino Control Commission questionnaires asking all casino applicants a wide variety of personal, familial, associational, medical, and criminal history questions.

Drug testing of employees and applicants to Fortune 500 companies is now common. Although there has been no reported litigation about drug testing of casino applicants, routine urine testing of all government job applicants has recently been held unconstitutional in a landmark lawsuit called O'Keefe v. Passaic Valley Water Commission, No. C-16230-88 (Chancery Div., Passaic Cty., NJ, Oct. 9, 1990), appeal pending.

†In Patterson v. FBI, 893 F.2d 595 (3rd Cir. 1990), the ACLU unsuccessfully challenged government surveillance and opening of the mail of a young boy who had written letters starting at age twelve to 169 countries around the world seeking information to develop his own encyclopedia. Many letters had arrived ripped and taped. The family learned of the government's interest when an FBI agent came to the house one day to inquire about the mail the boy had been receiving. The lawsuit sought access to, and then expungement of, the FBI's entire file on the boy, much of which had been classified as "secret" for national security reasons. The courts concluded that the FBI had acted properly, based on a secret FBI affidavit never shown to the Pattersons. (See "Writing Letters May Be Hazardous to Your Rights," page 50).

duces his passport, driver's license, car registration, insurance card, moving permit, green card, and casino ID card.

"Looks like everything's in order, but be sure to let me know if you get anything from the government or the Party," the man says.

As Ivan closes the door, he says: "Have a nice day," to show how American he is, but thinks to himself: "What a strange and friendly land. No one knows me, but everyone is interested in everything I do and wants to see everything I have. In some ways, it's just like home."

Embodying the Spirit— Justice William Brennan

Some have the title. Some hold the pursestrings. Others lead by force of personality, example, or plain hard work. William J. Brennan, Jr., though never the Chief Justice in title, essentially led the Supreme Court for most of his thirty-four years there. He lacked the personal flair of William Douglas or the academic credentials of Felix Frankfurter, but from 1956 to 1990, he cajoled, persuaded, and pricked consciences with his intellect, charm, careful crafting, and most significantly, steadfast devotion to constitutional principles and the common person. His presence will be missed by both the average citizen he protected from government and public interest groups pursuing causes. His absence will also leave a new generation of lawyers who yearn for social justice without a role model and champion.

The "Brennan Court" brought the Constitution home to everyone. Probably its most enduring legacy was the application of almost all of the protections of the Bill of Rights to state, county, and local governments. Back in 1833, the Supreme Court had said that the Bill of Rights limits only the federal government,[1] which was small and distant, and affected few people directly. Hard as it is to believe, not until 1925 was the First Amendment applied to all non-federal governments,[2] and not until 1961 was the Fourth Amendment so interpreted.[3] The most basic right—a jury trial—was not to be a federal constitutional requirement in state criminal cases until 1968![4] Justice Hugo Black had struggled valiantly to achieve application of the Bill of Rights to state and local governments since 1947, by his arguments that all of its provisions were "incorporated" into the "privileges and immunities" of national citizenship and/or the "liberty" that the Fourteenth Amendment protects against state and local governments.[5]

Success, however, came only in the 1960's, with the so-called "selective incorporation" doctrine and William Brennan's consensus-building skills. Selective incorporation required the Court to decide, one by one, which rights were so fundamental to our society and system of law that they must be considered part of the "liberty" of which citizens cannot be deprived by any government without "due process of law." By the end of the 1960's, all of the provisions of the Bill of Rights, except the right to jury trial in civil cases, the right to a grand jury indictment in criminal cases, and the protection against excessive bail, had been "selectively incorporated" and thereby applied to all non-federal governments. Even those who now urgently call for limiting the Bill of Rights to the "original intent" of those who wrote its provisions are not seeking to undo this recent but now basic tenet of constitutional law—that the same rules apply to City Hall as to Congress.*

The "Brennan Court" also gave life to abstract principles. Freedom of speech now insures the right to express the most reviled of views, including the burning of the flag that represents freedom itself. (See "Flagging the Burning Issues: Disrespect and Offense," page 46.) Freedom of the press was given practical meaning when Brennan clarified that newspapers could not be sued simply because they published articles or ads that inadvertently misstated some facts about public figures. (See "It's Scandalous What Some Think Is Slanderous," page 62.) Brennan dusted off the hoary English writ of habeas corpus and brought it roaring back as the guarantor of the criminal procedural rights that he had helped to make applicable to the states. (See "*Law v. Justice*: A Twisted Case," page 195.) Rural America's equivalents of the old English rotten boroughs—political districts that

---

*As a result of incorporation, this book is, to be precise, about the Fourteenth Amendment as well as the first ten amendments, which are known as the Bill of Rights. Also some rights, such as the rights to travel, to marry, to choose whether to complete a pregnancy, and to refuse medical treatment, have been found by the Supreme Court to be part of the liberty protected by the due process clause or unenumerated rights secured by the Ninth Amendment. (See "The Right to Die: New Laws Are Needed," page 118; "Rethinking Juvenile Curfews: Whom Are We Protecting," page 241; and "Why Can't Love and Justice Coexist?" page 246.) For simplicity's sake, I refer essentially interchangeably to constitutional rights, the Bill of Rights, and civil liberties. The term "civil rights" is used to refer only to protections, both constitutional and statutory, against discrimination. (See Chapter IV, page 121.)

had lost most of their people but none of their political power—were forced into the twentieth century by Brennan's assurance in the initial one-person, one-vote case that an urban citizen's vote would have the same weight as all others.[6] Minorities, progressive employers, and academics were reassured in their search for diversity and equality by Brennan's plurality opinion in *Bakke*, the first affirmative action case, and women were given non-patronizing equality as a result of his pioneering decisions on women's rights. (See "We Still Need Affirmative Action," page 146.) And surely, Brennan's view, although technically still a dissent, of the need to protect the personal dignity of victims of misfortune and medical technology, like Nancy Cruzan, will ultimately prevail. (See "The Right to Die: New Laws Are Needed," page 118.)

Many of us who chose the law profession in the 1960's did so because of Justice Brennan's assurance that the law, and in particular constitutional law, can be a positive force for social change. He did not fail us. In the face of a frequently apathetic public and unsympathetic legal establishment, he showed that devotion to principle is possible throughout a career. His life's work affirms that the Constitution was meant to endure and to shield the rights of servicewomen, accident victims, minority voters, pregnant teenagers, and schoolchildren alike.

Obviously he could not singlehandedly restrain the tides of reaction. Yet his persistence will be rewarded. Growing student activism, homelessness, disillusionment with politicians, and a deep recession signal another period of social upheaval and regeneration, like the 1930's and the 1960's. Society will again be called upon to redeem its constitutional promises—this time to AIDS victims, crack babies, the homeless, the structurally unemployed, the disabled, and the forgotten. The Brennan legacy will be there to guide the redemption. I hope future law students will read enough "old" cases to know that the path less travelled was gloriously followed by Bill Brennan, and that has made all the difference.

Constitutional Rights Are for Everyone, Every Day

New Supreme Court cases are important for all of us, as well as fun to crow or carp about. But it is vital that we not forget that the life of constitutional law is its day-to-day impact on ordinary people who are not in the spotlight of newspaper headlines or congressional hearings. In that spirit, I thought that it would be enlightening to chronicle briefly some of the hundreds of citizens' problems that one encounters and tries to remedy in the day-to-day work at the American Civil Liberties Union. I recite only facts confirmed by the government entity involved or by appropriate documentation.

• A citizen who passed the relevant civil service test is asked to take a urine drug test for appointment to the position of—water meter reader.

• A disk jockey is arrested in a bar, by an officer who had been listening while on duty in the parking lot, for dedicating to the local police chief a song called "I-95," in which the singer refers to a discourteous driver by a vulgar expression. The charge is "harassment" or, as more specifically stated in the criminal court complaint: "repeatedly committing acts with the purpose to alarm or annoy members of the police department."

• The mayor imposes a 30-day "emergency" curfew, forbidding all persons, adult as well as juvenile, who are not residents of a specified section of town—which happens to be a low-income housing project—from being there after 7:00 p.m. unless they have a specific prior invitation from a resident. A man is arrested while distributing to

11

residents of the area at 7:00 p.m. on a sunny June evening a flyer with a copy both of a newspaper article noting the ACLU's criticism of the curfew and of the First and Fourteenth Amendments.

• A well-known peace group, which has held peaceful protests in town in the past, is required to post a $1 million insurance policy for a march and rally memorializing persons recently killed in Central America because an earlier rally on the same subject by an *unrelated* group had produced an alleged "near riot." The town attorney admits that he did not know how many, if any, arrests had been made at the prior event, what damage, if any, had been caused, or whether any claims that would be covered by the required insurance had been filed because of the earlier event.

• After stopping a car coming off a bridge ramp for a possible motor vehicle infraction, a police officer orders the young driver out of the car and directs him to drop his pants for a strip search on a public street at 2:00 p.m. on a sunny Saturday afternoon. Nothing was found and the youth was released.

• A police officer who passed the physical and written civil service tests and background investigation is removed from the police academy four days after appointment because he was found to be—over 35!

• School bus drivers who are obligated by law to submit fingerprints for criminal record checks before being re-licensed are also required to waive any possible claims against the government in case the records are disclosed by the government, inadvertently or otherwise.

• A school dress code is adopted banning the wearing of "tattered clothing," presumably by rich and poor students alike.

• A student is suspended for wearing a T-shirt that says "To Hell with the Devil."

• A passing driver, who stops to help after observing an accident, takes pictures of a state trooper's car backing into a car parked on the side of the road. He is arrested for taking pictures on the highway without permission.

• Three gay men are denied an apartment because the landlord fears that his family, who will live in another apartment in the same building, will catch AIDS from them.

The purpose of this listing is not to tout the success rate of the ACLU, although, in fact, we were able to obtain relief in all but one of these cases. Rather, these incidents highlight four realities of the interplay of government and citizen. The first is the incredible diversity of circumstances in which the Constitution comes into play, most of which were not envisioned by the Framers, who did not have cars, AIDS, cameras, drug tests, or T-shirts. Second, it is important to remember that the government and the Bill of Rights affect ordinary citizens in all walks of life—bus drivers, tenants, school children, disk jockeys, drivers, and police recruits, as well as peace activists.

Third, I note with incredulity that governments are still doing such petty, rigid, and thoughtless things in the last dozen years of the twentieth century. Too often government policymakers fail to consider whether a rule against slogans on T-shirts, a ban on taking pictures on the highway, or a requirement that applicants give up claims against the government for disclosing application information makes sense in general. Likewise, too often the police or other bureaucrats fail to consider whether such measures should be applied in the particular circumstances they confront.

Finally, public officials, with frustrating frequency, fail to consider the constitutional implications of their policies and actions. Probably no court case ever decided that the precise phrase "To Hell with the Devil" is protected by the First Amendment when worn by an adolescent in a public school. Nevertheless, high school principals should have some appreciation of First Amendment principles and some obligation to consider not just what the parents or school board will think, but what the Framers would have expected. (See "Students Learn From Free Expression and Due Process," page 75.)

The Constitution is a blueprint for governing, not an inconvenience or obstacle to good government. From police chief to pollwatcher, job descriptions should include "apply the Bill of Rights with care at all times."

When Will the Government Ever Learn?

Not thinking about the Constitution is bad enough. But ignoring a directly applicable court decision goes beyond carelessness. In law school I was taught that if a court with binding authority in the jurisdiction had already decided an issue, the matter was closed, continuing to act in violation of the ruling was unlawful, and attempting to relitigate it was frivolous, unless one had a good-faith basis for seeking reconsideration. That concept was referred to by the Latin phrase "stare decisis," which translates roughly as "to stand by matters already decided," or sometimes by the English expression "the rule of law." I don't think I misunderstood. But increasingly, as far as civil liberties are concerned, governments seem to think that it does not matter what was decided before or how directly relevant it is and that they have no obligation to inform themselves or their employees of developments in the law.

A few examples will suggest the nature of this problem:

• In August 1986, the United States Court of Appeals for the Third Circuit (the highest federal court, other than the United States Supreme Court, with authority over matters from Pennsylvania, Delaware, the Virgin Islands, and New Jersey)* struck down a town ordinance requiring the fingerprinting of persons who want to canvass

*There are thirteen federal appeals courts covering the fifty states. Each is referred to as a circuit, from the days when the judges would literally "ride circuit," going by horse from place to place to hold court. Appeals from the circuit courts go to the United States Supreme Court.

14

door-to-door as a violation of the First Amendment.[7] (See "Talking Politics Door-to-Door," page 59.) In February 1987, the United States Supreme Court refused to review that ruling.[8] In July 1988, seventeen months later, a desk police sergeant in the town that lost the case told members of the very citizen organization that won it that he would not process their canvassing applications without fingerprints. When informed by the group of the court decision, the sergeant said that he had received nothing in writing and that he had only the ordinance to go by. A telephone call from the ACLU to the town attorney finally led to instructions to the town clerk and police to stop taking fingerprints and to return those already taken.

• A town recently issued a summons to the owners of a single-family home, which they had been renting out to four single women for a year without incident. The town accused the owners of violating a zoning ordinance that prohibits more than two individuals unrelated by blood or marriage from living together. The state supreme court had held ten years earlier that a virtually identical ordinance that limited occupancy to no more than four persons unrelated by blood or marriage violated the state constitution's protection of privacy.[9] That ruling had already been applied by another court in the same state in a published opinion issued one year earlier to prevent application of a comparable ordinance to bar ten college students from living together.[10] The ACLU successfully defended the homeowners against the summons.

• A small township recently issued summonses to two mothers for permitting their sixteen-year-old children to be out in a public place after 10:00 p.m. in violation of a local curfew ordinance. The mothers had given the boys permission to camp out in a tent in the backyard of the home of one of the boys' fathers, in anticipation of leaving early in the morning on a school trip. Courts have generally invalidated non-emergency curfews, even if they do not contain the more questionable approach used in this town of holding parents responsible for their children's violations without having to show that the parents knew where the children were. The most recent major decision invalidating a curfew, which happened to be in the same state, had come only a year earlier in an ACLU-sponsored case involving boys under seventeen out too late at a Chinese restaurant.[11] (See "Rethinking Juvenile Curfews: Whom are We Protecting?" page 241.)

The ACLU succeeding in having the charges against both mothers dismissed and persuaded the town not to pursue juvenile delinquency charges against the boys.

• A flamboyant mayor announced that he would not grant a permit to a group of gay activists to hold a rally on the sidewalk in front of City Hall. Almost fifty years earlier, the United States Supreme Court had told the even more flamboyant Mayor Frank Hague that he could not deny a rally permit to labor organizers from out of town.[12] Only a few years before the recent incident, a unanimous Supreme Court had re-affirmed the *Hague* decision and applied it to protestors who had been improperly kept away from the sidewalk in front of the Supreme Court building in Washington.[13] A permit was issued one hour after a phone call from the ACLU to the town attorney reciting these basic precedents.

• In a matter given national press attention, a woman moving out of a town was issued a summons for violating a local ordinance that prohibits moving into or out of town without a police permit. The application must state where the person is moving to and becomes a public record open to inspection. Moving is prohibited on Sundays and after sundown. The permit costs $5. The penalty for violation is a $500 fine and/or ninety days in jail. Over 120 years earlier, the United States Supreme Court had struck down a Nevada statute levying a $1 tax upon every person leaving the state, because it violated the constitutional right to travel.[14] In the 1970's, the Court struck down, as improperly burdening that right, various requirements that one live in a particular state or locale for an extended period before being able to register to vote, get an abortion, or become eligible for welfare or health care.[15] After intervention by the ACLU, the charge against the woman was dropped and the town promised to repeal the ordinance.

Explanations for these and, unfortunately, many other examples I could describe from across the country are of two basic types: either the government officials involved are not aware of the law or, if they know the law, they don't care.

The first problem often derives from ignorance by municipal or school board attorneys of current constitutional law. Although these attorneys often take courses or otherwise remain up to date on zoning and school law, they do not consider constitutional requirements to be of comparable importance. When states impose mandatory continuing legal education requirements upon practicing lawyers, as some already have, they should require all lawyers, but especially municipal and school board attorneys, to study constitutional law with an up-to-date text covering current cases! Alternatively, the local League of Municipalities, school board association, ACLU affiliate, and others with expertise should join in developing programs and procedures to alleviate the knowledge gap about current constitutional requirements for those advising governmental bodies regarding ordinances and key policy decisions.

The ignorance problem can exist, however, as the desk sergeant example above illustrates, even when the town attorney knows the law. Rarely does the town attorney insist or even advise the governing body that it must amend its ordinances to reflect constitutional deficiencies or that it must inform its employees in the interim that they are not to enforce invalid provisions. The desk sergeant's ignorance of the federal appeals court's ruling on the very fingerprinting provision that he was enforcing is, unfortunately, typical.

The prevailing view seems to be that constitutional law is not "law" in the same sense that statutes and ordinances are. The supremacy clause of the Constitution—which provides that the federal Constitution supersedes all inconsistent state and local laws—appears to have been inverted. Local governments act as if the Constitution is not to be followed unless expressly incorporated into state or local statutes or ordinances. Even that inverted approach might be acceptable if it were accompanied by the view that statutes and ordinances must be immediately revised to conform to the Constitution. As the examples above show, that often does not happen.

The second problem—the "who cares" or "let's see what we can get away with" attitude—is even more serious. From mayors and town attorneys to principals and police officers, government officials often take the view they can do anything unless expressly barred by a court. Thus they will adopt a curfew, deny a parade permit, or censor a school newspaper without worrying or caring if it is unconstitutional, until someone like the ACLU sues and gets a court order to stop it. The political hay to be made from both taking and defending popular but constitutionally defective positions is apparently too great to resist.

17

In part to change the incentives and counter this attitude, Congress passed in 1976 a law requiring state and local governments to pay the attorneys' fees of persons who sue and prove constitutional violations.[16] This has helped but is not enough for two reasons. First, the law does not cover violations of state constitutions, as in the example of the summons for having four unrelated people living in a home. Second, it does not apply in the many situations, like the homeowner, curfew, and moving permit charges, where the issue arises when the municipality prosecutes in criminal court for violations of patently unconstitutional ordinances.

Several remedies are needed. First, we need laws that award attorneys' fees both for civil actions won under state constitutions and for successful criminal defenses based upon the unconstitutionality, under any constitution, of the statute or ordinance underlying the prosecution. Such laws should help to make politicians aware of the countervailing costs, both in money and attendant bad publicity, that accompany unconstitutional grandstanding.

Even more importantly, we need to re-train our government officials to understand the basis and nature of their power. Rather than being limitless and subject only to after-the-fact correction by the courts, their authority is derived from and delimited by the federal and state constitutions. In the Preamble to the Constitution, "we the people" gave our representatives power to "promote the general welfare" only in a manner consistent with the parallel obligations to "establish justice" and "secure the blessings of liberty." We need to insure that mayors and council members as well as judges learn, or re-learn, that basic civics lesson.

Can We Risk a Constitutional Convention?

Q. *What's a Con-Con?*
A. A constitutional convention to propose constitutional amendments for ratification by the states, called by Congress in accordance with Article V of the United States Constitution. Such a convention must be called if two-thirds of the states (currently, thirty-four states) petition Congress for such a convention.

Q. *Have we ever had one?*
A. No. All of our twenty-six constitutional amendments were proposed by Congress and then ratified by the states, which is the other method for amending the Constitution set forth in Article V. There have been several prior efforts to call a constitutional convention, but none of them has been supported by the necessary two-thirds of the states.

Q. *Who's proposing a convention now?*
A. Different groups are always calling for such action on various issues. But right now the ones furthest along are advocates of a constitutional amendment to require a balanced federal budget.

Q. *Why?*
A. They are fed up with the President's and Congress' inability or, perhaps more accurately, unwillingness to balance the budget. They have tried several times to get such a balanced budget constitutional amendment through Congress but so far have been just barely unsuccessful. In 1982, the Senate approved the amendment by the necessary two-thirds vote, but the House did not. The 1986 effort failed in the Senate by only one vote. In July 1990, the House failed by only

19

seven votes to give the necessary two-thirds approval. Therefore, these groups have for the last fifteen years been trying to get the amendment adopted through the alternative route of a Con-Con.

Q. *Where do things stand now?*
A. Between 1975 and 1983, thirty-two states passed a resolution calling for such a convention. If two more states adopt such resolutions, Congress will have to consider several key procedural questions in deciding whether it must call a convention. First, must the thirty-four state resolutions calling for a convention be identical in their wording? The first thirty-two on this issue have not been. Second, must or should Congress consider a state's resolution if it subsequently voted to rescind it? In 1988, Alabama and Florida voted to withdraw their earlier resolution calling for a convention. Twelve other states are considering such action. Scholars agree that rescission is permissible, because Article V was meant to prevent casual amendments and to ensure concurrent agreement of a significant majority of the country in light of prevailing social, economic, and political circumstances. Third, is there a maximum time period within which all such resolutions must have been passed to trigger the congressional obligation under Article V to call a convention? This effort has extended over fifteen years, whereas Congress has often given states only seven years to ratify constitutional amendments that it has proposed. This issue is similar to the second and should be governed by the same considerations—namely, the need to insure a *concurrent* supermajority on the issue given *current* circumstances.

Q. *Who's opposed?*
A. Many people. In New Jersey, for example, when the issue was brought up in 1988, the opposition was a statewide coalition of some twenty-seven groups ranging from religious and labor groups to the Daughters of the American Revolution and the National Organization for Women.

Q. *Why would civil libertarians be concerned with a balanced budget amendment?*
A. We're not. The concern is with the method of adopting the amendment—that is, calling a constitutional convention rather than having Congress propose the amendment for state ratification, which is the procedure used for all other amendments in the last 200 years.

Q. Why would civil libertarians be opposed to a constitutional convention, when the first such convention produced the Constitution, which they glorify, and when the Constitution itself provides for such a convention?

A. That's a good question.

First, it is important to remember that the first constitutional convention did not produce the Bill of Rights, which most people view as the jewel in the crown. Rather, the people demanded adoption of such individual protections as the price of ratification of the original Constitution, which was the convention's workproduct.

Second, Article V, as noted, established two ways of amending the Constitution: by congressional proposal with two-thirds of each house concurring, or by a constitutional convention called by Congress when petitioned by two-thirds of the states. In either case, proposed amendments must be ratified by three-fourths of the states (at present, thirty-eight states). The Framers of the Constitution were understandably uncertain how the new government would work and whether some revisions might soon be necessary. Clearly there was concern that Congress might stymie important initiatives once it was firmly entrenched in the new capital. To insure that the people could effect major reform even if Congress proved a roadblock, the Framers established an end-run procedure—the Con-Con.

History has shown their fears to be unfounded. Congress has proposed all of the twenty-six constitutional amendments that have been adopted in our first 200 years. Congress has been willing and able to propose many substantial changes—including the post-Civil War revolution of the Thirteenth, Fourteenth, and Fifteenth Amendments, which eradicated slavery and sought to guarantee racial equality. It has been willing to try a radical social experiment—Prohibition—and then undo it when it failed. Moreover, the original concern about an unresponsive Congress was substantially reduced by the Seventeenth Amendment (itself proposed by Congress), which requires direct popular election of the Senate. Indeed, the balanced budget amendment now at issue was passed by the Senate in 1982 and only narrowly defeated by the House then and in 1990.

Civil libertarians are concerned about how the convention delegates would be selected. Would they be elected or appointed and would the one person-one vote principle be applied to any election? And how would the convention be conducted? For example, would the deliberations be open to the public and the press? Article V leaves all of these questions unanswered.

Most importantly, however, civil libertarians are concerned that a constitutional convention could turn out to be a "runaway" proceeding, going far beyond its original purpose by seeking to amend many other things in the Constitution. For example, the current "drug war" climate or recent AIDS hysteria might lead a convention to suggest repealing or drastically modifying the Fourth Amendment, which prevents unreasonable searches and seizures. The abortion controversy of recent years makes that issue a likely target. The recent push for a constitutional amendment against flag-burning shows that the First Amendment, too, might be fair game.

These fears are far from new. In 1788, one year after the convention that wrote the Constitution, James Madison, who would the next year draft the Bill of Rights, wrote vividly of his concerns about any future constitutional convention. He expressed fear that:

> election into it would be courted by the most violent partizans [sic] on both sides; it . . . would be the very focus of that flame which had already too much heated men of all parties; would no doubt contain individuals of insidious views, who under the mask of seeking alterations popular in some parts . . . might have a dangerous opportunity of sapping the very foundation of the fabric. . . . Having witnessed the difficulties and dangers experienced by the first Convention . . ., I should tremble for the result of a Second.[17]

Q. But how could such a convention address civil liberties issues if it is called solely for the purpose of proposing a balanced budget amendment?

A. There are no rules for how such a convention would be conducted. Congress has never called one, nor has it passed general legislation to govern such conventions in anticipation of the need to call one, although many respected leaders and organizations have suggested such legislation. Nor is it clear that Congress, even with advance legislation, could control the convention, a constitutional super-body, from considering amendments other than the one mentioned in the document convening it, such as the balanced budget amendment. Who could stop a convention from considering and proposing other amendments? Would the Supreme Court consider that a dispute it could hear? Would Congress or anyone else have legal "standing" to bring such a challenge? Should we risk the political spectacle and constitutional gridlock of Congress seeking a court injunction against a popularly elected constitutional convention?

There is also a more specific risk. Many of the state resolutions call for a convention to propose an amendment that would "require a balanced federal budget and a limitation on the rate of increase of federal spending." With such a mandate, couldn't a constitutional convention propose an amendment that would require that the budget be balanced, in part, by barring appropriation of any federal funds: a) for health facilities that perform abortions; b) for aid to states that allow flag-burning; and c) for aid to school districts that do not require prayers in school, that bus children for purposes of integration, or that teach Darwin's theory of evolution or refuse to teach creationism? Such a convention might not appear "runaway" in form, because the amendment would appear focussed on balancing the budget, but it surely would be in substance, because it in fact would address social policies not mentioned in the resolutions requesting the convention. It would thus evade Article V's intent of activating the extraordinary machinery of such a convention only when there is widespread consensus about the need for a particular change. This example shows that, even if a constitutional convention were technically to stick to its designated subject matter, which one cannot confidently predict given the lack of formal controls, it would be impossible to ensure that it would not roam at large in unrelated issues unless the exact text of any proposed amendment were set forth in the state resolutions requesting the convention and in the congressional document convening it.

Q. What should advocates of a balanced budget amendment do?
A. If all that is desired is a balanced budget amendment, I suggest that they conduct a campaign to persuade current members of Congress or elect new representatives who will propose it as a constitutional amendment to the states for ratification, the same way that we have amended our basic charter since the start of the Republic. After the close House vote in July 1990, proponents of the balanced budget amendment need change only seven representatives, or their votes, to get approval there. And in 1986 they were only one vote short in the Senate. Given the anti-incumbent mood of the country, especially on budgetary matters, such a campaign might well be successful.

23

An alternative, which is also now being considered, is to modify Article V of the Constitution to provide a third means of amending the Constitution without calling a convention. As of 1990, three states—Virginia, Ohio, and South Dakota—have approved resolutions calling for an amendment to Article V that would permit a constitutional amendment to be adopted if three-fourths of the states propose it and Congress does not affirmatively vote to disapprove it within two years.[18] This would give the states and the people the ability to get around a congressional roadblock without calling a convention that might consider numerous amendments with no relationship to the grievance that prompted its convening.

In short, I say can the Con-Con and go the old route or find a new and safer way.

A Civil Liberties Lawyer on Jury Duty

It was with mixed emotions that I received notice in September 1987 that I was to report for jury duty in New Jersey's Essex County Superior Court. On the one hand, ever since seeing as a boy the movie "Twelve Angry Men" with Henry Fonda and Lee J. Cobb, I had wanted to take part in a jury deliberation. Also, because I was a lawyer and had become directly involved in court administration, I was particularly interested in observing the jury selection process first-hand. I was also eager, as too few citizens are, to perform my civic duty and was confident that I could be a fair juror. On the other hand, I knew to a virtual certainty that, given my position then as Legal Director of the American Civil Liberties Union of New Jersey, I would be excused from any case for which I was chosen. My prediction proved true, but I was glad that I was called and generally impressed by how well the process worked.[19]

In most states, as in mine, the process starts when you receive a form in the mail checking whether you are qualified to be a juror and have any basis to be excused. In the past such forms were sent only to persons registered to vote, but to insure greater representativeness of juries, many states have started using driver license lists as well. Because of the skewed effects of using voter registration rolls, Michigan has gone so far as to use only lists of licensed drivers and non-drivers with state personal identification cards.[20] A jury qualification form that I received when I lived in California in the early 1980's asked me to return it only if I claimed to fit one of the five criteria for exemption: not being a United States citizen or a resident of the court's jurisdiction, not having a good understanding of English, being a peace officer, or "not possess[ing] natural faculties or ordinary intelligence or [being] decrepit!"[21]

On the Monday morning that I was summoned to appear, some 750 jurors gathered on the fourth floor of the courthouse for orientation. A slide show was shown to the entire group emphasizing the importance of the jury function and outlining how a jury is picked and a trial conducted. I thought the presentation was inspirational without being maudlin and informative without being condescending. Its one defect was that almost all the participants portrayed in the slides were white, and, with the exception of a few jurors and court reporters, all men. There should have been a much greater diversity of actors.

This is particularly important in a county like Essex, which is headquartered in Newark, because the citizens called to jury duty who observed the slide show were themselves very diverse. They were very different from the elite, "blue ribbon" panels of the old days, which were typically composed of politically connected, older, wealthy, white men. Between 40 and 50 percent of the jurors at the courthouse on the week I was there were African American. At least half were women. Ages varied from 18 to 75 and all towns in the county were represented. Moreover, there were persons from all walks of life—secretaries, plumbers, salespeople, accountants, and even a police officer. The vast majority were employed and part of the great American middle class. None of the unemployed jurors were on welfare; in that respect, the jurors were unrepresentative, especially of the city in which the court sat.

The courtroom participants I observed were more diverse than society at large. Of the first twelve jurors called to the box in the first case I observed, six were African American, of whom five were employed men. (I did not get to see the final composition of that jury after the lawyers had completed their challenges, as I was one of those challenged and sent back to the central jury room.) Of the eight attorneys I saw (being called to four courtrooms in my two days of jury duty), three were African Americans and two were women. Of the four judges, one was a woman. My two days of jury service can hardly substitute for hard overall statistics. For example, employed African American men are far from five-sixths of the adult African American population; indeed, recent data suggests that as many as 25 percent of young African American men are currently in prison or on parole or probation.[22] African Americans are also very far from constituting three-eighths of the legal profession. (See "We Still Need

Affirmative Action," page 146.) And women comprise no more than 10 percent of the judiciary in this country.[23] Yet it seems clear that we have made meaningful progress towards the goal of insuring a fair cross-section of our society among jurors as well as other courtroom participants.

Jury panels of fifty were called out to courtrooms when needed. There was a big demand on Monday morning, but thereafter it was sporadic. As a result, we spent a good amount of time waiting in the central jury room. Nevertheless my experience was far better than the horror stories one often hears of jurors sitting around for days without being called to a courtroom. I was in a courtroom involved in the jury selection process almost half of the hours that I was on jury duty, not counting lunch. Indeed, if a call came and no complete panel was available, the jury control staff would call out the numbers of all available jurors excused from different panels who were sitting in the central jury room and send them out together as an ad hoc panel to the requesting judge.

Jury utilization has improved nationwide because of the introduction of shorter tours of duty. When I was called, my county required one week of duty or, if selected, one trial, whatever its length. (Because of holidays, I served only two days.) Now it is down to two days or one trial. In about a quarter of courts around the country, the obligation is only one day or one trial.[24] This makes for less waiting around, although it also leads some jurors to create excuses as they get to the end of their one afternoon of jury duty.[25]

Once in the courtroom, we would be addressed by the judge, who would explain the general nature of the case, introduce the lawyers and parties, name possible witnesses, and in some cases, ask some very general questions of the entire panel, such as whether they would give greater credence to the testimony of a police officer. Then the wheel would be spun and the appropriate number of jurors called forward—fourteen in criminal cases and eight in civil, thereby providing two alternates in either case.

This is a big change. Until 1970, everyone assumed that twelve jurors were constitutionally required in all cases. In that year, however, the United States Supreme Court ruled that a criminal jury of six was adequate to satisfy the Sixth Amendment's guarantee of an impartial jury.[26] Later, after sociological studies showed that smaller juries are less representative of minority groups, less likely to foster effective

27

group deliberation, and may be less accurate in their results, the Court was to rule that five people was too small a jury.[27] Many states, like mine, have retained twelve-person juries in criminal cases under either their state constitutions, statutes, or court rules. However, most places have adopted six-person juries in civil cases. Although this move is a cost- and time-saver, we ought to think carefully whether, even in civil cases, we are forfeiting too much of the value of having a cross-section of our society decide how and when people should pay for their transgression of society's rules.

Once the required number of people were in the jury box, the judge would either ask the general questions, if that had not been done earlier, or would request certain individual information. In some cases, the judges would ask only for the name, town, and occupation of the juror and his or her spouse, while in others they would also inquire about the number, age, and occupation of the juror's children. In criminal cases, the jurors were also asked whether they or any close relatives or friends had ever been a crime victim or been arrested; in civil cases, the question was whether one had been in an accident or involved in a civil lawsuit. Follow-up questioning would sometimes be at the side of the judge's bench so only the judge, lawyers, and court reporters could hear the answers; other times it was done in open court. Questioning was always serious and courteous; at no time was a juror embarrassed or harassed.

Increasingly throughout the country, judges, rather than the parties' lawyers, conduct this questioning, which is known in the law as "voir dire," from the French words for "to see" and "to say." Lawyers object because they feel that, with their knowledge of the case and the perspective of their client, they can more effectively elicit answers that will indicate prejudices that would render a juror unacceptable. Judges, however, feel that it takes too long for lawyers to pick a jury. My own sense is that judge questioning works fine in routine cases but should be at least supplemented by attorney inquiries in sensitive or controversial cases.

Once the questioning was done, the lawyers could decide whether to "challenge" a juror. There are two kinds of challenges. A challenge "for cause" is one based on a claim that the juror has disclosed a legally impermissible bias, such as a greater belief in the testimony of police officers than that of other witnesses, or an unacceptably close connection to the parties, lawyers, or events of the case. There is no limit to the number of challenges for cause that a party may make, although the judge determines whether any challenge is valid.

In addition, each party gets a fixed number of opportunities to eliminate jurors without having to give a reason and without control by the judge. These are called "peremptory challenges." Peremptories have a long if not always noble history. In Roman days, the Lex Sevilia of 104 B.C. authorized the prosecutor and the defendant to propose 100 prospective jurors each and then for each to strike fifty from the opposing side's list.[28] It has ever since been assumed that, to insure a fair jury, parties must be able to remove those jurors whom the parties sense will not be open-minded, even though they cannot formally articulate the basis for that feeling.

As with all discretion, the completely unfettered discretion of parties and lawyers to reject jurors on such hunches can be and has been abused. Claims of racially biased use of peremptory challenges most typically arise when prosecutors excuse all or most African Americans from juries in criminal cases where the defendant is African American. Such abuses led the Supreme Court in 1986 to reaffirm that the intentional exclusion of minorities from juries, by this as well as by other means, violates the equal protection guarantee of the Fourteenth Amendment. It overruled a prior decision of the Warren Court that allowed such claims to be heard only when the defendant could show a pattern of racial exclusion over many cases. Instead, the Court now requires prosecutors to explain to the judge the reason for excusing each minority juror whenever the number and race of jurors excused and the circumstances in any one case indicate discriminatory use of peremptory challenges.[29]

To many of my fellow jurors, the challenge process seemed overly sensitive and hence foolishly wasteful of fair jurors. Very few people were excused by the judge "for cause." Most were excused by the lawyers without explanation, by use of a peremptory challenge. Lawyers for criminal defendants regularly challenged persons who had been, or were close to, crime victims while prosecutors challenged those who had been involved in the criminal process themselves. People who had had car accidents and been involved in lawsuits were regularly dismissed from civil juries. My colleagues on the panel thought that some of these criteria were too broad, given the frequency of such occurrences in modern life, and eliminated too many open-minded and worthwhile jurors. I tend to agree, especially with regard to the car accident-civil lawsuit point, although as an attorney I appreciate the need for unexplained, free-wheeling peremptory challenges, barring racially discriminatory abuse. Mostly, I think the jurors were simply frustrated that they did not get to sit on a case. I was impressed by how seriously all jurors took their job and how eager they were to serve. If they were excused more than once, they became understandably frustrated at sitting around in the jury control room, especially as the second day stretched on and there were fewer calls for jury panels.

My number was called three of the four times I was in a courtroom—in two criminal cases and one civil case. As expected, I was excused all three times. In the criminal cases, I underwent extensive examination by the prosecutors about my experience in teaching and practicing criminal law and my work at the ACLU, in particular any lawsuits alleging police misconduct. But in neither case did the judge find any cause to excuse me and thus the prosecutors were forced to use peremptory challenges to eliminate me, as did the insurance defense lawyer in the civil case. I fully understood those decisions, as did my juror colleagues, many of whom were smiling knowingly when the lawyers finally announced that I was excused, even though I truly felt that I could be a fair and impartial juror.

An interesting parallel situation was the only police officer on the panel, who was finally excused from a criminal case for cause, after extensive questioning, because he had admitted he would give greater credence to the testimony of a fellow officer. The jurors on my panel, myself included, wondered why so much time was spent with other questions since he had stated his disqualifying view at the very outset. Significantly, in light of my comments above about diversity, the officer was African American.

Because I was excused each time, I never heard any jury deliberations. Indeed we generally have far less information about jury deliberations than about jury selection because the law makes deliberations strictly confidential, subject to very narrow exceptions. In some states, lawyers are forbidden by ethics rules from speaking with jurors at all. An experiment in the 1960's by two prominent scholars who were allowed to hide microphones and tape jury deliberations led, after an ensuing public furor, to rules prohibiting observation or taping of deliberations under any circumstances.[30] In addition, all states and the federal courts forbid jurors from testifying about their deliberations or mental processes and will consider challenges to jury verdicts only if there is evidence of improper external pressure—such as a threat or bribe—or introduction of information not provided at trial—such as the comments of a sheriff or of a juror who visited the scene of the crime.[31] Thus we know about jury deliberations only from the occasional news interviews with jurors and from fictional movies like "Twelve Angry Men."

In sum, from my own experience as a juror, I was impressed by the diversity and dedication of the jurors, the efficiency of the court staff, and the professionalism of the judges and lawyers. Further improvements are possible in reducing juror waiting time, such as the one-day/one-trial system or a procedure for calling potential jurors the day before to confirm whether they need to come to court. I thought the selection process worked as well as could be expected, although I concluded that it makes little sense for lawyers and police officers to be called to jury duty as they will, for good reasons, almost inevitably be excused. Notwithstanding the improvements already implemented, the key reality remains that our jury selection process is intentionally slow and costly because our ideals of representativeness and impartiality are lofty and hard to satisfy. However, after witnessing the process close up, I still think it's worth the trouble.

A Civil Liberties Agenda for the 1990's

As we begin the third century of the Bill of Rights, it is good for all of us, including the Ivans who just got here and those of us who work regularly in the Constitution's vineyards, to pause from our daily tasks, take a step back, and consider the broad picture. Where are we now and what most needs our attention in the future? I suggest that we should focus on five major areas in the coming years.

Protect Privacy in a Shrinking World

As technology provides ever easier and more subtle means of gathering information about people and as the planet gets increasingly crowded, privacy becomes increasingly significant. That vital "right to be let alone" was first articulated in American law by Justice Louis Brandeis and his brother-in-law Samuel Warren in their famous article 100 years ago, at the beginning of the second century of the Bill of Rights.[32] It was prompted by outrage at the "indecent" coverage by the "yellow press" of Warren's fashionable high-society wife.

When Americans lived on an open frontier, the environment itself—forests, meadows, ranches, farms, mountain ranges, and lakes—provided privacy. People were more concerned with finding companions and developing community cooperation to deal with the weather, dangerous animals, natural calamities, bandits, and displaced native people. Protecting privacy was secondary. Now that we live so near each other, often separated only by paper-thin apartment walls, now that our conversations can be overheard by wiretaps and tiny voice-activated tape recorders, our bodily functions can be scanned by chemical tests, our activities can be monitored by zoom lenses and one-way mirrors, and all the information about us can be traded and

32

sorted by lightning-fast computers, we need to reassess whether the law adequately protects our privacy.

The Supreme Court's initial approach to protecting personal privacy in the face of intrusive technology seemed to make sense. In the famous 1967 case of *Katz v. United States*,[33] a gambler challenged his conviction because the evidence against him came from a wiretap placed on the outside of a glass-enclosed public telephone booth on the street, from which he had placed bets. The Court explained that the Fourth Amendment protects people, not places and therefore courts must look to "the reasonable expectations of privacy" of ordinary citizens, rather than the traditional privileges of private property, in deciding what is protected by the Constitution. The Court ruled that Katz had a reasonable expectation of privacy with regard to the conversations he had in the booth, even though he did not own the phone booth, he was visible to the public and police through the glass doors, and the wiretap did not intrude into the physical boundaries of the booth. Because of that expectation, the Court concluded, the government violated Katz's Fourth Amendment rights when it listened to his calls without first obtaining a warrant from a judge.

Subsequent decisions have, however, undercut that approach. For example, a later Supreme Court majority ruled that, because garbage bags placed at the curb might be torn open by dogs, children or scavengers, the person who puts them there has no reasonable expectation of privacy in their contents and, consequently, the police may open and search them at will. (See "Do We Expect Our Garbage To Be Inspected by Police?" page 91.) In a similar vein, a lower court recently ruled (and the Supreme Court declined to review the decision) that citizens have no reason to expect privacy from police overhearing their conversations when using a cordless rather than a traditional wired telephone.[34] Such rulings simply fly in the face of common understandings of when to expect and how to preserve privacy. It is time to re-think the law to ensure that, even in the twenty-first century, every human being will be assured that zone of seclusion needed to relax from the pressures of the world, nurture close relationships, and pursue personal interests.

Protect Rights Against Private As Well as Government Intrusion

Privacy issues highlight the need to reconsider the line traditionally drawn in constitutional law between actions taken by private entities, which are not regulated, and actions taken by governmental entities and officials (known in constitutional law as "state action"), as to which constitutional protections apply. Thus, at present, the government cannot fine a person even fifty dollars without a court trial and a public school cannot suspend a student for ten days without some kind of a hearing, reflecting the principle of due process. However, a private school, even one receiving almost all its funding from the state to teach special education students placed there by the state, can fire its teachers or suspend its students without giving them any explanation or any opportunity to contest the charges.[35]

The state action/private action distinction reflects the historical origins of the Constitution—the revolution against the Crown. But increasingly, as private commercial entities have grown to have as much power as governments and to employ the same methods that provoked colonial concerns, the line has become fuzzy.

A supervisor's surveillance of an employee, just like a principal's discipline of a student, has the same impact on the affected individual whether the authority is acting for a private or public entity. Employers, private as well as public, now seek drug tests, fingerprints, and complete physical exams from applicants. Banks and insurers, like state licensing boards, scour one's financial past. Credit agencies, like police doing background checks, ask neighbors about alcohol use and moral character. On-the-job surveillance may include listening in on telephone conversations, monitoring employee restrooms, searching lockers, and requiring polygraphs. Ever-present computers permit free exchange of all this data among private as well as public actors.

Similarly, crucial rights of public expression are as readily squelched by private interests as by the state. The privately owned shopping mall serves the same social and commercial functions today as did the publicly owned downtown sidewalks of three decades ago. Surely the need for communication among citizens about current affairs is not diminished because stockholders rather than taxpayers hold title to the marketplace.

Courts in several states have begun to grapple with these realities. Because the federal constitution has been limited, as noted, by a fairly narrow definition of state action, these courts have turned to their state constitutions to provide protection against actions by private parties. New Jersey, a leader in this development, has already applied

34

its state constitutional right of free expression to a private college campus, overturning the conviction for trespass of a Socialist Worker Party pamphleteer on the Princeton University campus.[36] Courts in California led the way in applying free speech rights to shopping malls.[37] Recently, random drug testing in private industry was invalidated as against the public policy of the New Jersey Constitution. (See "Constitutional Rights Should Apply At Work," page 110.)

What these courts are undertaking, and what I suggest that all of us need to start doing, is to identify the core values protected by the federal and state constitutions—such as protecting personal privacy against unjustified intrusions, insuring fair play when imposing penalties, and guaranteeing freedom of thought, belief and expression—and then to apply them whether threatened by a fast food chain or the chief of police. We should invert the comment of Eisenhower's Secretary of Defense Charles Wilson: what's good for the Defense Department is good for General Motors.

Exorcise Subtle Racism

Constitutional law no longer tolerates slavery or even separate drinking fountains, but racism is still the scourge of our society. I'm not just talking about the blatant racism of a Howard Beach or Bensonhurst attack. I'm also referring to the more subtle problem of judges assuming that the African American in the courtroom who is dressed in a suit is the criminal defendant rather than his lawyer, and of the press play about allegations—which proved to be false—that an African American stranger murdered a white woman named Stuart in Boston. I am thinking also about the unimpeachable study showing that nothing but race can explain the striking difference in the frequency with which the death penalty is applied to African Americans who kill whites as compared to whites who kill African Americans and the Supreme Court's acceptance of this established jury racism. (See "Racism at the Gallows," page 182.) We need to develop legal doctrines to address this evil that are as sophisticated and humane as the racism is subtle and insidious.

Guarantee The Right to a Home

All rights are meaningless if one does not have the energy, time, and ability to exercise them. Society generally recognizes this through its longstanding and substantial commitment to education: the provision of common knowledge about the world necessary to develop one's individuality and to participate in the economic and political system. For millions of our fellow citizens, however, both education and civil liberties are peripheral, as they struggle daily simply to survive their environment. Much like our frontier pioneers, modern hot-air-grate dwellers cannot afford to be concerned with the niceties of protecting privacy in their hostile environment.

Until now, a significant rule of constitutional law has been that although the government may not infringe directly upon our basic rights, it has no obligation to take affirmative steps to ensure the exercise of those rights. Thus the state, at least as of this writing, must allow abortions, but it need not provide money or public hospital services for poor women who cannot otherwise obtain them.[38] Likewise, the state may not directly harm children, but it has no obligation to protect children whom it has placed in homes from known threats from their caretakers.[39]

This arbitrary line between direct and indirect infringement of rights must be re-thought in an increasingly interdependent and state-controlled economy and community. It is true that no single public official, federal, state or local, consciously chose to force thousands of citizens to live on the street. But our governments collectively did choose our zoning laws, housing codes, eviction laws, banking and mortgage financing regulations, rent control ordinances, tax rules, and massive cutbacks over the last decade in mental health facilities, public housing construction, and rent subsidies. One must ignore reality to say that homelessness is not at least in significant part the result of government actions. (See "Why Homelessness is a Civil Liberties Concern," page 158.) We need to hold government responsible for the composite impact of its laws and actions and thus render our federal and state constitutions genuine guarantors of those fundamental civil liberties that we have treasured these past 200 years.

Rethink the Drug War

Just as our housing, taxing, zoning, and banking policies have produced homelessness and its attendant civil liberties problems, our drug policy has developed its own constitutional fallout. A drug war, like any other war, produces a mindset that both justifies otherwise unacceptable means and rejects disagreement as disloyal. (See "Declaring War on Undeclared Wars," page 227.)

Our current drug war, like the prior ones, has eviscerated the Fourth and Eighth Amendments. The public and political pressure to catch drug dealers has led both law enforcement officials and courts to bend or break all the rules established by the Fourth Amendment for police searches and seizures—downgrading probable cause to reasonable suspicion and then dropping even that. (See "What Ever Happened to Probable Cause?" page 104.)

In addition, the "zero tolerance" push to prosecute anyone having even the slightest involvement with drugs (see "Should We Tolerate "Zero Tolerance?" page 95) and the reflexive demand for mandatory minimum sentencing laws have filled our jails and prisons to bursting. In the 1980's, the American prison population exploded; from June 1989 to June 1990 alone, the prison population grew by 80,000 to reach a record total of 755,000.[40] We now have the highest incarceration rate in the world—426 of every 100,000 residents are confined—well exceeding the rate in South Africa and the Soviet Union, even though the crime rate has dropped since 1980.[41] Not surprisingly, the growing appetite for incarceration is not matched by a comparable willingness to increase corrections budgets. The predictable result is overcrowding and the attendant inadequate space, exercise, hygiene, medical and psychiatric care, and other conditions violating the Eighth Amendment's ban on cruel and unusual punishment. The prison systems in nearly forty states were under court orders by early 1991 based on determinations that the overcrowded conditions were unconstitutional.[42] Quite apart from the constitutional defects, the failure to fund prisons adequately renders it impossible to undertake the kind of education, vocational training, and psychological treatment needed to return the offenders to a productive and law-abiding existence.

Even more disturbing than the constitutional damage inflicted is the fact that the drug war has failed. More drugs are coming into the country and more people are involved with them. Economic productivity is sapped, educational efforts are undermined, and the social fabric is strained. In response, many responsible voices, from a federal judge to numerous law enforcement personnel, have begun advocating legalization of drugs. Like many others, I am very torn and undecided about such proposals. But whether or not we completely give up the criminal deterrent, it is clear that we need to reorder our priorities. We have never had sufficient treatment capacity for all those needing it—whether self-referred, brought in by families or employers, or directed by the criminal process. We have spent far less on researching drug treatment than on developing better guns for police. We have only recently begun to incorporate drug education into our school curricula. Quite simply, we have never tried a coordinated, fully funded education, prevention, and treatment approach to the drug problem. The substantial benefits in restored civil peace and civil liberties would make it worth a serious try.

Both of the last two agenda items—guaranteeing shelter and providing adequate drug treatment—will cost money. The "peace dividend," much discussed at the end of the Cold War in late 1989, never really developed, in part because of the Persian Gulf crisis. Hopefully it will materialize in time as we re-assess our military needs. But whatever the level of government expenditures, we must assure that civil liberties concerns are prominent in the setting of budget priorities. Should we spend money on tactical police force equipment or on prison rehabilitation programs? Should we cut the capital gains tax or fund housing for the homeless? The power of government to provide for the general welfare and common defense is defined by all the provisions of the Constitution, including the Bill of Rights. We need to make the Bill of Rights a line item in every budget.

Each era has its special civil liberties challenges, apart from the ongoing struggles to preserve freedom of conscience and expression, ensure equality of treatment, and maintain fair procedures. In our time, the challenges derive from the shrinking of our world and our growing interactions and interdependence. We must learn to preserve individual privacy and to master the demon of racism that taints social intercourse if we are to live close to one another. We must also find controls over the growing private power centers and the devastating drugs flooding our country, which now impact all aspects of daily life. Similarly, the expansion of government regulation of economic life requires that the state be held responsible for the foreseeable, unfortunate outcomes of its complex interactions with its citizens. The world may be smaller, but the problems seem more complex. I hope that our 200-year-old blueprint will be up to these challenges.

II

FREE EXPRESSION

Almost everyone takes freedom of speech and press for granted. They shouldn't. The British, from whom most people think we got those freedoms, have been struggling recently with court injunctions against newspapers and books. Artists in this country are facing funding cut-offs and criminal prosecutions. People who write critical letters to the editor are getting sued for libel. Citizen groups are having trouble canvassing door-to-door in the evening or without being fingerprinted. Protestors have been required to post millions of dollars in insurance. And after the Supreme Court's recent decisions treating flag burning as protected speech, a majority of Congress wanted to amend the First Amendment.

The problem is that, while everyone likes to express their own opinion, no one likes to be criticized, especially not public officials. The brilliance of the First Amendment is that it is what judges call "content-neutral." That means it protects all expression from government interference regardless of the subject matter, speaker, or point of view. The lesson that all of us, but especially government, must re-learn constantly is that this protection extends to, in fact is precisely meant for, speech that is critical or even disparaging of the government, the flag, the police, the public schools, and other sacred institutions. The essays in this chapter are designed to remind us where the First Amendment came from and how it must be applied if we are to be true to its lofty purpose.

Mother England's Not-So-Free Press

There is a tendency among Americans, particularly lawyers and judges, to wax eloquent about the English* origins of our most precious liberties. Apart from the Magna Carta, which actually redistributed power between the king and his feudal lords, one of the most frequently cited documents is the English Bill of Rights. It was adopted in 1689, a full 100 years before our Bill of Rights, the bicentennial of which we are now so proudly celebrating. Alas the publicity is out of line with reality. I recently moderated a program in London comparing British and American approaches to press coverage of national security issues. The program highlighted not only the irrelevance of the English Bill of Rights to their daily life, but also how much less protection their citizens and press have than we do. In short, Americans who express dismay over restrictions on press freedom here should not look to Mother England for help.

The three starkest differences are in the ready availability in England of: court orders (injunctions) against publication of "state secrets"; criminal contempt proceedings against those who print material that was banned in a court action even though the publishers were not parties to that proceeding and thus not restrained by the court from publishing; and criminal prosecutions of both civil servants and the press for leaking and publishing government information. The contrasts are best highlighted by the most famous recent case in England—the controversy surrounding the book *Spycatcher*. It may read like a Grimm's fairy tale, but it really is true.

---

*For convenience I use the terms "English" and "British" interchangeably, although I recognize that the Scottish, Welsh, and Northern Irish constituencies within Great Britain are not English.

41

Spycatcher is a book by Peter Wright, a retired twenty-year veteran of MI5, the British security service for internal matters that is roughly equivalent to our FBI. The book describes numerous operations of the agency, including its electronic surveillance of foreign embassies in London and its investigation of left-wing groups in the United Kingdom. More dramatically, the book describes a plan by MI6, the English equivalent of the CIA, to assassinate President Nasser of Egypt, suggests that one of the directors of MI5 was a Soviet agent, and explains how some MI5 members plotted to destabilize the government of British Prime Minister Harold Wilson. As detailed in one court opinion, most of these allegations had previously surfaced in books written years earlier by others.

Because Wright lived in Australia and intended to have the book published there, the English Attorney General first began proceedings in Australian courts to prevent publication. The case was based upon the theory that Wright had breached a lifelong duty of confidentiality to the government, which derived from his employment with MI5. Publication was enjoined by the Australian court in 1985; that order was not lifted for two years.

Meanwhile two prominent newspapers in London, the *Observer* and the *Guardian*, published articles in June 1986 about a forthcoming hearing in the Australian case and included outlines of some of the allegations of the unpublished manuscript. The British government went to court in England and obtained an injunction restraining those two newspapers "from publishing or disclosing any information obtained by Mr. Wright in his capacity as a member of MI5 or from attributing any information about MI5 to him."[1] An appeal failed to dislodge this injunction. Thus, had I tried to publish this essay in England in 1986, I would have been enjoined from doing so by a court!

In April 1987, three other British newspapers published articles about the book describing some of the more sensational allegations. These papers had not been parties to the injunction proceeding and had therefore never been served with the court order preventing publication. Nevertheless the Attorney General asked to have them held in contempt, claiming that they should have known about that court order. The Court of Appeal ruled that they could be held in contempt if they simply had knowledge of the injunction, and they were later thus convicted. At this writing, the final appeal of those convictions is still pending before the House of Lords. Thus again, had I been writing in England between 1986 and 1988, this piece would have been a basis for a contempt conviction even though I had neither been in court nor ordered not to write it! So much for the concept of due process and the right to one's day in court, which we derived from the Magna Carta and the English Bill of Rights.

Meanwhile it was announced that the book was being published in America by Viking Penguin, a subsidiary of an English publishing house, in July 1987. Andrew Neil, editor of the *London Sunday Times*, obtained a copy of the book in America, smuggled it into England, and published the first of a series of excerpts in the *Times* on July 12. The next day the government moved to hold the *Times* in contempt. On July 15, the Court of Appeal issued the contempt ruling involving the other newspapers noted in the prior paragraph.

At that time, the *Observer* and *Guardian* moved to dissolve the original injunction because of the American publication of the book and the availability in England of imported copies. (Inexplicably, the British government never sought to ban importation of the book.) The Vice-Chancellor vacated the injunction, because "the law could, I think, be justifiably accused of being an ass and brought into disrepute if it closed its eyes to that reality." But the Court of Appeal reversed and the House of Lords also upheld the injunction pending a final trial of the case, simply because the Attorney General had "an arguable case for a permanent injunction."[2]

The House of Lords, which is Britain's highest court as well as the upper house of Parliament, decided the case on the merits in October 1988. The Law Lords, as they are known, vacated the injunction at that time only because "general publication in this country would not bring about any significant damage to the public interest beyond what has already been done."[3] They accepted the government's theory of a lifelong duty of confidence and the appropriateness of injunctions, except when, as in this case, widespread publication elsewhere rendered such orders futile. They also ruled that the *Sunday Times'* serialization in July 1987 was unlawful and directed the *Times* to pay to the government all profits from that issue.

Lest I be accused of one-sided criticism of the British courts and government, I should note at this point that this last order in the *Spycatcher* case—requiring payment of profits derived from publication—is the same remedy used by the United States Supreme Court at the request of our federal government in a case in 1980 called

43

Snepp v. United States.[4] That case was brought by the government against a former Central Intelligence agent who failed to submit his book about the American evacuation of Vietnam, *Decent Interval,* to the CIA for pre-publication approval. As in England, the Court here accepted the government's position that the papers an agent signs when first hired create a lifelong obligation of confidentiality that requires pre-publication submission of any writing throughout his or her life to prevent disclosure of classified material. Strikingly, the profit penalty was imposed in that case even though the CIA admitted to the Supreme Court that the book as published had, as the author always claimed, revealed no classified information whatsoever.

Surprisingly the *Spycatcher* saga did not involve what had been the most infamous and regressive of British government censorship tools—the Official Secrets Act. This law, in effect in some form for over 100 years, made criminal any disclosure by a civil servant, or publication by an outsider, of any information obtained in the course of official duty in the British government! Everyone agreed that Wright would have been prosecuted under this act had he still lived in England. But the act is not limited to national security secrets; until its recent narrowing, the British often wryly claimed that a civil servant could be prosecuted under the act for disclosing the number of cups of tea served in the Home Office. In the most famous recent real case, a civil servant was prosecuted because he gave a report to a member of Parliament about the sinking of a ship during the then recently concluded Falkland Islands war. Fortunately, in an act known as "jury nullification," or rejection of the law, the jury refused to convict him even though the judge told them that his actions breached the technical boundaries of the law.

As a result of outrage over that prosecution, the Official Secrets Act was amended in 1989. In its new form the act prohibits disclosure only of intelligence, military, diplomatic, and criminal investigative information and in some instances requires the government to show "damage" from the disclosure. However, prosecution of the press is still possible, no defense that disclosure was in the public interest is permitted, and "damage" is defined to include not only actual injury to the national security but the *likelihood* that release of *that kind* of document would adversely affect the work of the agency.[5]

Although even in its revised form this statute seems drastic, a recent ruling of a federal appeals court in the United States renders the American Espionage Act and the theft-of-government-property statute very similar to the British Official Secrets Act. In *United States v. Morison*,[6] the Fourth Circuit Court of Appeals upheld the conviction of an American naval intelligence officer for passing top secret American photos of a Soviet military installation to *Jane's Defence Weekly* (ironically a British journal) because it might have revealed American photographic spying capabilities. The court upheld a jury charge that the government need prove only "that the disclosure of the photographs would be *potentially* damaging to the United States," refused to narrow the statute to cover only disclosure to foreign agents, and rejected a First Amendment claim on behalf of journalists who receive such information. The Attorney General has since threatened to use the theft-of-property law against civil servants who leak information as well as those who pass photos, documents, or other tangible objects.[7]

The outlook within Britain is dreary and, despite the *Snepp* and *Morison* comparisons noted, still bleaker than here. They still do not have a written constitution, despite recent discussion of the benefits of following the American model. The English Bill of Rights is of no help because it is treated as just another law, which cannot supersede conflicting statutes or court decisions even though it is hundreds of years older. Yet there is hope on the horizon. The European Community has adopted a Convention on Human Rights and created an enforcement structure including both a Commission and a Court of Human Rights, which sit in Strasbourg, France. Individuals and entities, such as the British newspapers, may file petitions alleging that their national law conflicts with the European Convention, just as citizens of a state in our country may complain to the federal courts that a state statute conflicts with the federal constitution or a federal statute. The British government, which has accepted the European Convention as binding, has lost almost every time it has appeared before the European Court. Indeed, the *Spycatcher* affair is now before the European Commission. Thus Britain may after all, end up with a written constitution protecting freedom of the press, but it will be one imported from the Continent.

The future may be encouraging and European, but the present is bleak and British. *Spycatcher* confirms that like us, Mother England needs to recapture the spirit of the Magna Carta and its Bill of Rights. Maybe, as during our revolution, we can again lead England back to the principles it first taught us.

Flagging the Burning Issues: Disrespect and Offense

Most Americans, including many public officials, just don't understand the First Amendment. This is obvious from the uproar and the attempt to amend the Constitution following each of the Supreme Court's two recent flag-burning decisions. It is also highlighted by the 1990 obscenity prosecution in Cincinnati of an art gallery that displayed the controversial Mapplethorpe photography exhibit and the Florida obscenity prosecutions the same year of the rap group 2 Live Crew and the store owner who sold its sexually explicit records. Similarly illustrative was the Senate's initial approval in 1989 of Senator Helms' amendment barring the National Endowment for the Arts from funding "indecent material, including . . . material which denigrates the objects or beliefs of the adherents of a particular religion or nonreligion" or "denigrates, debases or reviles a person, group or class of citizens on the basis of race, creed, sex, handicap, age or national origin."[8]

Many Americans apparently think that the First Amendment is primarily designed to protect the right to send letters to the editor or to Congress and similar polite forms of political commentary. It is not always successful even in that regard. (See "It's Scandalous What Some Think is Slanderous," page 62, and "How Can You Petition When The Doors Are Closed?" page 70.) But in any case that is not its primary function. You don't see the chief executive officers of Fortune 500 companies, the chairs of the Republican and Democratic National Committees, publishers of major metropolitan dailies, senior law partners, Grandma Moses, Norman Rockwell, or PTA presidents out on picket lines cursing the government or burning flags. There is a reason for this. They are part of the establishment and thus are protected in their speech by the political or cultural power structure. They have far more persuasive and direct ways of making their views known.

The First Amendment is designed for those on the outside—the powerless, the oppressed, the disaffected, the ignored, or just simply the minority. As the civil rights movement and Vietnam War protests reminded us, people take to the streets when the ballot box and the corporate board room are not working for them. In the incident that led to the first decision on flag-burning by the Supreme Court, Joey Johnson and his Revolutionary Communist Party colleagues burned an American flag outside the Republican National Convention in 1984. They did so because they had no position inside the convention and felt this was the only way of calling public attention to their dismay with government policies. Likewise, the young African American artist Dread Scott did not create his flag-on-the-floor artwork, which was displayed in Chicago at the time of the flag-burning controversy, because he was the idol of Chicago art lovers. And certainly, 2 Live Crew is far from a pillar of the cultural establishment.

Quite simply, because such groups and individuals do not control either political or media power levers, they are often frustrated by their inability to communicate their views. They move towards more outrageous expression to get attention and be heard. They find it necessary to shock and offend. They show disrespect because they feel it. The First Amendment, believe it or not, was written for them.

Two very different establishment groups have recently confirmed this understanding. In August 1989 a special committee of the American Bar Association, composed of law school deans, a former secretary and a former deputy secretary of state, a former internal revenue commissioner, a former United States attorney, and a former solicitor general, unanimously urged Congress to abandon efforts to outlaw desecrating the flag. The committee said:

> The American flag commands respect and love because of our country's adherence to its values and its promise of freedom—not because of fiat and criminal law. . . . It is just when people take great offense because of disrespect shown to an honored symbol that the right of free expression needs protection, not prosecution.[9]

In the same month the directors of six major arts organizations that then received funding from the National Endowment for the Arts—from the Chicago Art Institute to the American Dance Festival—published in the *New York Times* their views on what works in their fields could have been banned under the Helms amendment. They noted everything from Shakespeare's "Merchant of Venice" and Moliere's "Tartuffe," which denigrate religion, to D.W. Griffith's movie "The Birth of a Nation" and all Tarzan and Western movies, which denigrate ethnic and racial groups. Typical is the comment of the general director of the San Francisco Opera:

> Dealing as it does with the most extreme human emotions, even the standard operatic repertoire would come under fire if the Helms restrictions were indiscriminately applied.[10]

If you are skeptical about the insights of American bar or art leaders on these points, it is worth noting the approach of the Chinese government. In the same month as the preceding comments and two months after the Chinese government brutally squelched the democracy movement in Tienanmen Square, the *People's Daily*, the Chinese Communist Party newspaper, accused "a small group of thugs" of using freedom of press to confuse readers and to "cook up rumors and instigate attacks on the Party and the people." It warned that "the press . . . must take a clear-cut stand in supporting correct political directions." Meanwhile, the works of ten writers were banned outright and the Propaganda Department sent investigators into news organizations to find and punish those who "sympathized" with protestors.[11] The following year the government proposed a new press law that requires the press to uphold the leadership of the Communist Party, Marxist thought, and socialism.[12] Clearly the Chinese government understands the core problem—that speech, if unregulated, will frequently be critical, disrespectful, and offensive.

The First Amendment rejects the Chinese response to this challenge. As a Vietnam veteran who now works for a state government told me, it is insulting to say that American soldiers shed blood to protect a colored piece of cloth, purchased for a few dollars in a discount store, from being torn or singed. Did they also die, as noted recently by a former federal employee, to prevent the American flag stamp from being canceled or postmarked?[13] No, they fought so that we would all be free to express our dissatisfaction with our government without fear of reprisal, in whatever manner our political situations, creative skills, and frustration levels dictate.

Writing Letters May Be Hazardous to Your Rights

There are some stories that are simply too wild to be believed. This is one of them. Unfortunately it is a true story. Even worse, it is about our government.

In 1983, when he was twelve years old and in the sixth grade, Todd Patterson had an idea. Not content with his local library's resources for a school assignment, Todd decided to create his own encyclopedia of the world. He wrote letters to all 169 foreign governments seeking information about each country. He mailed the letters in envelopes from his father's domestic laboratory supply business, which was conducted out of the family home.

His international correspondence caught the eye of some agency of the United States government. Some of his foreign mail arrived in damaged condition. Strange clicks on the telephone made his father suspicious; finally, he said into the phone: "If you want to know something, come and talk to us." Two days later, in the fall of 1983, an FBI agent appeared at the Patterson home. Todd's mother showed the agent his correspondence, and Todd, who was not home at the time, later spoke with the agent. Also Todd voluntarily notified the agent the following summer when he was invited to visit the Soviet Mission in New York City.

Over the years, at least fifty pieces of mail have arrived at the Patterson home torn, opened, or otherwise damaged. Once Todd received an envelope from the Soviet Mission in New York City which was resealed and stamped: "Received in damaged condition by the Postal Service." Inside was an envelope from Sweden addressed to a total stranger in a nearby town. In response to Todd's inquiry, the Director of the Postal Service's Mail Classification Office said he had no explanation for the damaged mail. The FBI insists that its investigation ended after the agent's 1983 home visit. But there is a 1985 FBI memo and a 1988 news clipping in Todd's FBI file, and foreign mail occasionally still comes to the Patterson home in damaged condition.

In 1986 an employee of the father's company picked up his telephone, which was connected to the business phone by call-forwarding, and heard a voice say "Operator, this is not the phone I want tapped."

In 1987, Todd, then sixteen, learned of the Freedom of Information Act (FOIA) and requested a copy of his FBI file. It was first denied, but after an administrative appeal six pages were released which were heavily blacked out for reasons of "national security."

In May 1988, Todd sued the government with the help of the American Civil Liberties Union. The main goals were first to uncover the full contents of Todd's FBI file pursuant to FOIA, and then to have the file destroyed under the federal Privacy Act, which prevents the government from gathering and maintaining records about the exercise of First Amendment rights. Todd wanted the file destroyed so that his intended future career with the Foreign Service or the State Department would not be impaired. A claim was also brought directly under the First Amendment and mail tampering statutes against both the FBI and the as yet unknown agency of the federal government that initially intercepted the mail.

Todd's struggles with secret government were re-doubled once he got to court. First, the FBI refused to provide any significant information or documents, relying on a court-created legal doctrine, the "state secrets privilege," that allows the executive branch not to disclose military and national security secrets in court. The FBI did release some more pages from his file—at last count the total was twenty-four pages—but most of them were blacked out and marked "classified" or "secret." One that was not blacked out, but still stamped "secret," was a *New York Post* article about the filing of Todd's lawsuit in 1988!

Second, the trial judge decided the case in secret. Judge Alfred Wolin, a Reagan appointee, first upheld the government's refusal to provide any information under the state secrets privilege, which sounds like and reminds one of England's Official Secrets Act. (See

"Mother England's Not-So-Free Press," page 41.) He then reviewed Todd's unedited FBI file alone in his chambers, along with a secret FBI affidavit explaining why it was afraid that release of the file would reveal foreign intelligence sources or investigative methods. Based on his own review of the file and affidavit, the judge ruled for the government on all claims, concluding that the FBI acted lawfully, there was nothing derogatory in the file about Todd, and the FBI's conduct had "negligible First Amendment implications."[14]

Although admitting that "at first blush, the investigation appears ludicrous," Judge Wolin found that national security precluded disclosure of the file under the Freedom of Information Act. Most amazingly the judge also ruled that retention of the file for over five years after the innocent truth was discovered by the FBI did not violate the Privacy Act's explicit ban on government *maintenance* of files about Americans' exercise of First Amendment rights that were not relevant to a legitimate law enforcement function.[15] He stated that the "regulations which authorized the activities undertaken by [the FBI] in this case did not impermissibly chill plaintiff's First Amendment right of free speech."[16] Further he concluded that there was no evidence that any mail had been opened and suggested that "the distance the mail traveled, the size and content of the envelopes, and the national origin of the mail are the far more likely culprits in assessing why plaintiff's mail may have arrived in damaged condition."[17] In any case, he ruled, the state secrets privilege precludes Todd from finding out if the judge was right.

The Third Circuit Court of Appeals in Philadelphia pursued the same "trust us" approach to justice on the appeal of that decision, but added another secrecy twist. They, too, reviewed the file and FBI affidavit in secret and assured Todd that there was nothing to worry about. They, too, did not explain why maintenance of now six-year-old records about a twelve-year-old boy was relevant to a current legitimate law enforcement function. They, too, failed to explain why they required the government to show only "relevance," when the Privacy Act's legislative history and the implementing guidelines from Nixon's own Office of Management and Budget defined a stricter standard. But unlike the trial court, the appeals court did not even consider the First Amendment claim. It concluded that because the state secrets privilege precluded discovery of the name of the federal agency accused of intercepting and opening the mail, the Pattersons

could never serve it with court papers. Thus the court had no jurisdiction over the agency and could not consider the First Amendment
claim against it.[18]

In October 1990, the United States Supreme Court announced—
albeit in open court—that it would not review this case.[19]

It is distressing and ironic that a court action intended to discover
the nature and propriety of secret government action (which would
be known as "covert action" if done overseas) should be resolved
through secret proceedings. A young man, pursuing the ideals of our
country through the methods prescribed by our Constitution, seeks
to learn about the world in which he is growing up by writing letters
for information. He then follows the laws of his country in asking his
government whether it has any files on him that would hinder his
chances of serving his government when he grows up. Thereafter he
asks the courts, which he was taught constitute an independent branch
of government, to determine what is going on and they respond:
"Trust us! The government has shown us everything and all is in
order." Due process must mean more. Whatever the technical justifications for this ruling, we must ask what lessons this young man
and others around the country will derive from this approach.

Of even deeper concern, however, is the courts' view that there
are legitimate law enforcement reasons for, and "negligible First
Amendment implications" from, the government unearthing, investigating, and then indefinitely keeping substantial, classified files
about the admittedly innocent international correspondence of an
American citizen. Do they mean that the First Amendment does not
protect letter-writing to other countries or that FBI monitoring has
no impact on a citizen's activities? In this ever shrinking and ever
more interdependent planet of ours, in which my industrial smoke is
your acid rain, and in which entire cities can be obliterated by in-
advertence or overreaction, it is vital that the peoples of the world
get to know each other and their differing cultures, social mores, and
governmental systems. Could one really doubt that knowing the FBI
will conduct on-going surveillance would adversely affect, or as we
say in constitutional law "chill," citizens' willingness to try such tentative, exploratory, non-commercial communication?

The First Amendment protects a most fragile component of human behavior—the exploration of ideas—one for which few are willing
to shed blood, forfeit careers, or take on the full force of the law

enforcement community. They shouldn't have to. Although the Supreme Court refused to wrestle with the threat to our national security posed by a curious twelve-year old, it is imperative that Congress, the only branch not yet besmirched by this case, re-examine the role of the FBI relative to domestic political activity and draft a formal statutory charter that safeguards free pursuit of ideas as well as domestic tranquillity.

Charging for Free Speech

There is no such thing as a free speech. Almost all public expression has some cost, whether it is the expense of publishing a book such as this, xeroxing flyers to announce a rally, or renting a hall for an organizational meeting. An increasing number of towns and cities around the country have tried to add a new cost by requiring sponsors of public rallies or marches, as a condition of obtaining an event permit, to purchase insurance and/or promise to pay any claims against the city as a result of the event. Because the sponsors of such events are often small, ad hoc groups with minimal funds, these requirements may amount to a denial of permission to hold the event. Because of their limited resources and controversial views, these groups also have few alternative means of presenting their ideas to the public. The First Amendment's profound concern for robust public debate on all issues of public importance, regardless of the viewpoint presented, requires that we scrutinize such demands for insurance carefully.

The main question I always ask in such cases[20] is: why is the town requesting insurance? I have never received a satisfactory answer. Of course, the response is usually "to prevent damage to persons and property." But what damage, by whom, and to whom?

The first area to separate out is damage to the demonstrators themselves, such as what happened when Martin Luther King walked over the bridge in Selma, Alabama, or through the Chicago suburbs. Our law has long rejected the idea of a "heckler's veto," that is, letting opponents silence the speaker through hostile and improper conduct, such as heckling or throwing rocks. Likewise, we can hardly let opponents create insurmountable financial burdens by convincing city hall that the marchers must buy insurance for what the opponents might do to them. Opponents should not be able to raise the ante by raising a ruckus.

Similarly, demonstrators cannot be asked to insure against police misconduct or negligence. Courts have regularly held that municipal duties, such as the obligation to maintain public streets in safe condition, cannot be delegated to private parties. And the Bill of Rights is meant to control police misconduct, not its victims. Both insurance principles and constitutional concerns for deterring government misconduct preclude such a shift in financial accountability.

We thus reach the primary concern in requiring insurance: to cover damage resulting from the intentional or negligent conduct of the participants themselves. Municipal demands for insurance, like those seeking indemnification, reflect apprehension that the town might be held liable for the participants' conduct. This fear is, quite simply, groundless. In no case, including the many unpublished decisions I have found and the cases that did not go to court that I have been involved in or heard about, has there been any evidence of towns ever having been held liable for the behavior of public demonstrators, and no insurance association was able to produce any such instance at my request.

This is predictable for at least two major reasons. Court decisions and statutes throughout the country leave towns immune from liability for the conduct of private groups or persons acting with government authorization, whether it be a barber license or a hunting permit, because such persons are clearly not employees or agents of the government. In addition, the statutes that give up the ancient "sovereign immunity" of the state and permit some lawsuits against the government for acts of its employees, almost invariably retain immunity for failure to enforce the law, for example by failing to provide adequate police protection. Thus town attorneys, while understandably anxious to protect their clients in these times of exploding insurance and liability costs, have simply overreacted in this area.

Finally, there is the question of requiring participants to obtain liability insurance for their own conduct, much as drivers are required to have car insurance, not to protect the town but to insure that injured parties are compensated. Although there is a superficial appeal to this analogy, it quickly breaks down. Rallying and marching are not intrinsically dangerous activities, as driving is. Moreover one must ask, under the First Amendment, why are marchers forced to provide insurance, but not other people in public who are not driving cars, such as pedestrians in busy downtown intersections, business messengers on bicycles, or football players in the park? It is illogical to suggest that planned activities supervised by police after advance notice and the opportunity to prepare and regulate, such as protest marches that must seek permits, are more likely to produce injuries than unplanned events. I, for one, would feel much safer at a protest rally of 10,000 than at a Sunday afternoon football game with ten college chums.

But even if it were true that planned activities are more likely to produce damage, the basic First Amendment problem is that, by requiring a rally permit applicant to obtain insurance, towns are imposing financial liability simply because of political association. Common sense suggests that when sponsoring organizations have peaceful purposes, any injuries or damage will most likely be caused by rowdy, last-minute joiners over whom the sponsor will have little, if any, control, rather than by those deeply involved in the event's planning. These spontaneous troublemakers would not be considered employees or agents of the sponsoring group under traditional personal injury law, which makes an organization responsible for the negligence of its employees. In any case, the First Amendment imposes far more stringent requirements than ordinary law for imposing liability on a group. Moreover, insurance by its nature requires advance payment. Thus towns are asking current peaceful members to pay, regardless of their own conduct, for the possible improper acts of those who might choose later to associate with their cause.

The Supreme Court has addressed a closely related problem in a 1982 case called *NAACP v. Claiborne Hardware, Co.*[21] In that case, the Court held improper, under the First Amendment, Mississippi's attempt to hold the NAACP, which organized an economic boycott to protest racial discrimination, liable to the local merchants for damage to their stores or businesses. The damage resulted from improper conduct, such as threats or actual violence, by a few participants. To impose group liability, the Court said, the First Amendment requires a showing either that the group had unlawful goals that the misbehaving individual knew of and sought to advance, or that the group had specifically authorized the individual's improper conduct in advance or expressly ratified it afterwards. The Court in no way altered either the rule that ordinarily makes individuals financially respon-

57

sible for what they themselves do, intentionally or negligently, or the obligations of groups dedicated to violence. But because of the First Amendment, it simply would not allow liability to be imposed on a political sponsor with peaceful intentions but a few raucous followers. If an organizing group cannot be held responsible in such a setting after violence actually occurs, surely a requirement for advance payment of an insurance premium based on mere speculation or fear of violence is not permissible.

But even if insurance could be required in theory, there are enormous problems in practice. What does one do with a reviled group like the Nazis to whom no one will sell insurance, as actually happened in the famous case in Skokie, Illinois? What about a group that literally cannot afford the insurance, even if some broker would write a policy? The few court decisions in this area that specifically address these concerns have held it unconstitutional to require insurance when literally none can be obtained, either as a result of prejudice or cost.

In sum, there is no legitimate need for insurance and the burden is misplaced. Rather than impose unnecessary or unreasonable insurance burdens, our federal, state and local government officials should be sitting down with public event sponsors to map out reasonable routes and plan intelligent use of crowd dividers, police escorts, and monitors. They should then train the police on how to separate the troublemakers from the citizens peacefully exercising their First Amendment rights. We know it can be done because it already is being done every week in towns across this country.

Talking Politics Door-to-Door

As our national elections become ever more electronic, it is important to remember that in local elections and a wide variety of non-electoral campaigns, most politicking in this country is still done in person. Despite the lure of thirty-second spots, phone banks, and glitzy mailings, one of the most common and inexpensive technique for personal political contact is still the door-to-door canvass. Certainly that is true for the less-well-financed community and grass-roots organizations. Although Jehovah's Witnesses won the right to proselytize in person in a series of Supreme Court cases in the 1940's, the comparable right of political groups is again in question. Towns throughout the country are seeking to impose time restrictions and new licensing requirements on political canvassers. The recent spread of citizen action groups has engendered new constitutional consideration of the subject.

The most common regulations imposed by towns are a 5:00 p.m. curfew on residential canvassing and a fingerprint requirement for those wishing to go door-to-door. The most frequent challengers are citizen groups that depend on daily contact with a large number of individuals for their financing and political organizing. The most important decision is *New Jersey Citizen Action v. Edison Township*,[22] in which a federal appellate court struck down 5:00 p.m. curfews and a fingerprint rule from six communities as violating the First Amendment. The key questions are: Why are the regulations enacted? Why can't the political groups live with them? And why does the First Amendment prohibit them?

Both the curfew and fingerprint requirements reflect a growing fear of crime. The evidence, however, is that neither rule protects against crime and that this obviously legitimate goal can be achieved by means that intrude far less on the political rights of canvassers. Some towns suggested that burglars might pretend to be canvassers. But most burglaries do not occur in the evening when people are at home, but rather during the day when the house is vacant. Legitimizing door-to-door visits only during the day hardly undercuts the burglar. None of the many citizen group canvassers in the case mentioned above had been arrested for a crime—except, in a few instances, the "crime" of canvassing after 5:00 p.m. Comparisons of demographically similar towns with and without canvassing curfews show no significant differences in crime rates and any changes in the crime rates in towns that have imposed canvassing curfews are consistent with the downward national crime trends.[23]

Fingerprinting, of course, is a good way of finding people with prior criminal records. But it only works if you have access to the records. In the *Citizen Action* case, it was shown that for years the towns could not get the FBI or the state police to process the fingerprints they received from permit applicants. Thus local police could only check them against their own local arrest records for criminals they would have known about anyway. The towns' police experts also confirmed that there was no noticeable impact on crime when FBI and state police processing of applicant fingerprints stopped.[24]

In any event there are far less intrusive alternative licensing requirements, not objected to by political organizers, that will effectively deter the participation of criminals. Most prominent are requirements that the canvassers register in advance with the police, that they provide the police before starting with maps of their canvassing routes, and that they wear an identification badge with a picture if that is deemed helpful. By these means, both the police and the public will know who is canvassing where and, thus, who is not a burglar. A police expert for the towns said that police "can be almost positive that nothing is going to be done" by a registered but unfingerprinted canvasser.[25]

Towns that impose a curfew also cite the need to protect privacy. The evidence shows, however, that as many as two-thirds of the people approached at home between 8:00 and 9:00 p.m. (which is the latest hour that citizen groups will canvass even without a legal restriction) sign petitions and close to 40 percent of them make financial contributions. At no time of day or evening are more than 5 percent of people approached overtly hostile to canvassers and there is no noticeable increase in hostility as the hour gets later.[26] The government is not normally allowed to impose uniform restrictions to satisfy the preferences of a small minority, and this situation should be no different. People who are annoyed can always post "No Trespassing" or "No Solicitors" signs and enforce them by calling the police, if they want to protect their quiet and privacy. In any case a canvassing curfew cannot prevent the privacy intrusions effected by telephone calls from political, commercial, and charitable solicitors who can afford to use that technique.

How important is the right to canvass in the evening? To put it plainly, canvassing groups cannot survive otherwise. In the world of two household breadwinners, few adults are at home before 5:00 p.m. on weekdays. Saturday canvassing does not provide sufficient time to reach a targeted community or to afford the full-time employment needed to attract and retain canvassers. Phone and mail canvassing do not produce immediate cash and thus can only be used by groups with established bank accounts. Mailings, moreover, are expensive. Shopping center solicitations do not allow one to focus on voters or residents of a particular town or district. In short, there are no adequate alternatives to home canvassing for many small or newly formed groups or for those with a specific geographic focus.

The First Amendment, quite simply, does not permit infringement upon peaceful political activity where, as here, the restrictions do not significantly advance the government's legitimate goals—in this case, reducing crime and protecting privacy, alternative rules serve those interests more directly, and there are no adequate alternatives to the regulated behavior.

I share the annoyance of many when my dinner is interrupted by the doorbell or the telephone. I do not like, in any case, to be pressed for a contribution or signature without an opportunity to reflect. But I am also not prepared to turn my back—or slam my front door—on a fundamental premise of our society: that our world and our government would be better if people would talk to each other about common problems and possible solutions.

It's Scandalous What Some Think Is Slanderous

Sometimes I think I am naive. Every time I hear about another libel suit against a citizen speaking out or writing to the editor, I say to myself: "It can't be; there must be a mistake." Every time I read the legal documents, I must pinch myself to realize I'm not dreaming. Once I even called a senior partner of a firm on whose stationery such a complaint was typed to tell him to check who stole the firm's letterhead. Every time the ACLU gets one of these frivolous matters thrown out, I wonder whether there shouldn't be some penalty or other deterrent for the lawyers, if not for the public officials, who have all sworn to uphold the Constitution. Certainly more than a quarter century after *New York Times Co. v. Sullivan*,[27] the leading case setting constitutional limits on slander and libel actions, it should be considered settled law.

I wish I had only a few examples:

• Student editors of a college newspaper are sued by a college administrator because of a spoof classified ad using her name that was published in the annual April Fool's Day issue.

• A tenant organizer is sued by a major local landlord for statements made at a public hearing of the town council considering an ordinance relating to tenant rights.

• A former county employee is sued by the county administrator for allegedly distributing an anonymous newsletter criticizing the county government and the administrator in particular.

• A local police union sues a community group leader for writing a letter to the editor of the local paper critical of unnamed police officers for moonlighting as security guards and for harassing young people in town.

• A principal and three teachers sue a parent and grandparent because of critical comments about the school quoted in the press and included in a letter written to the school.

• A landlord already determined by the judge to have racially discriminated in renting apartments sues the plaintiff's expert witness and the canvassers who did a survey of the tenants in one of the landlord's developments because of the report they prepared for use in the case.

• A union dissident is sued by the union for harassment and making false statements about the leadership.

• A company sued for environmental violations brings a libel counterclaim against the environmental group which brought the suit for having distributed a leaflet listing the company as one of the "Dirty Dozen."

• A student reporter and school coach are sued by a local athletic club for remarks about the club by the coach quoted in the high school newspaper. The reporter in turn brings the student editor of the paper into the lawsuit.

The ACLU has obtained dismissal or withdrawal of the first seven cases; the last two are still pending at this writing.

None of these is a close case. The law has been clear now for over a quarter century that neither a government official nor a public figure can win a slander or libel suit under the First Amendment without proving that the statement was both false and made with knowledge of, or at least "reckless disregard" for, its falsity. True statements of fact and opinions not amounting to assertions of fact are absolutely protected by the First Amendment.

The problem, which is evident from my examples and the statement of the law, is that although suits like these clearly cannot be *won*, there is little to stop them from being *brought*. Defending such a lawsuit to the point of dismissal or favorable judgment often entails substantial and costly pretrial depositions and exchanges of information called "discovery" and preparation of extensive legal briefs.

The part-time student organization that partially funded the April Fool's spoof edition in the first example spent $90,000 in legal fees before the case was finally dismissed. A pending lawsuit also imposes substantial anxiety and uncertainty upon the letter-writer or speaker. Most importantly, knowledge that such lawsuits can be brought and that even defending against them successfully is very costly and time-consuming will deter, or "chill," some citizens from speaking out at public meetings or writing to the local paper—activities that the First Amendment was designed to foster.

The only restraints now in effect are the laws or court rules (Rule 11 in federal court) that permit courts to impose monetary penalties on lawyers as well as parties for filing frivolous lawsuits or engaging in frivolous proceedings after a suit is brought. Lawyers working in the public interest sector, typically legal services and civil rights attorneys, have generally been hesitant to seek sanctions under provisions like Rule 11. This is primarily out of fear that regular invocation will backfire and lead to misuse against those bringing controversial civil rights litigation or actions based on novel constitutional theories. The history of Rule 11 bears this fear out; sanctions have been imposed disproportionately upon lawyers representing civil rights plaintiffs.[28] Moreover, many public interest lawyers believe that people should not be deterred from bringing their grievances to court even if they entail unusual or novel legal theories.

These concerns seem inapplicable, however, to the kind of libel cases outlined above. Those cases are in no sense efforts by conscientious litigants seeking, as did the civil rights movement in the 1960's, measured modification or principled reconsideration of constitutional rulings. These are lawsuits brought by individuals with no doctrinal or philosophical motivation and no likelihood of success. The sole purpose is to punish or intimidate those who have spoken out publicly in ways that the plaintiff does not like. Public interest lawyers are rightfully fearful of the misuse of sanctions and understandably urge repeal of such provisions. But if, as is likely, such rules remain in effect, the public interest bar should reconsider whether their careful application to litigants and lawyers who step entirely outside the limits might not, in the long run, produce greater compliance with constitutional principles by all. Certainly the current state of affairs is not tolerable for those who believe in the rule of law and the free public exchange of ideas.

Racial Slurs: Free Speech or Discrimination?

Public debate is rarely elegant. Street corner speakers and rally orators don't use the $200 words or smooth expressions of a William Buckley. This is because their words reflect deep emotions about controversial matters. They often express disrespect, disgust, disappointment, or moral outrage. Tolerance of such harsh criticism is the price of free expression.

But free speech is not absolute. Threats of violence are punishable as assault, and misrepresentations to consumers can be the basis for civil and criminal penalties. Some movies are so offensive and without artistic merit that they may be banned as obscene. Intentional falsehoods that smear another's reputation are condemned as libel. Drawing the line on protected speech is most difficult, however, when the words are opinions, not facts, and threaten emotional, not physical, injury yet undermine another of our society's fundamental constitutional values: eradicating racial and religious discrimination.

The most famous recent example of this conflict of rights was the American Nazi Party's attempt in the late 1970's to hold a rally in the village of Skokie, Illinois. Skokie was almost 60 percent Jewish and many thousand residents were survivors of Hitler's Holocaust. The marchers were few in number, but they threatened to wear Nazi uniforms and swastikas. Skokie denied them a permit, relying upon a specially adopted ordinance that banned any assembly that would:

> portray criminality, depravity or lack of virtue in, or incite violence, hatred, abuse or hostility toward a person or group of persons by reason of reference to religious, racial, ethnic, national or regional affiliation.[29]

The town contended that it could ban this virulently hateful display because it would cause irreparable psychic damage to the numerous Holocaust survivors in town.

The ACLU represented the Nazis and challenged the ordinance and the denial of a permit. This decision, consistent with the ACLU's long standing commitment to free speech, cost the organization many thousand members who could not stomach this particularly obnoxious and insulting form of political speech.

The courts agreed with the ACLU, struck down the ordinance, and ordered the town to issue a rally permit. The courts recognized the intense emotional injury that exposure to this display could inflict upon Holocaust survivors. Nevertheless, they noted that no one was forced to observe the event and, given the advance publicity, survivors in town would hardly risk stumbling upon it inadvertently. More importantly, the courts reiterated the traditional First Amendment requirement that listeners who find speech or art obnoxious must shield their eyes or ears rather than ask the government to ban the expression.

This issue has come up again recently as a result of university efforts to ban racist slurs. These policies are a reaction to the disturbing growth in the use of racist epithets in flyers, speeches, graffiti, and comments in classrooms, dorms, and elsewhere. The increase in such language reflects both long-simmering racist attitudes and a greater willingness to express them and act on them openly. Such slurs can be particularly inhibiting to racial minorities who may be few in number and already feel isolated within the university and especially frightening to those living in dormitories near those expressing these hateful views.

This conflict of free expression and racial equality rights is particularly intense in the university setting. Academics are deeply devoted to complete freedom from scrutiny or penalty for any intellectual inquiry or expression, capsulized in the phrase "academic freedom." Accordingly they exalt tolerance and free expression as the highest university virtues. At the same time, universities have been in the forefront of societal efforts to overcome past discrimination and diversify the classroom and workplace. They deeply believe in judging people only by their intellectual abilities and not by the color of their skin. Consequently, they strive to make minorities comfortable and accepted in the university setting so that they may concentrate on and excel in their studies.

No one can question the motives of the universities that have developed policies banning racist and other insulting speech. The issue is whether they have appropriately balanced the significant competing academic and constitutional interests.

The most famous attempt failed. The University of Michigan adopted in April 1988 a policy that subjected students to discipline for:

Any behavior, verbal or physical, that stigmatizes or victimizes an individual on the basis of race, ethnicity, religion, sex, sexual orientation . . . and that

b. has the purpose or reasonably foreseeable effect of interfering with an individual's academic efforts . . . or

c. Creates an intimidating, hostile or demeaning environment for educational pursuits, employment or participation in University sponsored extra-curricular activities.[30]

Any one could file a complaint under the policy, which could lead to a formal hearing and sanctions ranging from a reprimand to removal from university housing, suspension, or expulsion. In August 1988, the university announced that it was withdrawing subsection (c) because of the need for clarification.

Shortly thereafter, the university issued a guidebook explaining what the policy banned. Examples included not only "racist graffiti on the door of an Asian student's study carrel" but also:

A male student makes remarks in class like "women just aren't as good in this field as men" thus creating a hostile learning atmosphere for female classmates.

Students in a residence hall have a floor party and invite everyone on their floor except one person because they think she might be a lesbian.

You exclude someone from a study group because that person is of a different race, sex, or ethnic origin than you are.

Your student organization sponsors entertainment that includes a comedian who slurs Hispanics.

A few cases were pursued under the policy. In one, a complaint was filed and a hearing held because a social work student stated in class that homosexuality was a disease and he wanted to develop a counseling plan for changing gay clients. The student was acquitted. However in two other incidents, the university required apologies and informal counseling, in one because a student in business school read a limerick ridiculing a famous athlete's sexual orientation and in another because a teacher complained when a dental student said he had heard, as it turned out from an African American roommate, that minorities had difficulties in a particular dentistry course.

The policy was challenged in court by the ACLU on behalf of a biopsychology graduate student who was studying controversial theories on biological differences between sexes and races that he feared might be perceived as "sexist" or "racist" and therefore subject to discipline under the policy. The court found the policy both too vague, in that it failed to warn students of exactly what words might be punished, and too broad because it included constitutionally protected speech that the state-run school had no power to prohibit.

As the court in Michigan recognized, there is a longstanding doctrine in First Amendment law that "fighting words" are not protected by the Constitution, just as obscenity, incitement to riot, and libel are not protected. Fighting words had been defined by the Supreme Court in a 1942 case as "those which by their very utterance inflict injury or tend to incite an immediate breach of the peace."[31] This has turned out to be an even narrower category than its wording might suggest. Insults, even vile ones, shouted at police officers have not been punished under this rule.[32] Display of the swastika in Skokie did not qualify. Indeed, since that first case, the Supreme Court has never upheld a conviction for fighting words. Its rulings have clarified that to insure that speech is not punished merely because it is unpopular or uncomfortable, only those grossly insulting and provocative words spoken one-on-one to an individual in a setting in which a violent reaction is unavoidable can be banned.[33]

Perhaps a vile and provocative racial slur directly shouted at an individual minority student during a confrontation in a dormitory hall could be sanctioned under the "fighting words" doctrine. But given the close quarters and the clear intent of communicating to a specific individual, such a statement might well violate more general laws or rules against intimidation or harassment. As the court in Michigan reminded us, however, we must be careful to distinguish between general statements about other groups, however insulting, and specific personal attacks.

University bans on racist speech are not the answer for several reasons. First, as the Michigan case illustrates, they almost inevitably face serious First Amendment limitations; to be constitutional, they may outlaw only a few of the racist expressions that rightfully disturb us. Second, they are unnecessary to address many other common incidents: all graffiti are prohibited by criminal law and student codes, regardless of their message, and all threats and unwanted physical contacts are illegal, regardless of their motivation. Third, such policies do not address, and are not needed to address, serious racially motivated violence, which is prohibited by regular criminal laws and subject now in several states to close law enforcement scrutiny and enhanced penalties.

Finally, and most importantly, such policies do not address the underlying racism, which is the real problem. As the American Jewish Committee has outlined in its recent thoughtful publication, *Bigotry on Campus: A Planned Response*, the entire university community must be mobilized to deal with racism comprehensively. Everyone from the board of trustees to the resident counselors in the dormitories must clearly and regularly articulate and enforce the policies against racial discrimination. Faculty and staff, including housing staff, must be diversified to establish a role model for the students. Sensitivity training must be provided for students as well as dormitory counselors and other staff. Public forums should be held both to discuss the issues directly and to present prominent speakers of all backgrounds. Cultural differences should be celebrated, by ethnic fairs and the like, not just noted or tolerated. Racist and sexist theories or comments in class should be challenged, analyzed, and rebutted.

In sum, we need to eliminate by word and deed both the appearance and reality of racial intolerance, even while recognizing that we must tolerate most of the disgusting language of the few and hopefully increasingly isolated bigots in our midst.

How Can You Petition When the Doors Are Closed?

If one were to ask the average citizen what the First Amendment protects, the answer would most likely refer to one of four well-known clauses: those guaranteeing freedom of speech, press, and religion, and the one prohibiting the "establishment" of religion. Less well-known and less frequently invoked is the right "to petition the government for a redress of grievances." Its fame is limited because everyone, including the government, takes it for granted and because it is often seen as included within freedom of expression. Actually it has its own force and vivid history. Unfortunately the government occasionally overreacts and clamps down on critics even when exercising this most basic, direct, and usually peaceful method of political protest.

To get a flavor of its purpose, one must know some history. In 1790, reacting to a gathering of 150,000 people presenting petitions, the English Parliament prohibited public meetings of more than fifty people to petition the King unless the meeting was held in the presence of a magistrate with authority to arrest everyone present! Using a comparable approach, the United States House of Representatives adopted in 1836 a rule tabling without discussion all petitions on the subject of slavery, including, of course, the many urging abolition of slavery. In 1840, the House amended the rule to simply prohibit *receipt* of any petition on the subject. It took former President John Quincy Adams, then a member of the House, four years to convince the House to repeal that rule.[34] Clearly the petition clause responds

70

to the natural tendency of even democratic governments to hear only what they want to hear.

Two famous instances of petitioning restrictions have reached the Supreme Court. Once, during the civil rights struggle of the 1960's, a few hundred young African American demonstrators marched peacefully in groups of fifteen from a church to the South Carolina State House grounds in Columbia, where all three branches of state government were headquartered, to protest segregation. The demonstrators walked single file or two abreast around the grounds. About 200 to 300 onlookers gathered. Although the police later admitted that there had been no threats by or against the protestors and that they were not blocking pedestrian passage, the police ordered the group to disperse. The testimony was that they responded with "boisterous, loud, and flamboyant conduct," which included "listening to a religious harangue" from one of the ministers and "loudly singing the Star Spangled Banner."[35] A total of 187 people were then arrested for breach of the peace. The Supreme Court noted that a protest at the seat of government is the quintessential form of political expression and overturned the convictions as violating the First Amendment, relying on both the right to petition clause and the free speech provision.

In 1980, the Supreme Court was confronted with an Air Force rule that prohibited people in the service from circulating petitions to members of Congress or other public officials without approval of their commander. The petition in question, which was addressed to the secretary of defense and members of Congress, concerned Air Force grooming standards. Air Force Reserve Captain Glines had given the petition to a sergeant, who had obtained eight signatures on it. Glines was removed from active duty and reassigned to standby reserves. The Court upheld the restriction, refusing to apply the protections of the First Amendment, including the petition clause relied upon by the dissenting justices, with full force to the military. The Court amazingly also decided that the rule did not violate a federal statute that expressly safeguards the right of people in the armed services to communicate with Congress for redress of grievances, concluding that the law protects only an individual letter to a soldier's own representative, but not a collective petition. This narrow interpretation ignores the political reality that collective action is more effective than individual effort and that the petition clause speaks to the right of the "people," not just of individuals, to demand a change in government policy.

In 1988, we experienced in New Jersey a dramatic example of similarly arbitrary restraint on public petitioning in the classic civilian setting. A number of citizens, including clergy and members of well-recognized community organizations, went to the state capital to call upon the legislature to increase the funding for welfare grants, which had not been increased in eleven years. The protest was given impetus by a recent state appellate court decision—ironically, resulting from the government's failure to respond to a petition by over 100 community groups—that the Department of Human Services must calculate and certify to the legislature each year the current financial needs for basic subsistence to permit the legislature to determine the appropriate level of welfare grants.[36] After holding a press conference, the group followed its previously announced schedule and went in mid-afternoon to the State House Annex where the legislature was meeting, both to observe the legislative session and to lobby individual lawmakers.

They were met at the door by a state trooper who told them they could not enter. They were not told why. Requests to see a supervisor were unavailing; only more troopers showed up. When one assemblyman, a former speaker, came out and invited the fifty individuals in as his guests, he was treated no better. The answer was "no" and without explanation.

As legal director of the American Civil Liberties Union of New Jersey, I received telephone calls from the scene from two participants. My immediate call to state police headquarters produced an explanation that there had been a sit-in that day in the rotunda of the neighboring State House and the troopers were trying to avoid an escalation of the situation. I was assured that the persons I was in touch with need only ask a trooper to see a supervisor to be informed of the situation. After I so advised them, the protestors calling me went up to three separate troopers but each simply said "no, you cannot speak to a supervisor."

As it turned out later, five or six people from another *unrelated* group, seeking greater aid for the homeless, had been sitting in the office of the deputy to the governor in the State House since noon that day, seeking an appointment with the governor. No one had sat in at the rotunda and, indeed, the group that I was dealing with, which was barred from the neighboring annex, was told by the troopers to go into the rotunda to wait! Most importantly, no one had been accused of doing anything improper in the annex at the time that the doors were barred, and the persons sitting in the governor's staff office were not ordered to leave until 7:30 that evening (at which point those who refused were arrested).

The legislative leaders who met with the state police superintendent later that week seemed satisfied by his promise that in the future he would keep them informed of any decisions by himself or others in the executive branch to close off the legislative branch of government from the public, even though he did not offer to consult with them or allow them to make the decision. As a result of ACLU letters and a meeting we had with the attorney general and the state police superintendent, the policy was later changed to require consultation with, and deference to, the preferences of the leaders of the legislature, which was to be viewed as the "tenant" of the building for which the state police provided security. Legislative preference could be ignored only if the state police were convinced that a significant and imminent physical danger existed. The right to petition the legislature peacefully was restored.

These facts bespeak an obvious and classic violation of the fundamental right to petition the government for redress of grievances. Obvious because one cannot deprive individual citizens of their constitutional rights because of a mere suspicion that they might abuse the right or because someone else has violated the law. Classic because the most typical government error is overreaction, sweeping up both the innocent and guilty. Even assuming that six people in the governor's office had abused their right of access by overstaying their invitation, there was no basis for the state troopers to exclude fifty other law-abiding persons at a different site on unrelated business, especially since they had been specifically invited in by a legislator.

Even when there is a legitimate basis for exclusion, for example if there is a bomb threat or hostage-taking within a building, the government owes the public an explanation. This is not simply a matter of courtesy. In the above instance, the state troopers' arrogant silence only compounded the violation: it engendered distrust and hostility. Indeed, the absence of a government explanation will often make citizens believe that their rights are being violated even when they are not, occasionally leading to unnecessary or inappropriate reactions.

Because we have a government of, by, and for the people, citizens have a right to come to the seat of their government to voice their concerns. Absent a true emergency, the sign outside all government offices should always read: "Your Government: Open for Business." And we must constantly remind our representatives that the First Amendment defines part of their business as listening to our grievances.

Students Learn from Free Expression and Due Process

• A principal in Hazelwood, Missouri deletes two entire pages from a high school newspaper because they contain stories of three students' experience with pregnancy and discuss the impact of divorce on students at the school. The United States Supreme Court rules that the First Amendment rights of the student journalists were not violated because the paper is sponsored and funded by the school and thus the school principal is the publisher who has editorial control.

• Two teachers and a PTA president develop an innovative musical to teach geography to elementary schoolchildren, for which half the student body auditions. A small group intervenes, claiming that because the play refers to thirty-three countries and two times thirty-three is sixty-six and Satan's number is 666, "even a cursory reading shows clear implications of voodoo and witchcraft." Also the inclusion of characters from China, India, Japan, and the Soviet Union is faulted because "these are all Eastern religion-believing countries." The principal calls off the production.

• One-paragraph long, primarily descriptive reviews by a student of the movies "Rain Man" and "Mississippi Burning" are removed from a junior high school newspaper because the movies are rated "R."

• A group of high school students are told that they may not call their after-school club the Young Republicans Club because the name is too political, and they receive critical comments from teachers when they rename it the Young Conservatives Club.

• Books such as *The Naked Ape* by Desmond Morris, *Down These Mean Streets* by Piri Thomas, and *Slaughterhouse Five* by Kurt Vonnegut are ordered removed from a New York high school library by the school board because they are "anti-American, anti-Christian and just plain filthy," after several board members attend a conference of a conservative parent organization.

• Principal Joe Clark, acclaimed by President Reagan as a model educator, summarily suspends sixty students because he believes that they are too old and are not making sufficient progress in school.

• A ninth grader is suspended and ordered to take a urine test based on the allegation of another student that the first student had given him a bag with a white substance some three weeks earlier. Within days, the urine test comes back negative and the chemical test of the white substance shows it to be chalk and Tylenol. Nevertheless, the school authorities sign a juvenile delinquency complaint charging a drug offense, which is later dismissed. A hearing is not held until the boy has been out of school for forty-one days, at which time the board of education acquits him of all charges except "bad judgment."

The common theme in these events is not simply that they all occurred in public schools. It is that the school authorities in each instance justified their actions as furthering the educational goals of the institution. Surely many would agree that it is sound policy not to allow high school students to remain in school indefinitely, regardless of their age or academic progress. Further, no one will dispute that drugs in school undermine a productive educational atmosphere, and most would agree that suspension and even criminal prosecution may be appropriate tools for dealing with some drug offenses in school. Likewise, most people would consider it necessary, given the lesser experience and less mature judgment of high school student journalists, to give faculty advisers of school newspapers some degree of control to prevent libel, obscenity, and invasion of privacy.

But the real question is whether these legitimate educational goals can and should be advanced through means that trample on students' constitutional rights. Not only are free expression and due process constitutionally guaranteed to high school students, but I suggest that ignoring those rights is counterproductive and ultimately destructive of our schools' educational goals.

The constitutional point is quite clear. Over twenty years ago, the Supreme Court held that high school and junior high school students had a constitutional right to wear armbands in school to protest the country's participation in the Vietnam War and therefore could not be disciplined for doing so.[37] The Supreme Court also ruled more than fifteen years ago that students have constitutionally protected interests both in receiving mandated public education and in their personal reputations that entitle them to the protections of the due process clause for even ten-day suspensions from school for misconduct.[38] Almost ten years ago, the Court ruled that the New York school board in the example above could not, under the First Amendment, remove books from the school library if it was motivated by a dislike for their contents or pressure from political opponents of the books, rather than by neutral pedagogical reasons.[39] In 1984, the Court confirmed that students have constitutionally protected privacy rights in school that prevent unreasonable searches by school personnel of students or their property while investigating violations of either school rules or criminal law.[40]

The Court's most recent student rights decision in the Hazelwood student newspaper case described at the outset[41] is both short-sighted and unprincipled—in short, bad constitutional law. The majority tries to avoid the clear impact of the Court's earlier armband case by creating a new and artificial distinction between student expression that receives some school support, such as a school newspaper, and that which does not, such as an underground student newspaper or armbands and T-shirts worn by students. The more appropriate distinction, and the one previously thought to govern, is between assignments given by teachers to students as part of the established curriculum, on the one hand, and all forms of student-generated expression on the other. It is enough for present purposes to note that even the Court majority in *Hazelwood* did not question the continued viability of the armband case or the application of constitutional rights to public school students.

What is truly distressing is, as the dissent notes, "the civics lesson" which the *Hazelwood* decision and the other instances noted at the beginning of this essay provide to students. We teach them, especially in this period of the Bicentennial, of the glories of the Constitution and Bill of Rights. We invite special speakers in, hold special assemblies, and create special lesson plans to explain the Constitution. We give them pop quizzes on the specifics of the First, Fourth, and Fifth Amendments. We explain patiently that even a person accused of the most heinous murder is entitled to the presumption of innocence. But then, when school authorities suspect students of drug offenses or are not satisfied with their academic performance, they summarily suspend the students without notice, a hearing, or even a chance to explain whether the facts are actually as the principal suspects they are. Or, when the principal does not like the tone or subject of a particular newspaper story or movie review, he simply removes the page, without consultation and without reliance on an established, neutral rule derived from sound journalistic, pedagogical, or legal principles.

This kind of behavior can teach our students only one of two things—that the school authorities do not care whether they are violating the constitutional rights of the students, or that the teachers and principals do not really believe in the rights that they so proudly teach the students. I am confident that neither government abuse nor government deception is the kind of civics lesson we want students to learn. It would be a wonderful object lesson if, instead, accused students were given written notice, had a chance to consult with their parents, a counselor or other students, could put on their witnesses and ask questions of accusing witnesses, and then hear a reasoned decision by a neutral decisionmaker. Wouldn't the lesson be just as good, and the school's legitimate interests as fully served, whether the student were found guilty or not guilty? Wouldn't we likewise teach student editors much more if, instead of abruptly removing an unsatisfactory article, the principal or faculty advisor sat down and explained to them the law of libel or privacy, why the piece as written violated it, and how they could re-write the story and still get across the key facts and their opinions without violating other people's rights? Life in school is a microcosm of life in society, for which school should be preparation. If we were simply to practice in school what we preach there, students would quickly capture the spirit of the Bill of Rights and carry that vital civics lesson with them for life.

III

PRIVACY

There are two problems with privacy: we are not sure exactly what we mean by it, and it is not mentioned in the Bill of Rights.

People invoke the term "privacy" to cover a variety of concepts. To many people, privacy means the right to be left alone—for example, to walk or drive *in public* without being stopped by police. But it also signifies the right to do things in private—that is, without the presence of others. An extension of this aspect of privacy is the desire to keep information about oneself from other people—whether it is illegal activity, delicate medical conditions, family history, or school grades. Finally, the courts have used the term to cover the power to make key personal decisions on one's own—most prominently, the decisions whether to terminate a pregnancy and whether to refuse medical treatment. These concerns are related, but there are important differences that we need to consider carefully.

Though the word "privacy" is not used in the Constitution, many provisions bear upon these concerns. Most prominent is the Fourth Amendment, which protects "the right of the people to be secure in their persons, houses, papers, and effects against unreasonable searches and seizures." The Fifth Amendment states that no one can be compelled to be a witness against him or herself in a criminal case. The Sixth Amendment permits the accused to have the assistance of counsel in a criminal case, and almost certainly was meant to incorporate the English and colonial respect for the confidences between a defendant and his or her lawyer. Even the never-invoked

Third Amendment speaks to privacy in providing that "No soldier shall, in time of peace be quartered in any house, without the consent of the owner." And, of course, the First Amendment protects the rights to express oneself, assemble, and practice one's religion without government interference.

As good lawyers and practical politicians, the Framers recognized that any laundry list of specific rights might be thought to be exclusive, so they added the Ninth Amendment which confirms that "The enumeration in the Constitution of certain rights shall not be construed to deny or disparage others retained by the people." After the Civil War, the people added the Fourteenth Amendment, which not only protects the unspecified "privileges and immunities of citizens of the United States" from infringement by state and local government but also prevents deprivation of "liberty" without "due process of law."

Clearly then, the Founders were concerned with safeguarding many aspects of what we call privacy. They also recognized that rights can rarely be absolute: the Fourth Amendment does not ban all police searches but only those unreasonably undertaken without a warrant and probable cause. The breadth and generality of the Ninth and Fourteenth Amendments also reflect a recognition that particular points taken for granted then may not have been mentioned or that changes in society will require differing emphases. Our task is to ferret out and articulate the meaning of these provisions and the scope of the various concepts of privacy in the ever shrinking, overcrowded, and technologically intrusive world of our generation.

Legal Roadblocks to Traffic Roadblocks

One of the more publicized law enforcement efforts and the one that ordinary citizens are most likely to encounter, after the airport metal detector, is the roadblock. Its best-known purpose is to check for drunk drivers. However in recent times, as part of the war on drugs, some police agencies have tried to use the technique to catch drug users or traffickers. Roadblocks in general, and their expansion beyond the original drunk driving rationale, raise very serious civil liberties questions. I will address first the general constitutional objection to this technique, which is based on privacy theory and the fact that roadblocks are an inefficient means of catching offenders. I will then address the specifics of roadblocks—their location and timing and the procedures used. Concerns about the privacy intrusions and the risks of abuse have led many state courts to impose some limits on roadblocks. Such limits are based on interpretations of state constitutions that are more protective of individual rights than the United States Supreme Court's unfortunate recent ruling that the Fourth Amendment generally permits drunk-driving roadblocks.

First, what's wrong with a roadblock? A roadblock or fixed checkpoint, like a metal detector check or a random drug test (see "Job Tests, Not Urine Tests," page 98), intrudes upon the privacy and freedom of all involved, without the slightest suspicion about any particular individual, in order to catch any offenders who may be in the affected group. In principle it is no different from searching all homes in a neighborhood to uncover weapons, as was done in some cities during riots in the 1960's, or searching all student desks, bookbags, and pocketbooks to find a missing watch. We all know that such general searches will uncover something, because in any given population there will almost certainly be someone who has violated some law or

81

rule. But the Fourth Amendment expressly limits police efforts to uncover evidence of crime, not because the Framers were against detecting crime but because they feared unchecked government. It is important to recall in this context that one of the royal practices that provoked our Founders to revolution was the common use of general warrants and writs of assistance to search commercial establishments for customs violations. Such documents were issued without any basis for suspecting that any specific offenses had been committed in the particular locales to be searched.

In more recent times, as fear of crime has grown, the public has appeared more willing to forgo Fourth Amendment rights if doing so might increase safety. The widespread acceptance of routine airport metal detector searches is an example. They have proven popular and have passed constitutional muster for two reasons. First, they are minimally intrusive. No questions are asked and the machine checks only for metal and beeps only if one is carrying a significant amount of metal. If there is no beep, one's walk down the corridor is hardly slowed at all. If the machine beeps, one is given a chance to remove innocent items, such as keys, a watch, or coins, that might have triggered the machine's response. If the detector still beeps, the follow-up search is performed with only a hand-held metal detector. In any case, one need not disclose anything or permit any kind of a search, even the initial detector check, because one can simply walk away without entering the protected section of the airport. Second, metal detector checks are very effective—even the smallest weapons are readily detected. As a result, plane hijacking has practically been eliminated since these searches were implemented.

In contrast, drunk-driving roadblocks are far more intrusive than metal detectors, yet are both expensive and unproductive. High-speed travel of passengers as well as the driver is halted, a visual search of the car's interior is effected, and occupants must answer police questions or face adverse inferences and various physical tests. These intrusions require a substantial investment of police time. They cannot be conducted by one or two officers alone, as ordinary observation of moving traffic can. For safety reasons, the area must be clearly marked and cordoned off. Sufficient staff must be available to pull over and investigate those drivers considered suspicious after the initial inquiry and to arrest and process those found intoxicated, without interrupting the roadblock routine.

The results have not justified the costs. In the only controlled experiment, one Maryland county implemented DWI (driving while intoxicated) roadblocks while a neighboring county with comparable demographics and travel patterns did not, relying instead on traditional police observation of traffic. Alcohol-related accidents in the checkpoint county decreased ten percent, but the control county saw an eleven percent reduction in the same time period. In fact, while fatal accidents in the control county fell from ten to three, the number in the checkpoint county went up from three to eight in the same year.[1]

In a Michigan roadblock case that went to the United States Supreme Court, it was proven that nationwide only about one percent of drivers stopped at sobriety checkpoints are arrested for drunk driving.[2] On the one occasion that Michigan had implemented its roadblock program prior to the court case, two DWI arrests were made by nineteen officers operating the checkpoint after stopping 126 drivers. No estimate was offered of how many DWI and other offenses would on the average have been observed and prosecuted by nineteen officers on ordinary highway patrol during the same time period. Indeed, Michigan admitted that the goal of its checkpoints was to deter drunk driving not by making a large number of arrests, but rather by creating a public *perception* that there was a high risk of arrest. The evidence shows, however, that the deterrent effect of widely publicized roadblocks is short-lived, with drunk-driving figures quickly returning to previous levels. The conclusion drawn by many experts, including a National Highway Traffic Safety Administration study and many police officers, is that drunk-driving roadblocks are not cost-effective.[3]

The Supreme Court, in finding the Michigan DWI roadblock constitutional, did not dispute the figures. It simply ruled that a one percent "catch" rate was effective enough to satisfy the Fourth Amendment, regardless of what the alternatives might have accomplished. In contrast, a number of state courts have considered the relatively high expense and low rate of arrests from roadblocks, as compared to normal traffic patrol, in concluding that warrantless roadblocks violate their state constitutional protections against unreasonable searches and seizures.[4]

Even if one discounts the statistical evidence and allows DWI roadblocks generally, as the Supreme Court has done, one must consider numerous questions about when, where, and how roadblocks should be implemented. Several state courts that have allowed road-blocks have sought to minimize the intrusions and the risks of abuse of discretion by requiring careful police planning and oversight. Pro-visions include specific justification of the location and time selected, advance notice to the public, close supervision to insure that a routine is maintained (for example, pulling over every tenth or twentieth car) and the length of detention limited, and accurate record-keeping to permit judicial review.[5]

The requirement that authorities explain their choice of the lo-cation and time of drunk-driving roadblocks is central. The justifi-cation must be in the form of specific evidence that the proposed location is the site, at the time of day or night when the roadblock is to be conducted, of significantly more of the offending behavior than occurs elsewhere or at other times. This can rarely be shown except for roadblocks set up very close to bars at closing time.

A good case study is the attempt several years ago to set up road-blocks on the George Washington Bridge linking New York and New Jersey. The official purpose was to identify drivers under the influence of drugs. The location was picked on the theory that many people were going from New Jersey to Washington Heights at the northern end of Manhattan to buy "crack" or other drugs, were consuming them immediately, and then driving home under the influence.

The theory was not, however, borne out by the facts. Of course, there are always a great many cars crossing the bridge; hence, at any time, given the nature of our society, there are likely to be some drivers on the bridge who are drunk, drugged, or otherwise impaired. But the police had no evidence of a sudden increase in, or even a substantial existing problem with, drivers under the influence of drugs at the bridge. Indeed, by slowing all cars to a crawl, the police were depriving themselves of the best evidence of that offense—visual ob-servation of erratic driving. The only support for selecting the bridge as the roadblock location cited by the authorities to the media, and later to the courts, was the prevalence of crack buying in Washington Heights and the increasing number of cars with New Jersey license plates seized in drug arrests.[6] In practice, the roadblocks produced mammoth traffic jams, affecting up to a million interstate travelers on one night alone, though only nine arrests were made, and not all for drunk or drugged driving.[7] To avoid repetition of such traffic back-ups, the authorities moved the roadblock on the second night of the operation to a point on a highway one mile north of the bridge. In court they admitted they had no evidence suggesting a high proportion of impaired drivers at that location or even that a majority of drivers crossing the bridge took that road.[8]

Given the ineffectiveness of roadblocks in general, the lack of specific evidence suggesting that the bridge was a site of more than average drunk or drugged driving, and the availability of cheaper, more direct, and more effective ways of detecting such driving, the logical conclusion is that the authorities were using these roadblocks for reasons other than preventing that hazard. Perhaps they thought the procedure would create good public relations, or they were really looking not for bad drivers but for drug dealers. But no court, at that point or since then, has authorized or approved the use of roadblocks for either of those purposes. In fact in June and July 1990, several years after the New York-New Jersey bridge roadblock, two federal judges in California struck down as unconstitutional the federal authorities' explicit attempt to broaden its immigration checkpoint at San Clemente to look for drug offenders, even though the evidence of drug trafficking there was quite strong.[9] These rulings flow from the fact that the Fourth Amendment does not allow general searches to find criminal offenders.

Even if roadblocks could be aimed at drug offenders, the choice of location was still inappropriate. Assume that Washington Heights was or is a center of "crack" dealing. That would in no way suggest, and both common sense and traffic studies would refute, that most or even many people driving across the George Washington Bridge are in possession of that drug. The vast majority of cars on the bridge do not originate in Washington Heights. Also, once dealers and purchasers know of the roadblocks, they will surely take other routes. In any case, as already noted, roadblocks have been shown to be an inefficient use of police resources for detecting traffic offenses; with regard to drug possession, they would logically be less effective because the observations during a stop are even less likely to produce evidence of such a crime. Moreover, if many drug transactions were actually occurring in Washington Heights, roadblocks on the bridge would not catch the large percentage of buyers going elsewhere after the transaction.

Direct observation of the drug sale locale would, on the other hand, reap many more drug arrests, just as observation of staggering tavern patrons going to their cars will catch far more DWI offenders than stopping every fifth car on a nearby highway. Not surprisingly, when the courts invalidated the roadblocks on the bridge, New Jersey police began just such observations, calling the license plate numbers ahead to colleagues on the other side of the bridge where they could intercept only those cars and make the appropriate arrests.

Finally, even if we are satisfied that roadblocks are justified at some locations and times, we must still consider how they will be conducted. Will the public be given advance notice of the roadblocks? Can one make a U-turn to avoid the time and inconvenience of going through a roadblock? What questions will be asked of drivers and passengers? Who will be asked to get out of the car? When will the driver be asked to walk a straight line or touch his or her nose? Whose cars will be searched? Who will be asked to take a breathalyzer, urine, or blood test?

In a 1979 case called *Delaware v. Prouse*,[10] in which I was co-counsel for the citizen, the United States Supreme Court struck down random car stops for license and registration checks. The ruling recognized that the breadth of discretion afforded the officer on the scene risked discriminatory or selective application, for example stopping only African Americans, long-haired hippies, or young people. Similarly, do officers really stop exactly every tenth or twentieth car at a roadblock or are they influenced by the appearance of the car or the driver? Perhaps increasing use of video cameras on police cars would help insure compliance with the scheduled routine.

But even if the stops at a roadblock are truly routine, there is still substantial risk of abuse in the discretion left to the individual officer to decide how long to detain the car, what questions to ask, when to require the driver to get out of the car, and when to require sobriety tests, including the involuntary taking of a blood sample. For example, because a roadblock prevents visual observation of erratic driving, the officers have little to go on, other than dilated pupils or unsatisfactory answers, in determining whether they have stopped a driver under the influence from whom they should request a blood sample. Yet at night most drivers will have dilated pupils because of the limited light. The whole idea of the Fourth Amendment is to have an objective, uninvolved judicial officer, not the police officer on the spot who is concerned about arrest statistics, decide what particular intrusions are justified as to each individual. The Fourth Amendment does not permit police, based on a hunch, to use such intrusive means as compelled blood-taking to develop evidence for an arrest. Rather it requires independent, objective evidence amounting to probable cause to believe that an offense has occurred—and typically a judge's concurrence with that judgment in the form of a warrant—*before*, not after, intruding upon constitutionally protected privacy.

I am confident that the driving public, conscientious police authorities, and state courts, which are charged with interpreting state constitutional protections independently of how the Supreme Court interprets the Fourth Amendment, will come to see the dangers inherent in roadblocks and reject their use for drunk driving as well as for drug offenses. We will all be better off, and in this context more successful in catching criminals, if we return to the tried and true method of having police observe citizens' behavior and then interfere with someone's liberty, travel, and privacy only when they have a sound reason to believe that the individual they are stopping is guilty of a particular offense.

Going Too Far: Police Strip Searches

Here are four hard-to-believe but true stories.

• Late on a rainy night, a car is pulled over for driving too slowly. A routine check reveals an outstanding warrant for the driver for seventy-five dollars in unpaid traffic fines from a nearby city. The driver and her husband have with them only forty-five dollars in cash and some merchandise they just bought for their business. The police say that's insufficient and that the driver will be detained until she posts_ the full amount in cash or is picked up by the authority (some twenty-five miles away) that issued the warrant. The local police station to which she is taken has no overnight facilities so she is taken to the nearest county jail where, like all incoming inmates, she is photographed, fingerprinted, strip-searched, and then subjected to what is known in legal jargon as "a body cavity inspection." No exception is made because she is having a menstrual period at the time. The next afternoon she is picked up by police from the city that issued the warrant, pays her fines, and is released.

• In the middle of a sunny Saturday afternoon, a young driver is pulled over by a police officer at the end of an exit ramp from a bridge. After the usual document check, the driver is frisked, the car is searched, and then the driver is told to drop his pants. Nothing illegal is found and the driver is released.

• Seven persons are arrested for disorderly conduct for demonstrating on the lawn of city hall about the city's failure to reopen a homeless men's shelter. A relative and a lawyer friend come to the stationhouse to post bail. Just prior to being released, the four women, but not the three men, are strip-searched. At trial all are acquitted.

• A young woman canvassing at night for a community organization (see "Talking Politics Door-to-Door," page 59) is arrested for canvassing without a permit when she misreads her street map and inadvertently approaches a few homes in the town next to the one that had issued a permit. While awaiting processing to be released without bail, she is strip-searched. Nothing is found.

Is this the way police should be treating our citizens? A sense of common decency, quite apart from any sophisticated understanding of constitutional requirements, tells us that the answer should clearly be "no." Fortunately the law is now beginning to reflect the sense of outrage felt by the affected citizens in these cases.

In the first case described above, a federal judge ruled that strip-searching of all arrestees, without any reason to suspect that they had contraband or dangerous weapons on them, was unreasonable and violated the Fourth Amendment.[11] She held the county that ran the jail liable even though it was enforcing a state corrections department regulation requiring strip-searching of all new inmates. Thereupon the county settled, paying substantial damages to the plaintiff and attorneys' fees to the ACLU, which brought the case. In the bridge ramp situation, the ACLU supplied the police with the testimony of two eyewitnesses to the sidewalk strip search, who happened to be off-duty newspaper reporters. After an internal investigation, disciplinary charges were brought, leading to the suspension of the offending officer for sixty days without pay. In the third case, the New Jersey Inmate Advocate's Office, a state agency authorized to represent inmates in disputes with authorities, brought a lawsuit against the city claiming violations of both the Constitution and a state statute expressly limiting strip searches. The suit resulted in damages for the women and a new city policy precluding strip searches under such circumstances. In the fourth case, the canvasser was acquitted and then sued and obtained damages for the strip search.

The Constitution does not mention strip searches. The history books do not indicate that even the highly offensive redcoats engaged in such degrading practices. But the Fourth Amendment prohibits unreasonable searches and it therefore falls to our current society, applying its evolving standards of decency and privacy, to define unreasonableness. Certainly strip-searching is appropriate in some cases. One could hardly fault the police for fully disrobing either an inmate who had just held guards hostage with a knife or a person arrested for armed robbery who was seen stuffing something down his pants just before arrest. But the fact that a strip search may be justified in such situations does not mean we should have the same rule for all persons however briefly detained by police and for whatever reason.

Recognizing the need for a more discriminating approach, seven federal appellate courts, responsible for cases coming from the majority of states, have held routine strip-searching of minor offenders, such as traffic offenders, to be unconstitutional.[12] In New Jersey the legislature enacted several years ago the unusual statute noted above, which prohibits strip searches and body cavity searches without a warrant, consent, or probable cause to believe weapons or contraband will be found on the person. The law permits strip searches for any arrestee who is to be confined in jail, but only if the person has first been afforded "a reasonable opportunity to post bail." To make that requirement meaningful, the law also requires the use of a "bail schedule," which is a list, created by judges in advance, of bail amounts for different offenses that arrestees or their families can post between arrest and when the person is brought to court and has bail set on an individual basis.[13]

Unfortunately, the second, third, and fourth incidents noted above, which occurred in New Jersey after the statute was passed and after several of the decisions already mentioned were issued, demonstrate that police do not always promptly implement changes in the law, either constitutional or statutory. Indeed as of this writing, the largest city in the state still does not use the bail schedule for minor offenders mandated over five years ago by the state law. As a result city authorities must be detaining and strip-searching some minor offenders in violation of their rights. The task now is for the relevant authorities in each state—the administrative offices of the courts, presiding judges, attorneys general, prosecutors, and municipal police departments—to educate themselves and their staffs about the plain law that police cannot simply order citizens stripped routinely, at whim, or for minor offenses. The Fourth Amendment's rule of reasonableness is a rule of human decency, now as it was 200 years ago.

Do We Expect Our Garbage to Be Inspected by Police?

In May 1988 the United States Supreme Court ruled, in a case called *California v. Greenwood*,[14] that the Fourth Amendment does not require the police to have a warrant, probable cause, reasonable suspicion, or even an inarticulate hunch before opening and searching anybody's garbage placed at the curb for collection. I share the suspicion of Justice Brennan in dissent: "that members of our society will be shocked to learn that the Court, the ultimate guarantor of liberty, deems unreasonable our expectation that the aspects of our private lives that are concealed safely in a trash bag will not become public."[15] Reflecting that reaction, which is based on the knowledge that our trash can reveal much about our personal, social, financial, and political affairs, two state supreme courts have already come to the contrary conclusion under their state constitutions.[16] I suggest not only that the Supreme Court grossly misapplied its existing interpretation of the Fourth Amendment but that the approach itself is flawed and fails to reflect societal values and understandings. We must take a fresh look at the problem in order to protect individual privacy meaningfully in the real world.

In *Greenwood*, a police officer, suspecting that Greenwood was involved in narcotics, asked the neighborhood trash collector to keep separate and turn over to her the plastic garbage bags that Greenwood left out on the curb in front of his house. Based on what she observed after reviewing the trash, the officer obtained a warrant to search the house, which produced evidence that led to the prosecution. Greenwood and the other person arrested in his house sought to overturn

91

their convictions because the evidence used against them was what the law calls "the fruits" or result of the initial search of Greenwood's trash, which was undertaken without a warrant.

The Court started its analysis with its current doctrine that the search "would violate the Fourth Amendment only if [the defendants] manifested a subjective expectation of privacy in their garbage that society accepts as objectively reasonable."[17] It grudgingly admitted that, by placing their trash in opaque bags left on the curb only briefly before the truck was to pick them up and mix them with the trash of others, the defendants in that case "may well" have expected that the contents would not become known to the police or members of the public. But, the Court concluded, that expectation was not "objectively reasonable" in the eyes of "society."

This conclusion is based on what the Court stated is "common knowledge that plastic garbage bags left on or at the side of a public street are readily accessible to animals, children, scavengers, snoops, and other members of the public." The Court also observed that the individuals "placed their refuse at the curb for the express purpose of conveying it to a third party, the trash collector, who might himself have sorted through [their] trash or permitted others, such as the police, to do so."[18] Moreover, the Court reasoned that "police cannot reasonably be expected to avert their eyes from evidence of criminal activity that could have been observed by any member of the public, [because] what a person knowingly exposes to the public, even in his own home or office, is not a subject of Fourth Amendment protection."[19] In support of this proposition, the Court relied upon its own prior decisions that the police do not violate the Fourth Amendment when, without a warrant, they install a pen register that records all numbers dialed on a particular telephone or fly an airplane low over a fenced backyard. In those cases the Court had reasoned that the telephone company and any private pilot could have recorded or seen the same thing.[20] Finally, the Court supported its conclusion that "society" would not consider the expectation of privacy in one's trash reasonable by referring to the lower federal and state courts that had previously rejected the claim.

In so ruling, the Court clearly misapplied its own Fourth Amendment jurisprudence. The current rule, as the Court said, is that what one *knowingly exposes to the public* is not a subject of constitutional privacy protection. The Court had never before held that one does not have privacy rights against the police when one does *not* expose one's possessions to the general public but simply leaves them in a place where some other person might improperly invade the container. Surely police may not search a handbag left briefly on a bus terminal bench just because some child, beggar, or thief could as easily get into it. Recently, the Connecticut courts faced the question whether police could search the closed duffel bag, sleeping bag, and boxes left by a homeless man during the day in the heavy underbrush beneath a highway ramp, which was his temporary "home," because, as the state argued, he was an "interloper" on public property and his property could have been seen and examined by what the trial court called another "vagabond or knight of the road."[21] Likewise it cannot be that police may now jimmy open car trunks in urban areas just because it is well known that thieves do so regularly. It is plainly absurd to say that the police have a legal right to invade property because of the possibility that private citizens might do so illegally.

In any case the doctrine relied upon is itself flawed in two basic ways. First, the extent of our privacy from police intrusion should not be limited to the protection afforded against intrusions by private citizens, unless we were to apply the Constitution fully to private parties in all settings. (See "Constitutional Rights Should Apply at Work," page 110.) The Fourth Amendment was expressly written to create a sphere of privacy for individuals and their possessions safe from government invasion except when an impartial judicial officer finds substantial justification. At least in criminal cases, it was not, and should not be, tied to the less restrictive common-law rules governing invasions of privacy by private parties for several reasons. Law enforcement has more authority, staff, resources, and interest to invade our privacy than most private persons do. Its invasions often do more harm, typically through an ensuing criminal prosecution. And there rarely is an adequate remedy for police error; all that is done is to terminate the prosecution. Thus, we should be very wary of allowing the government to search in the first instance; at least this is what the Framers thought.

Second, opening our affairs to some for a particular purpose is not the same as laying bare everything to everyone. We are frequently called upon to provide significant personal information to a large number of private entities—employers, banks, landlords, insurers, and the like. We do so to obtain the basics of life or other benefits. Ironically in the case of landlords from whom we rent our homes, we do so, in part, to secure some privacy. We have little choice about it. We provide that information, however, only for the purpose stated. For example, the telephone company may need to record the numbers one dials in order to provide proper billing. That does not mean one has "knowingly exposed" all one's telephone dialings to "the public," not to mention all federal, state, and local law enforcement officials. Agreeing, or more realistically, being forced to disclose some facts to some people in order to live in our society does not, or at least should not, mean that we have waived all privacy rights against the general public or the police.

I suspect that the reason why many judges do not appreciate this problem, and thus why it is inappropriate for the Supreme Court to rely upon lower court judges' views in determining society's thinking, is that judges rarely have their privacy invaded by anyone, least of all by the police. Judges generally do not have arrest records and have not operated marginal businesses or filed suspicious tax returns subject to intensive investigations. Because of their position in society, they may not appreciate the substantial risks of arbitrary and selective enforcement of this newly bestowed discretion to search discarded property against those of the "wrong" color, neighborhood, or background. If judges are to speak about society's expectations, they should consider not their own experiences but those of the average citizen. Those of us who live in the real world know that what we place in plastic bags or trash cans at the curb for collection may reveal much of a legitimately private nature and thus is not meant for either public viewing or police perusal.

Should We Tolerate "Zero Tolerance?"

• The Coast Guard seizes a $2.5 million yacht, even though no one is arrested, because marijuana seeds totalling one-tenth of an ounce are found on board during a routine document check while the boat is in the hands of people leasing it.

• Federal prosecutors seek to freeze all assets of a person charged with drug dealing, as a result of which he cannot hire an attorney to defend him at trial.

• A military commander permanently bans from his base, with only twelve hours' notice, an emotionally handicapped seventeen-year-old son of a resident career Air Force officer as a result of drug charges brought by civil police that have not yet been adjudicated.

• A mother's car is taken by the police because her son's friend was charged with smoking a marijuana cigarette in the car, even though the mother was not present or even suspected of knowing about or encouraging the drug use.

• One city threatens to close down entire apartment buildings under a local ordinance unless the landlords evict the tenants of apartments in which a person is arrested for (but not yet convicted of) any drug offense. This applies even if only a relative or visitor, and not the actual tenant, is arrested.

• Legislation is proposed to allow confiscation of cars and other property "utilized in" the commission of misdemeanor drug offenses, such as possession of less than fifty grams of marijuana.

The issues in these and similar situations are not whether drug use should be illegal or whether violations of the law should be pros-

95

ecuted. Rather the questions are whether, when, on whom, and for what offenses should the penalty of forfeiture of property be imposed?

These questions are most dramatically posed by the recent trend, exemplified by the illustrations above, towards "zero tolerance." This is a policy that dictates seizure and forfeiture of all property even remotely involved in an alleged drug offense, regardless of the amount of drugs involved, the value of the property seized, or whether the owner of the property had any involvement in, or knowledge of, the criminal activity. Three key features of "zero tolerance" render it objectionable.

First, "zero tolerance" treats the innocent and the guilty alike. The tenant, the Air Force father, and the absent boat and car owners, who are not charged with, not to mention convicted of, any crime—not even aiding and abetting drug possession by the guilty party—are subject to loss of their property because of the alleged acts of others. Only two defenses are currently recognized by federal and most state laws: that the property was stolen; or that the owner not only was unaware of and uninvolved in the criminal conduct, but that he or she had done all that could reasonably be expected to prevent the pro-scribed use.[22] It is not enough just to tell one's tenants, lessees, or guests that drug use is not allowed on the property; rather the owner is asked to become a law enforcer. Such a burden is utterly unrealistic. Is one supposed to hire a chaperone to stay in the car twenty-four hours a day even though one has lent it to a friend or rented it out? More importantly, this approach distorts our traditional concepts of guilt and innocence and removes from the government its burden of proving guilt before punishment is imposed.

Second, "zero tolerance" undermines the fundamental relation-ships of trust among friends and family, which are essential to a civilized and caring society. Should a mother lose her car because she lends it to her seventeen-year-old son and one night he invites a friend into the car who smokes one marijuana cigarette? Should a father lose his apartment, where he is an orderly and prompt-paying tenant, because his son is convicted of drug possession? Should a child be permanently barred from his home, and thus his parents forced either to abandon their home on a military base or abandon their son, be-cause he was arrested on a drug charge while off base? Courts have recognized a constitutional right of families to live together and have extended it to unrelated persons living in a single housekeeping unit.

(See "Why Can't Love and Justice Coexist?" page 246.) Is it permissible for the government to override this fundamental right by equating one child's criminal charge with parental guilt and disrupting the familial abode? Common decency demands rejection of such government intervention.

The third major problem with "zero tolerance" is that the punishment is often way out of proportion to the crime. It makes sense to confiscate the Rolls Royce of the drug kingpin dealing crack out of his car. But the very same law is applied to confiscate permanently a $2.5 million boat because of a renter's possession of less than an ounce of marijuana. Using a more common example, an ordinary working person's only family car, worth several thousand dollars, is confiscated because a teenage son or his friend once smokes one marijuana cigarette in the car.

"Zero tolerance" is premised, like all harsh, mandatory, non-individualized penalties, on a deterrence theory. I suspect that, if genuinely enforced across the board in an even-handed way (which is a very significant but separate issue), such harsh intolerance for drugs, when coupled with sufficient publicity, might eventually reduce drug crime somewhat, at least in cars. But England long ago gave up the death penalty for all felons because juries often found the penalty so disproportionate and unfair that they would not convict even in the face of overwhelming evidence of guilt. Loss of a $10,000 car, not to mention a $2.5 million yacht, for a $50 infraction (a common fine for minor marijuana offenses) is the economic equivalent of the death penalty for a pickpocket. I believe that the public now, as then, will rebel against such grossly disproportionate penalties and demand a system of law enforcement for drugs, as for other offenses, in which the penalty fits the crime, respects family relationships, and is imposed only on the guilty.

Job Tests, Not Urine Tests

The recent proliferation of programs for testing the urine of employees for illicit drugs, despite a documented leveling-off of drug abuse in this country, is a disturbing phenomenon. The desire for a simple answer—a clean test—to a complex and frightening problem is readily understandable. But like any other quick fix, this modern form of loyalty oath must be analyzed closely by everyone concerned with the rule of law and the state of our freedoms. First, I will review the traditional civil liberties concerns: the reversal of the presumption of innocence, the intrusions on personal privacy, and the unfairness of erroneous accusations based upon unreliable test results. I will then address the factors that render these impositions unreasonable: the inability of urine tests to gauge job impairment, which is an employer's only legitimate concern; the discriminatory focus on only one of many causes of poor job performance; and the failure to use less intrusive techniques that do measure ability to perform a job.

Random or routine urine tests violate the most basic American tenets of freedom. They presume that all employees are suspect and must prove themselves clean. Like roadblocks (see "Legal Roadblocks to Traffic Roadblocks," page 81), they intrude upon everyone's privacy based not upon evidence of individual criminality or even impairment, but rather upon generalized assumptions about the likelihood of finding some guilty parties in a particular population. As one well-respected federal judge, H. Lee Sarokin, put it, in ruling that the sudden locking of firehouse doors and forced urine testing of all firefighters violated the Fourth Amendment:

> The invidious effect of such mass roundup urinalysis is that it casually sweeps up the innocent with the guilty and willingly sacrifices each individual's Fourth Amendment rights in the name of some larger

public interest. The City . . . essentially presumed the guilt of each person tested.[23]

This ruling should have been unsurprising not only to those of us who follow drug-testing litigation, but to all who are familiar with the Fourth Amendment. For what is an across-the-board urine testing program if not a general warrant, the very evil that stirred the colonists to revolt and prompted adoption of the Amendment? As the philosopher Santayana reminded us: "Those who cannot remember the past are condemned to repeat it."

Some would say that the current situation is different, either because the threat to our society posed by drugs is far greater than that posed to eighteenth-century England by colonists' customs violations or because public employees must expect more stringent scrutiny in light of the public trust they have accepted. But surely if the severity of the problem were the test, we would allow general searches of homes for an escaped murderer or missing machine gun cache. But we don't. As for the public trust, we should consider whether we would tolerate routine searches of pockets and handbags as government employees come to work or of lockers and desks while they are on the job. In an age when millions are employed by the government, performing jobs from janitor to general, we cannot simply invoke the public trust to excuse all intrusions regardless of their severity or justification.

Nor is the balance tipped because the intrusions are minor. Urine tests for drugs intrude upon individual privacy in three significant ways. First, they force the individual to perform the most private of bodily functions in front of a stranger. Most people do not perform that function in front of their most intimate friends or lovers, and urinating in public is a criminal offense in most places. Second, to insure accurate testing, the employee is required to disclose all medication, nonprescription as well as prescription, being used. This risks disclosure of a wide variety of physical and mental conditions that are very personal and of no legitimate concern to the employer, but which are often the basis for discriminatory action. Finally, the chemical screening of urine can itself reveal numerous conditions, such as pregnancy, diabetes, or epilepsy, that many would reasonably wish to keep private. Like discarded trash (see "Do We Expect Our Garbage to be Inspected by Police?" page 91), bodily waste products can reveal a great deal about our lives that we may legitimately wish to keep from others.

Arguably the intrusions would be more acceptable if they were reliable indicators of a problem. Unfortunately they often are not. Initial urine tests that are "positive" for illegal drugs may reflect ingestion of lawful substances, including antihistamines and poppy seeds.[24] In one famous instance, a woman who was unable to provide her employer with a sample because she had recently urinated, was offered a drink of bitter-lemon soda. The quinine in the drink produced a "positive" result when she urinated later; even the next day's "negative" did not deter the employer from firing her. Similarly, a supervisor in California taking allergy medication tested "positive" for cocaine. He was forced to spend a month in a hospital treatment program and to submit to regular urine tests thereafter, despite medical findings that he was wholly asymptomatic and that there was no indication of any drug use ever.

Such initial miscarriages of justice have become less frequent because of the development of more accurate confirmatory tests that do not register "positive" for such lawful substances. The most commonly used and reliable one is called GC/MS, or gas chromatography-mass spectroscopy. But even with that test, there is the risk of human error—such as failure to prevent contamination of the sample or failure to clean, calibrate, use, or read the machinery properly. In this regard, we do well to remember an early study by the federal Centers for Disease Control of laboratories doing urine testing for methadone programs. The centers sent the labs various samples for testing, some of which contained only water while others had had traces of illegal drugs inserted. The centers found the different laboratories across the country incorrectly reporting water samples as positive for drugs in 6 to 66 percent of the tests.[25] Likewise the Navy reported that 49 percent of the scientific records and 43 percent of the so-called "chain of custody" records of urine samples were not legally supportable. Similar problems are chronicled in the 1988 House Government Operations Committee report calling for strict federal standards for laboratories performing such tests.[26]

But we need to address the broader issue. Even if all the tests were always accurate, are the reversal of the presumption of innocence and the privacy intrusions justified? As every employer's expert admits, even the most accurately conducted and chemically precise

100

drug test cannot show that the individual was under the influence of the substance or impaired in his or her job performance at the time of the test. Significantly, the test will be negative even though the employee is severely impaired, if the drug was used shortly before the test and thus before the body has had a chance to digest it fully. For example, an airline pilot who snorts cocaine minutes before giving the urine sample and boarding the plane will test negative though she or he is almost certainly impaired. A positive test result also does not show that the individual is drug-dependent, or even a regular user, just as a single abnormal sugar level does not establish diabetes. Indeed, a urine test cannot even show how much of the drug was ingested nor precisely when it was taken. Quite simply, a "true positive" result proves only that the person has ingested some quantity of the substance at some point more than four to six hours before the sample was taken and within the last forty-eight hours (for cocaine) or four weeks (for marijuana).[27]

But an employer's only legitimate concern is with job performance: can the employee do the job safely and efficiently? The employer has the right to demand that the person is on duty for the hours for which paid and that the job gets done. Accordingly the employer may legitimately observe, supervise, and record employee timeliness and work performance. If a person is regularly late for work or falls asleep on the job, a humane employer would seek to determine its cause, whether it is alcohol abuse, drug addiction, too much late night television, fights with a spouse, or an emotional disturbance, and help the employee to resolve it in order to restore him or her to full productivity. There need, similarly, be no special focus on drugs if the employer takes a more traditional disciplinary approach. If the employee cannot perform adequately, she or he should be warned, disciplined, and, if necessary, fired. Conversely, if a person is always on time and is performing the work well, it should not matter to an employer if that employee had six beers or smoked marijuana at a party the prior Saturday night.

The distinction regularly drawn by employers and some courts between off-duty beer and marijuana use is that the former is a legal substance and the latter is illegal. Although this is obviously true, and is relevant to criminal investigations and perhaps to moral judgments, it is simply not a distinction relevant to a job performance analysis.

Quite simply, employers are not arms of the law enforcement community, but supervisors of production.

As such, employers should, in fact, be even more concerned with alcohol problems than with drug use. Although drug impairment is a serious problem, it is far from the major source of poor job performance. There are between ten and thirteen million alcohol-dependent adults in this country, but the latest figures show at most four million drug abusers. In 1989, the National Institute on Drug Abuse reported that, despite the sharp climb in the use of crack cocaine over the last few years, the overall use of illegal drugs has been decreasing for ten years and the decline has accelerated in the last five. From 1985 to 1988, the number of current users (at least once a month) of marijuana and cocaine dropped by 33 and 50 percent, respectively. The number of heroin addicts in this country is the same as fifteen years ago, and daily marijuana use among high school students has declined since 1979.[28] If employers are truly concerned about drug-related job impairment, why don't they regularly require executives returning from lunch to take breathalyzer tests? Unlike urine tests, breathalyzers are very accurate indicators of current levels of alcohol in the system, and thus of current impairment. They are also far less intrusive on privacy and less costly than drug urine tests. The failure to screen for alcohol impairment while investing so heavily in drug tests makes no practical or business sense and is unfairly discriminatory.[29]

Some will say—this is all well and good, but what should we do about employees, like pilots and bus drivers, whose work immediately affects the safety of others, thereby denying us the luxury of waiting until after the fact to learn of any inadequacies on the job? With regard to those in safety-sensitive jobs, as with all other employees, the first line of defense is the traditional approach of supervisor and co-worker observation, which has been used for decades to detect alcohol intoxication and other motor impairments.

But for those who work alone or in situations where supervision may not adequately protect us, we now also have available motor coordination and visual acuity tests that can immediately assess current ability to perform the job. For example, there are computer programs that simulate flying or driving and measure the operator's response time and accuracy.[30] Such tests pose no civil liberties problems. There is no privacy intrusion, no presumption of guilt, and no discrimination among differing chemicals and causes of impairment. And they pro-

102

vide far more accurate and relevant information about job impairment. We would all be safer if, instead of giving pilots urine tests (the results of which will not be available until two days after the flight and which would not in any case reveal cocaine snorted in the bathroom just before flight), we required them to pass a flight simulation test immediately before take-off.

In sum, I do not suggest that the drug problem is either minor or under control. Nor do I urge that we ignore either the safety or the productivity impact of employee drug use. Rather I propose that we focus on job performance, establish strict performance standards, employ close and sound supervision, and when indicated by job performance or the unsupervised nature of safety-sensitive work, use only non-intrusive tests directly indicative of job performance, rather than intruding needlessly and focusing narrowly and irrelevantly on the purity of one's urine.

What Ever Happened to Probable Cause?

If some employee drug testing is deemed appropriate, despite the points in the last essay, one must consider *when* such tests should be allowed. Most of the public as well as legal debate about drug testing has focused on whether testing may be done randomly or routinely—that is, without the employer having to establish some basis for believing that the particular individuals selected for testing are likely to have used drugs recently and to be impaired by that use. Most courts have concluded that, except for jobs with significant public safety consequences, some such evidence relating to the individual is necessary.[31] What concerns me almost as much is the debate's failure to focus on how much of a showing is sufficient. The question has implications far beyond drug testing.

All of the courts, including the Supreme Court, that have reviewed drug testing have agreed that a government directive to an employee to provide a urine sample for chemical analysis is a "search" governed by the Fourth Amendment and its state constitutional counterparts. Yet almost all of the courts that have invalidated drug testing programs, with the notable exception of the trial court in one of the cases that ultimately went to the Supreme Court,[32] have found that the government need only show a "reasonable suspicion" that the individual is under the influence of drugs in order to require a drug test. But the Fourth Amendment nowhere refers to "reasonable suspicion." Rather it speaks about "warrants" being issued based on "probable cause" to believe that the evidence sought will be found, and "particularly describing the place to be searched, and the persons or things to be seized."

My question is: what ever happened to probable cause, or for that matter, search warrants? The answer is that the Supreme Court has

104

embarked over the past few years on a radical re-writing of the Fourth Amendment, which should be of concern to anyone who treasures personal privacy and freedom from arbitrary government intrusion.

It used to be that search warrants, issued by judges after review of police affidavits, were required unless an emergency, known in the law as "exigent circumstances," made preparing an application for and obtaining a warrant either impractical or dangerous. In those cases it was sufficient if the information known to the police on the spot amounted to what the judge would have required: probable cause to believe that contraband, the proceeds of a crime, or other evidence of crime would be found in the place or on the person to be searched. Simply put, probable cause is information that makes it probable that the evidence sought will be found in the location to be searched. Recently however, the Court has abandoned that constitutional scheme. Instead it has taken to determining for one kind of search at a time whether, based on the Court's balancing of the authority's reason for doing that particular type of search against the individual's interest in privacy, the government must use the "probable cause" standard articulated in the Fourth Amendment, or need apply only the Court's watered-down "reasonable suspicion" rule. Of even greater concern, the Court has on recent occasions dispensed with even that lesser justification.

The origin of the problem, ironically, is a 1968 decision of the civil-liberties-sensitive Warren Court that was designed to limit, rather than expand, police power. In *Terry v. Ohio*,[33] the Court concluded that brief, investigatory police "stops" of suspicious persons that fell short of arrest and pat-down "frisks" for weapons that did not involve reaching into the inside of clothing were, respectively, "seizures" and "searches" protected by the Fourth Amendment. But because such actions were less than full seizures and searches, the Court chose to apply the more general admonition of the Fourth Amendment—that all such actions be "reasonable"—rather than the specific and demanding warrant and probable-cause requirements. The Court created a new rule that police need have only a "reasonable suspicion" of criminal behavior to undertake these less intrusive street confrontations. In an attempt to restrain even that limited authority, the Court explained that a "reasonable suspicion" is more than a "mere hunch," which might justify more investigation but not any restraint or search of a citizen. *Terry* was the first time that the

105

Supreme Court had approved a search without at least probable cause. But because it placed low-level police interventions under constitutional scrutiny for the first time, it was deemed by many to be a step forward.

The Burger-Rehnquist Courts have, however, perverted this newfound protection into a limitation on individual privacy. First, police were authorized to stop cars and travellers based on reasonable suspicion of any traffic or criminal offense.[34] Then in 1985, in its first case involving a search of public school students, the Supreme Court decided that because school administrators were acting as educators and substitute parents, not as police, and because they were primarily enforcing school rules, not criminal laws, the Fourth Amendment required only "reasonable grounds for suspecting that the search will turn up evidence" of a violation of either a school rule or the criminal law.[35] The non-criminal rationale was striking because, although the search in that case, known as *TLO* for the initials of the juvenile, was based on a belief that the student had smoked ordinary cigarettes, the assistant principal actually found marijuana, which resulted in the juvenile delinquency conviction being reviewed by the Court. *TLO* involved a search of a student's purse, but the Court left open the possibility that searches of lockers and desks, which are school, not student, property, might not even require reasonable suspicion.

Perhaps that decision could be excused because it involved children who have more limited constitutional rights. But then in 1987, in its first case involving the search of the office of a public employee,[36] the Court expressly engaged in a balancing test to determine the level of evidence needed for a search. The Court concluded that the important government interests in uncovering work-related misconduct and in recovering office files when the employee is out of the office outweighed the diminished individual privacy interest in an office setting. The Court consequently allowed a search of office desk drawers and file cabinets based solely on "reasonable suspicion" even when the individual was suspected of serious misconduct, in that case, misappropriating an office computer. The opinion left open whether the same rules would apply to searches of employee property, such as briefcases and purses, while in an office.

In 1989, the Court used its balancing test to permit routine drug testing of all railroad employees working on any train that is involved in an accident, even if management has no reason to suspect drug use by any particular individual but only has a hunch that someone in the workforce had made a mistake.[37] It then went even further and ruled that all United States Customs Service employees who seek positions that involve carrying guns or drug interdiction may be tested for drugs because of the government's overwhelming interest in preventing drug use by employees in such circumstances. The Court so ruled even though the evidence showed that the agency had no basis for believing that more than a very small percentage of customs employees were involved with drugs.[38] The government's position was so weak that Justice Antonin Scalia, hardly a radical civil libertarian, felt forced to dissent. He noted that the government could not recite "even a single instance in which any of the speculated horribles actually occurred: an instance, that is, in which the cause of bribe-taking, or of poor aim, or of unsympathetic law enforcement, or of compromise of classified information, was drug use." He chided the Court and reminded the public "that symbolism, even symbolism for so worthy a cause as the abolition of unlawful drugs, cannot validate an otherwise unreasonable search."[39]

After those rulings, one might still have surmised that this balancing test, with its watering down of even the "reasonable suspicion" requirement, was only to be used for civil matters such as employment and educational discipline, not in traditional police investigations of crimes. Unfortunately this hope proved founded. Only one year after the railroad and customs cases, the Court ruled in 1990 that police seeking to determine whether anyone was committing the criminal offense of driving while intoxicated could stop all motorists at a roadblock regardless of how they were driving. (See "Legal Roadblocks to Traffic Roadblocks," page 81.) Of even greater concern was the Court's cavalier comment that its balancing test, which allows the Court to decide how much protection to give individuals in each context, was available to determine the constitutionality of all police stops of motorists, presumably including those based on suspicion of more serious criminal misconduct. The drug testing and roadblock rulings show that the Court is prepared to balance away not only warrants and probable cause, but even the limited protection of "reasonable suspicion."

Some will rightfully ask: what is the big deal? What really is the difference between "reasonable suspicion" and "probable cause?"

And anyway, how can privacy rights be absolute if we are to have effective law enforcement?

I confess that the terms are difficult to define with precision. But clearly there is a difference. Think of a typical murder mystery. There is reason, often very good reason, to suspect a whole range of characters, who may have had a strong motive or recent access to the victim and the murder weapon. Rarely, however, until the very end is there a basis to believe that "probably" one of them did it.

Similarly there may be a whole host of circumstances—such as increased tardiness or absenteeism, fatigue or absentmindedness on the job, or inability to concentrate or tabulate—that would raise a suspicion, perhaps even a reasonable one, of drug use. But one would need substantial evidence of impairment—inability to walk, talk, or bend over straight, for example, plus glassy eyes or an eyewitness to an apparent drug transaction—before one could say that "probably" it was drugs, rather than a physical ailment, family dispute, or alcohol, that caused the poor work performance. Police and courts distinguish daily between the reasonable suspicion of a weaving car that justifies pulling over the car for investigation and the probable cause of alcohol smell, slurred speech, and inability to walk or count required to justify the involuntary taking of blood to check for evidence of intoxication. And certainly everyone can see the difference between requiring *some* evidence, however defined, that a particular individual did something wrong, and using only general assumptions about the behavior of entire workforces or motorist pools.

Of course, private rights are not absolute; there must be some balancing between law enforcement needs and individual privacy. But the Court has apparently forgotten that the balance has already been struck—by the Framers! The warrant and probable cause requirements allow intrusions into privacy, but only when clearly justified in the eyes of a neutral judicial officer, rather than the employer, principal, or police officer on the spot who believes she or he is hot on the trail of misconduct.

Even if the Court had the right to redefine the balance, which it certainly does not, it has acted erratically at best. Removal and chemical search of bodily fluids is considered by many to be as intrusive as a traditional search of a car, for which probable cause is still required, or a search of luggage, for which a warrant is still required. And it is certainly far more invasive than the simple stop and external clothing frisk first permitted in *Terry* under the reasonable suspicion standard. Yet the Court has required the police to use the probable cause standard for taking blood tests to check for alcohol levels, but has allowed drug testing based on reasonable suspicion or no individual cause at all. Societal concerns, however legitimate, over drug use or other pressing current ills should not lead us to accept quixotic judicial balancing and consequent dilution of the personal privacy guaranteed us by the express terms of the Fourth Amendment.

Constitutional Rights Should Apply at Work

How would you like to work at a place with the following policy?

> To insure a safe and productive workplace, Management prohibits using, selling, transferring, possessing and being under the influence of drugs and alcohol on the work site.

So far it sounds fine. But how about the next paragraph of the policy?

> To effectuate this goal, Management reserves the right to conduct searches or inspections of employees and their personal effects and vehicles located on the premises. These searches may be made without prior warning and may be conducted with the assistance of electronic devices, search dogs and representatives of law enforcement agencies. Management may require that an individual may at any time be required to give a urine or blood sample in order to determine compliance with this policy. A refusal to provide a sample means that there is a presumption of a violation of this policy. Any employee who violates or refuses to comply with this policy may be disciplined, including discharged.

Now I think most people would say it doesn't sound so great. Having one's car, handbag, locker, or jacket sniffed by dogs or opened by a supervisor, having phone conversations monitored, and being forced to give a blood or urine sample whenever the boss demands one sound too intrusive. As is common, most would agree on the goal of keeping the workplace free of drugs and alcohol but would differ on what means we should be willing to use to attain that end.

The quoted policy is a real one. If the employer had been the Social Security Administration, the state transportation agency, or the local tax collector's office, the policy would clearly be unconstitutional. Should it make a difference that it was in fact the employment policy of a privately owned oil refinery?

Although the impact of such a policy on employees is identical whoever the boss is, the constitutional connotations are very different. In general the federal Constitution and most state constitutions limit only the actions of the government and not those of private entities. In constitutional law, this is known as the "state action" requirement, whether the government involved is a federal, state, or local agency. Over the past two decades, the United States Supreme Court has narrowed the concept of state action. It has ruled for example, that even a private school receiving 99 percent of its money from the government to teach students with special educational needs who are placed there by public school districts is not subject to constitutional rules of due process in disciplining its teachers or students.[40] Using this approach, the drug search and urine testing policy of the oil refinery quoted above clearly would be found not to violate the Fourth and Fourteenth Amendments.

While the Supreme Court was narrowing the concept of "state action," a few states began to interpret some provisions of their state constitutions to apply in some private settings. For example, California, Massachusetts, Washington, and New Jersey have applied their state constitutional free expression clauses to insure access for peaceful political leafletters to privately owned shopping malls.[41] New Jersey has extended their reach to private college campuses as well.[42] The rationale is that those locations, which are open to the public, serve the same function of meeting and communicating with others as traditional downtown areas, as to which access is guaranteed by the constitutions. New Jersey has also extended its state constitutional equal protection provision to prohibit sex discrimination by private employers.[43]

Most noteworthy in this regard, California has ruled that its special state constitutional provision on privacy, which was passed out of concern for both business and government abuses, applies to private as well as public entities. The state has thereby limited drug testing by private universities, railroads, and book publishers.[44] No state has yet ruled, however, that private companies are subject to the same search and seizure restrictions that govern police conduct. (See "A Civil Liberties Agenda for the 1990's" page 32.)

One state court in New Jersey has, however, started to move in that direction in a landmark drug-testing case. An employee named Hennessey had worked for thirteen years with the oil refinery near the New Jersey-Pennsylvania border that had the policy quoted at the outset. He had consistently received favorable evaluations and was not suspected of or charged with any misconduct. Yet he was discharged immediately after he was randomly selected for a urine test and his test came back positive for marijuana and valium. The court held the random urine testing program, and hence the discharge, illegal.[45]

The *Hennessey* court did not say that the state constitutional provision on unreasonable searches and seizures directly applies to private employers. Rather, it came to that conclusion indirectly. It applied a rule of private employment law now used by almost all states: that even when there is no written contract setting out the grounds for discharge, and thus an employer would expect to be free to discipline or fire a worker "at will," a private employer may not fire an employee in violation of "public policy." The key step that the *Hennessey* court took was to find that the state constitution is part of the public policy of the state. Higher state courts had already held that random urine tests of government employees (those conducted without reasonable suspicion that the employee is currently impaired by drugs) violate the search and seizure rules of the state constitution. (See "What Ever Happened to Probable Cause?" page 104.) The trial court, therefore, found that a discharge under a comparable program in private industry violated the state's public policy.

This approach has been used once before with regard to another constitutional right. A federal appeals court had previously ruled that, because the First Amendment is public policy, a private employer in Pennsylvania could not fire an employee who disagreed with the company's legislative position for refusing to lobby on behalf of the company.[46]

It is refreshing to have courts remind the government and the public that our constitutions, like budgets, pollution laws, and criminal statutes, incorporate fundamental policy choices governing the public's affairs. The decisions are also important because they force us to consider to what degree the Bill of Rights should apply to private employers.

Clearly wholesale incorporation of all of the rules of the Constitution into every employment relationship would be both cumbersome and unnecessary. The Sixth Amendment's guarantees of speedy and public criminal trials, for example, are obviously inapplicable. But we should recognize that most of us spend many of our waking hours as adults at the workplace. How we are treated there is critical to our sense of self and to our experiences as political citizens. In particular, how secure our car is in the company parking lot, whether our hand-bags, briefcases, lunchboxes, or lockers are examined, whether our personnel and health insurance files are confidential, and whether we must provide urine samples are the most substantial personal privacy issues that most of us will confront if we never get arrested. In ad-dition, discharge from a job is the stiffest penalty that most citizens suffer, as few of us experience anything harsher from the criminal law than a speeding fine.

It is not surprising, therefore, that we have long had federal and state civil rights laws that apply the constitutional rule of equal pro-tection to minorities and women in the private workplace. (See "Civil Rights Law, If It Ain't Broke, Don't Fix It," page 135.) We also have state laws and now a federal one that sharply limit privacy intrusions through polygraph tests by private employers.[47] Evidence rules have long protected the privacy of medical and psychiatric patients against the inquisitive eyes of employers and others. Courts in most states have long permitted citizens to sue for unwarranted privacy intrusions by peeping toms, trespassers, overzealous investigators, and the like.[48] It is hardly a drastic step to extend to private employers the consti-tutional rules against random drug testing, a modern form of over-zealous, peeping-tom investigation.

We have already come quite far in implementing basic consti-tutional principles in the workplace and other significant areas of private life. It is time to recognize that, if the Bill of Rights is to have meaning in its third century for all of us, not only the oppressed and criminally accused, we must apply its basic rules of equality, privacy, fair play, and free thought and association to private as well as public employment settings. The Constitution is sound public policy for all.

The Abortion Debate Is Unresolvable and Avoidable

There is no satisfactory resolution to the abortion debate. If one believes that a human life exists from the moment of conception, then abortion is the taking of human life, equivalent to murder. If, on the other hand, a fetus is not considered to be a human being until delivered, then a woman who is pregnant, like one who has breast cancer, should have the right, legal and moral, to choose what to do with her own body and future, which is considered part of the constitutional right of privacy.

Medicine cannot help us in this debate. Science can learn how a fetus develops; it was recently revealed that integrated brain activity begins in a fetus at about ten weeks of pregnancy.[49] Science can also improve the applicable medical procedures, thereby lowering the risks of both delivery and abortion, and can insure the viability of a prematurely delivered fetus at an earlier stage. But science cannot determine when human life begins. That is a legal or moral conclusion, a conceptual labelling of a physical event, which for many is a matter of religious faith.

The dispute is on two levels. On the ethical plane there is significant dispute about the morality of abortion, with major religions in sharp disagreement. For example, a group called the Religious Coalition for Abortion Rights consists of Presbyterians, Episcopalians, Methodists, Lutherans, Unitarians, Reform and Conservative Jews, and an organization called Catholics for Free Choice.

The second controversy concerns whether a moral tenet should be enforced by law. The pro-choice position is that by legalizing abortion the state is not *requiring* anyone to violate her ethical views; anyone who thinks abortion is immoral may carry her pregnancy to term. The response to that argument is that the government does not allow people to murder, rape, or kidnap and thus should not countenance the equivalent of murder simply because some would like to engage in it.

The rebuttal to this analogy to traditional crimes is that the abortion situation is very different. There is an overwhelming societal consensus that murder, rape, and kidnapping are immoral. The legislation making them crimes is a product of that moral consensus. But with abortion there is no broad-based societal agreement. In such a setting, according to this view, the political majority should leave all individuals free to make their own moral choice rather than using the state to resolve the matter by enacting law that chooses sides in the moral debate.

Because the legal feud is grounded in sharply differing views of ethics, compromise seems impossible. That is why the ingenious recent proposal of Professor Sass at Georgetown University—that legal protection should extend to fetuses when integrated brain functioning begins—is doomed to failure, even though, in any other political or legal context, it would seem like a reasonable compromise.[50] Clearly this debate, which has so torn our nation, cannot be resolved to the satisfaction of the morally divided combatants. But I suggest it need not even occur.

Abortion is only considered if a woman who does not want to have a baby becomes pregnant. We would have little need to debate its morality and legality if women who do not want to have children did not become pregnant at all. As a matter of human decency and as the surest way of getting out of the abortion quandary, our society should therefore develop a completely safe, reliable, uncomplicated, and cheap means of avoiding conception. Such means should be available to all—which means without cost to those who cannot afford it. The failure to do so thirty years after the contraceptive pill was developed is astounding and has needlessly contributed to the painful abortion battles of the last twenty years, which have injured our judicial and political institutions as well as many individuals.

Given the advances of science in so many other areas of human biology, it is almost inconceivable that the safest birth control method available today—condoms—is the same that was available in the sev-

115

enteenth century. No doubt a major cause of the slow developments in this area is the sexist view that women should bear the burdens of contraception. No pill for men has been developed or seriously contemplated, although the male reproductive system is far less complex chemically than the female system. And condoms only came back into favor because of the AIDS epidemic; that is, men were willing to "sacrifice" to avoid pregnancy only when their very lives were at stake. In addition, fears of liability and bad publicity and concern for the marketability of the product have also contributed to the failure of this country to produce any new contraceptive devices since the IUD until Norplant was approved in late 1990.[51] Whatever the reasons for the delay, a safe, reliable method is long overdue.

I recognize that my proposal is not without controversy. The Catholic Church officially views any method of contraception other than abstention as immoral. But no other significant segment of society holds the view that contraception is immoral. Indeed the Church itself does not consider the use of contraception as seriously wrong as abortion; there are no claims that contraception is murder and no calls for making it illegal. And the contraceptive practices of devout, practicing Catholic couples over the past decades indicate that the Church's doctrine is not widely accepted even by its own members. Of course, as noted before with regard to abortion, the widespread availability of contraceptives does not mean that anyone will be *forced* to violate his or her moral views by using them.

There will also not be complete agreement about methods of distribution. For example, many parents are troubled by the proposals now floated throughout the country for having high school nurses or clinics offer contraceptives to students. And I am sure some would be upset at the idea of people on welfare receiving free contraceptives. But as in all human affairs, we must be realistic and make choices. The human sexual drive is enormously powerful. Young people and poor people will continue to have sex whether others like it or not and whether they have protection or not. If we take no steps, adolescents will get pregnant and then either seek abortion or become parents before they are emotionally and economically ready. Those who so vociferously condemn teenage access to abortion, with or without parental notice or consent, should consider whether teenage access to contraceptives is better or worse. The reality of nearly a million teenage pregnancies each year means that we must choose between access to contraceptives and access to abortion—we cannot avoid both.

The abortion debates are so destructive and so distorting of our political life and constitutional order that I am convinced we must find a way out soon. I believe that, in the absence of universal moral consensus, a legal ban is both bad policy, fundamentally unfair, and unconstitutional. But I think the focus of the debate is misplaced. We should all work together to minimize the need for abortions and thereby avoid the mud-slinging. If a safe, reliable, simple, and cheap contraceptive along with appropriate education about its use were readily available to all, the number of unwanted pregnancies would drop dramatically and the abortion fury would almost disappear.

The Right to Die: New Laws Are Needed

In June 1990, the United States Supreme Court rendered its first decision in a so-called "right to die" case. *Cruzan v. Director, Missouri Department of Health*[52] was the outgrowth of the request of the parents of a thirty-year-old women who had been in "a persistent vegetative state" since a car accident seven years earlier to stop all medical treatment and nutrition. The case is significant primarily because it confirmed what most other courts had assumed: that the Fourteenth Amendment's protection against deprivation of liberty without due process guarantees a competent adult the right to refuse medical treatment. Also noteworthy is its second conclusion: that this right includes the choice to refuse food and water as well as respirators and more traditional forms of medical treatment.

Yet the Supreme Court denied the Cruzans any relief. It recognized there there was no evidence to contradict the sworn testimony of Nancy Cruzan's mother, sister, housemate, and friend and the finding of the guardian appointed for the lawsuit—that she would not have wanted to live indefinitely in her condition. The Court also acknowledged that the Cruzans were loving parents with no improper motivation for seeking relief. Nevertheless the Court relied upon a legalistic nicety—that the state, none of whose officials knew Nancy Cruzan or her wishes in any way, may insist upon continued treatment (in a case like Nancy's for as much as thirty years), unless it is satisfied that there is "clear and convincing evidence" that the patient, while competent, specifically had an intent to terminate this particular treatment were she ever to be in this particular condition.

In short, Nancy Cruzan should have had the foresight, before entering her car that fateful January 1983 morning, to draft and sign a formal legal document known as a "living will," which indicated her wishes with regard to termination of medical treatment should she ever fall into a state where she could not express her wishes. It is the formal legalistic perception of this complex human, social, moral/religious, and medical problem by the Court's majority, with its serious and unfair consequences for the average citizen, that most startles and disappoints.

The question of whether a human being should be able to refuse available care or, more broadly, to refuse to continue living is enormously complex and sensitive. Here are some of the major dilemmas: Should we treat equally those who are terminally ill and those, like Cruzan, who are in what doctors call a persistent vegetative state that may continue for decades? Should the amount of pain being suffered, the current level of functioning, that is "the quality of life," or the length of time remaining matter? Should we distinguish affirmative treatment, such as chemotherapy, from simple pain relief, or ordinary from extraordinary measures, or formal "medical treatment" from artificial provision of food and water? How should we determine the "true" desires of a now-incompetent patient, or even the wishes of a legally competent and conscious patient constantly in intense pain? Should we distinguish, morally or legally, between withdrawal of health care and affirmative steps to end life? The last question has been brought to public attention most recently by the attempted prosecution and later state request for an injunction against a Michigan doctor who had provided a "suicide machine" to assist a fifty-four-year-old, mentally competent Oregon woman with Alzheimer's disease to end her life.[53]

The importance of the resolution of these questions to affected patients, their families, the health care profession, and society as a whole establishes the need for deliberate, broad-based public policy. Under our scheme of government, this is primarily the job of the legislature, the representative crucible for resolving competing societal interests. So far forty states and the District of Columbia have provided by statute for some kind of medical self-determination, although only thirteen states and the District authorize appointment of health-care proxies, persons designated in advance to make medical treatment decisions when the individual making the designation is unconscious or for some other reason unable to do so herself.[54]

But we must not lose sight of the fact that neither living wills nor health-care proxy forms will solve the problem. Missouri in fact has a living-will statute, yet Nancy Cruzan had not executed one. As Justice Brennan noted in dissent, only a small minority (recent surveys indicate between 9 and 23 percent) of Americans have executed a living will or comparable document setting out their instructions for terminating care. Yet two 1988 surveys, one by the American Medical Association and the other by Colorado University, show that the overwhelming majority of Americans (80 and 85 percent respectively) would want life support systems, including artificial hydration and nutrition, withdrawn from hopelessly ill or irreversibly comatose patients if they or their families requested it.[55]

People do not complete such documents for a variety of reasons. Unlike Supreme Court justices, most Americans are not legally trained and do not have easy access to legal services. Young people consider themselves invincible or immortal, or simply do not think about the physical accidents or injuries that require resolution of these issues. Most people do not plan their meals more than a day in advance, so we should not be surprised they have not decided years in advance which should be their last meal. Some of those who are good planners are terrified to contemplate death or suffering. In brief, there are many perfectly human and understandable reasons why most people would not complete a formal legal document, such as a living will or health-care proxy, even if their state law provided for it.

The law should humanely serve everyone, not only those with legally perfect documents. We have for centuries had procedures for dealing with the affairs of those who die without a written will and they do not require leaving the estate in limbo for decades. Of course, the state is rightfully concerned that we accurately determine what the patient wants, as one choice is irreversible. Requiring a legal proceeding to probe whether the family members seeking termination of care have improper motives is certainly one legitimate condition. Likewise, the law should protect minor children who have not yet formed their own opinions on the wisdom of withholding medical care from the religious views of their parents, an issue revived by the recent criminal prosecutions of Christian Science parents who refused medical care for their young children.[56] But we can readily satisfy all such concerns without closing legal doors on people's right to decide how they want to live and die.

IV

CIVIL RIGHTS AND DISCRIMINATION

In 1954, the Supreme Court ruled in *Brown v. Board of Education* that segregation of public schools was unconstitutional. Yet today most minority children still attend schools that are predominantly African American and Hispanic. The percentage of African Americans in colleges declined in the late 1980's, while the percentage in medical and law schools remains far below their proportion in the general population. Although the causes of these phenomena are varied and complex, these basic facts remind us that the civil rights struggles in education and elsewhere were not resolved with the *Brown* decision or the passage of the 1964 Civil Rights Act.

In addition to race or ethnic background, other personal characteristics over which the individual has no control, such as gender and sexual orientation, have also historically been the basis for invidious discrimination. Our society is only now coming to recognize that these attributes are similarly irrelevant to educational or employment qualification and their use is equally degrading. The law is therefore starting to reflect the understanding that it is as irrational and demeaning to be denied a job, insurance, or admission to a university or club because one is a woman, disabled, gay, or afflicted with AIDS as it is to be so treated because of the color of one's skin.

Even after society understands and rejects the inhumanity of discrimination, there are complex questions about the proper solutions.

May the state force even private clubs to admit women or others with whom they do not wish to associate? Should only the individual job or university applicants who have themselves been injured be given a remedy? Or is there a societal benefit in diversifying schools and workplaces by consciously including members of groups that have historically been excluded? If so, how should we go about doing that? This chapter considers both what forms of discrimination should be impermissible and what the remedies should be.

Fight AIDS, Not the People We Fear Have AIDS

AIDS is probably the most frightening public health problem since the bubonic plague. People are understandably scared and uncertain how to respond. Hysteria, however, always breeds overreactions that threaten our liberties. Consider, for example, the Palmer Raids of the 1920's, the McCarthy investigations of the 1950's, and the current drug war. The question is: how can we protect everyone from a deadly disease yet avoid needless injury to its unfortunate victims as well as those erroneously assumed to be infected?

One actual incident highlights some of the problems. Three men answered an ad for rental of an apartment. After discussions, they reached an agreement with the landlord concerning a lease. The landlord then asked if they were gay. They honestly responded that they were. He then asked questions about wild parties and drug use. Finally he asked about AIDS, and they told him, accurately, that they did not have AIDS. Later that afternoon he called back to say that he would not rent them the apartment because he did not want his family, who would be living in one of the other apartments in the small building, to get AIDS from them.

Upon receiving the men's complaint, the state civil rights agency sued to stop the discrimination. The judge initially ordered the landlord to rent the apartment to the three men. The judge ruled that AIDS is a handicap and because the refusal to rent was based on a belief (albeit inaccurate) that they were so handicapped, it violated the state law's ban on discrimination based on handicap.[1] The reasoning was that just as one could not deny people an apartment in light of the law's ban on racial, religious, or national-origin discrimination because one wrongly thought that they were African Americans, Moonies, or from Mexico (any more than one could if the belief were accurate), one cannot refuse to rent an apartment because one incorrectly believes that the applicants suffer from a handicap such as AIDS. The order was later dissolved when the men decided not to take the apartment under the circumstances. The ACLU thereafter sued and won money damages for the men to compensate them for the humiliation they suffered and the expenses they incurred.

The same kind of overreaction based on misperceptions about the disease is evidenced in the slew of legislation proposed throughout the nation to deal with AIDS. Two common bills illustrate the problems best. The first is a requirement that all applicants for a marriage license take a blood test for the AIDS virus antibody. Such a law was passed in Illinois in 1987 but repealed two years later when the legislature realized how few people were infected and how many residents were marrying in neighboring states to avoid the requirement.[2] The second requires AIDS testing of all persons arrested for sex and drug offenses. A comparable executive overreaction is the federal government's refusal for ten years to accept donation of blood from Haitians because of what initially appeared to be a relatively high incidence of the disease in that ethnic group.

In each case the action or proposal springs from ignorance of the facts. Simply put, only a minority of homosexuals and drug addicts and a very small minority of Haitians and heterosexuals getting marriage licenses have AIDS, although AIDS can be transmitted through sexual intercourse, shared hypodermic needles, and blood transfusions. AIDS cannot be transmitted by a handshake, a cough, a sneeze, or other casual contacts that occur in school, at work, or at home. Homosexuals, like heterosexuals, can use condoms and other means of protecting themselves and their partners from the risk of AIDS.

The blood test is not a test for AIDS or even for the virus that causes AIDS—the human immunodeficiency virus (HIV). Rather it detects the antibodies that the body develops when exposed to the virus. The test was designed to screen donated blood to avoid accidental transmission during transfusions and is now properly used very successfully for that purpose. Far more people have been exposed to the virus than actually have AIDS. As of November 1990, about 155,000 people in the United States had been diagnosed as having

AIDS. Tragically, over 95,000, or almost two-thirds, of them are already dead. Yet the government now estimates that over one million people in this country would test positive for the virus antibody.[3] Although scientists now believe that most people infected with HIV will eventually develop AIDS, they do not yet know the exact proportion, what characteristics or behaviors make it more likely, or how long it will take.

What then is government to do? Obviously it should invest substantial resources to find diagnostic tests, interim treatments, and ultimately a cure. Tragically, the Reagan administration ignored the problem through the first half-dozen years of the AIDS epidemic, and thus many thousands will have died needlessly by the time a cure is found.

Government should also educate all of us as to the current state of medical knowledge about the illness, methods of transmission, available protections, and possible forms of treatment. The example was set by Surgeon General Everett Koop, who courageously overcame the Reagan administration's indifference some years ago and sent an informational brochure about AIDS to every American household. Among homosexuals, education has proven extremely successful, leading to changes in behavior and a significant drop in the rate of infection.

At the same time, government should ensure that homosexuals, Haitians, and any other group thought, rightly or wrongly, to be a high-risk group are legally protected from irrational fears. Congress has taken important initial steps by adopting first the Fair Housing Act amendments in 1988[4] and then the Americans with Disabilities Act in 1990.[5] Following the approach of the court in the case noted above, these laws treat HIV infection (not just full blown AIDS) as a handicap or disability, and expressly make discrimination in housing, employment, and public accommodations for "being regarded" as having such a disability just as illegal as discrimination based on a correct belief that one is disabled.[6]

Likewise the government should set an example for the rest of society by avoiding knee-jerk reactions that only aggravate irrational fears and hate. Given the availability for many years of sound blood screening tests to detect infected individuals, the federal government's refusal to accept donated blood from Haitians did nothing other than increase ethnic and racial tension, as the government implicitly recognized when it finally terminated that policy in late 1990.[7] Similarly it makes no public health sense to test the blood of everyone getting married; everyone convicted of (not to mention those only charged with) a drug offense, including possession of cocaine or marijuana, which are usually not injected by needle; or everyone convicted of a sex offense, including sexual fondling, exposure, or soliciting a prostitute. Such broad-based testing that is not tied to behaviors scientifically verified as capable of transmitting the disease will foment fear and encourage ostracizing actions. It will also waste valuable resources that could be used for education, prevention, and treatment of those in need.

The government should lead society in addressing rationally and compassionately the unavoidable and complex problems such a disease presents. For example, we need to develop coherent and fair policies on whether all patients who will undergo invasive procedures should be tested for HIV antibodies and the operating personnel informed of the results. At the same time we must consider whether all health care personnel doing such procedures should be tested and their patients informed of the results. There are no easy answers, but hysterical generalizations will certainly not help.

In sum, let's fight the disease and not groups of fellow citizens who are similarly panicked by the threat of a horrible but conquerable disease.

Men-Only Clubs: Illegal Discrimination or Protected Association?

As more constituencies assert themselves in our increasingly complex society, various demands will inevitably come into conflict. A prominent recent clash has been between the claims of women to be free from sex discrimination in all aspects of public life and the claims of various all-male groups to be able to choose with whom to associate in their privately owned facilities and clubs.

Courts around the country, including the Supreme Court on two recent occasions, have had to grapple with claims by women seeking to be admitted to various public service organizations, including the Rotaries, Jaycees, and Kiwanis, as full members, rather than relegated to pancake-making auxiliaries.[8] Likewise, selective private clubs, where the business and professional elite meet over power lunches, have faced legislative and judicial challenges to their exclusive admissions policies.[9] One of the most famous of those attacks resulted in the 1990 ruling of the New Jersey Supreme Court that the student "eating clubs" at Princeton University must admit women, a full twenty-one years after the college itself first admitted women students.[10]

The key question in all these cases is what is a "public accommodation," in which the law has for almost three decades, since the 1964 Civil Rights Act and comparable state laws, prohibited sexual, racial, and other forms of discrimination, and what is a "private" establishment in which freedom to choose one's companions is secured. The distinction clearly does not depend simply on the nature of the owner. Naturally, all government-owned buildings are considered public. But many privately owned facilities—for example, buses, trains, their terminals, movie theaters, motels, restaurants, supermarkets, and malls—are also treated as public accommodations, because they hold themselves out as open to the public. Indeed by advertising they affirmatively seek out public attention and patronage. Once having opened themselves to the public, they may not, by law, restrict themselves to a certain segment of the public, whether designated by skin color, sex, or religion.

Some private facilities, of course, remain clear of such restraints. Certainly we need not admit all callers to our living or dining room, for each of us retains, in the privacy of the home, the right to select with whom to associate. (This no longer holds true once one publicly announces that one's home is for sale.[11]) A private service organization or dining club, some contend, is much more like a living room gathering of friends than, say, a political party avidly seeking supporters in public elections or a catering service that publicly advertises for wedding parties.

In grappling with this dilemma, the Supreme Court has, as is traditional in constitutional analysis, first identified the reason for government involvement—in this case the vital and constitutionally based interest in assuring equal treatment of women. But even when implementing the most compelling state interests, the government must not intrude more than is absolutely necessary upon affected constitutional rights. This is known as "strict scrutiny" or "the compelling interest test." For that reason, the Court has focused primarily on defining with precision the nature of the constitutionally protected right of private association, to which attaches the privilege to exclude people on any basis.

The Court has identified two different kinds of association that deserve constitutional protection. First is the right of "intimate association," which involves family and similar close personal relationships. Under this category, the Court has protected the right to marry and to choose which relatives to live with against burdensome zoning and welfare regulations. An example is a ruling that struck down a local zoning ordinance that prevented a homeowner from having both of her young grandsons live with her because they were cousins (children of different sons) rather than brothers.[12] Although the Court has refused to consider of constitutional dimensions the most private and intimate of male associations—homosexual relationships in the privacy of a home (see "Anti-Gay Prejudice Should Not be Public Policy" page 131), it has nevertheless considered carefully the intimate association claims of men-only social organizations and clubs.

After close scrutiny of the nature and operation of such groups, the Supreme Court and other courts have ultimately denied them this kind of constitutional protection. They recognized that groups like the Rotary Club, with almost one million members nationwide, the Kiwanis, with 8,200 clubs and over 313,000 members in two countries, or even the Princeton eating clubs, each with thousands of members across the country who mostly do not know each other and attend club functions only once a year, hardly have the kind of close, personal relationships that prompt constitutional protection of "intimate associations."

Second, the First Amendment protects "expressional association" —the right to form a group to advance a political viewpoint or practice a religious faith. No one would seriously suggest, for example, that the Ku Klux Klan could be ordered to admit blacks or Jews, as the very purpose of the association is to advocate the inferiority of those groups. Likewise the Catholic Church could not be forced to admit students of other religions to its parochial schools.

This associational interest also seems inapplicable here. The Kiwanis and Rotary clubs assert that they gather for the purpose of providing community service, including service benefiting women, and they have long allowed women to help them in some of those projects through "ladies auxiliaries." In addition these groups, which are generally composed of members of the business community, provide opportunities to make and enhance business contacts. A businesswoman interested in community service will certainly not undermine the goals of those organizations. Likewise the Princeton eating clubs are designed to let undergraduates eat and socialize in smaller, more pleasant settings than a mass mess hall and to make professional and business contacts with well-placed alumni. The clubs do not contend that it is inappropriate to socialize with women; indeed they regularly invite women to dinner and sponsor or attend parties with women.

None of these groups associate to express a political or religious view that women should not be in business, provide community service, or associate with men. They seek to deny women only the power and respect of membership, not the possibility of social interaction.

Whether we like it or not, our densely populated and highly interactive society forces us more and more into public settings. If our society is ever to achieve true equality, we must accept, indeed hopefully welcome, the premise that all dealings outside the truly private domain of the home must be free from arbitrary and hurtful biases. Only when we are genuinely in private or are directly expressing a political or religious view may we act on our baser instincts to treat others as less worthy. Perhaps in time we can even learn to restrain or eliminate those impulses as well.

Anti-Gay Prejudice Should Not Be Public Policy

Whether or not we express prejudices in private, the law generally prevents us from acting on them in public. This legal limit is in part a product of the fact that we all belong to some ethnic, racial, religious, or handicapped minority and thus are vulnerable to prejudice. This sensitivity creates some political counterweight against condoning most biases or enacting them into law.

But the prejudice against men and women with a sexual orientation at variance with that of the majority is different in three key respects. First, the source of prejudice is more personal and psychological. People feel directly threatened by a lifestyle that challenges their very identity. Second, the prejudice is framed in moral and religious terms. Being gay is often condemned as sinful. Even during slavery, when African Americans were thought by their owners to be less than human, their very existence was not considered immoral. Third, the vast majority of the public, at least 90 percent by even the estimates most generous to gays, have the same sexual orientation. There is, therefore, far less political protection against majority rule. As a consequence, one glaring defect in both constitutional and civil rights law remains: the lack of legal protection against the intense and widespread discrimination against gays and lesbians.

The lack of constitutional protection is a result of a Supreme Court ruling in 1986. By a vote of five to four in a case called *Bowers v. Hardwick*,[13] the Court ruled that the constitutional rights of privacy and equal protection did not prevent Georgia from prosecuting for sodomy two consenting adult homosexuals arrested in their bedroom when police entered for a wholly unrelated reason, even though heterosexual couples were never prosecuted for the acts of oral or anal sex banned by the law. The Court ignored its rulings providing constitutional protection for intimate associations (see "Men-Only Clubs: Illegal Discrimination or Protected Association?" page 127), and denied relief because of the long-standing historical, religious, and legal condemnations of sodomy. The controversy was rekindled in late 1990 when Justice Lewis F. Powell Jr., who provided the fifth and deciding vote in *Bowers*, stated publicly that he had originally planned to vote to invalidate the law and now believes that he erred in voting with the majority.[14]

The political scene offers little hope of changing the law except where there are substantial gay and lesbian constituencies. In various recent political campaigns, candidates have asserted that the state should not allow homosexuals to be teachers, camp counselors, or foster parents. Even where the majority is not seeking to make anti-gay prejudice into public policy, it has not sought to eliminate discrimination based on such views. At present neither federal nor state laws (except in Wisconsin and Massachusetts) prohibit discrimination in employment, housing, education, or public accommodations on the basis of sexual orientation.

Some headway has been made, however, because the civil rights laws, which routinely prohibit discrimination based on a handicap, have been interpreted to prohibit also discrimination based on a mistaken belief that an individual is handicapped and AIDS and HIV infection have been declared handicaps. Thus, mistakenly thinking that gay applicants for a job or apartment must have AIDS or HIV infection and rejecting them for that reason would violate the civil rights laws' prohibition on handicap discrimination. (See "Fight AIDS, Not the People We Fear Have AIDS," page 123.) But with the law interpreted this way, one may still discriminate against gays and lesbians as long as it is not because of a belief that they are infected with the AIDS virus. It is extremely difficult to establish what someone is thinking when they discriminate. Moreover, with the slowdown in the AIDS epidemic in the gay community and the public awareness that AIDS is at least as prevalent among drug users as among gays, AIDS may not be the only or even the main reason for discrimination based on sexual orientation. Certainly it wasn't for the many centuries before AIDS.

Potentially more far-reaching advances in the law have come from a recent decision of the New York Court of Appeals and a new San

Francisco ordinance. The court ruled in 1989 that gay partners may be considered a "family" entitled to the protection of the state's rent control law,[15] and as of February 1991, San Francisco allows unmarried couples to register with the city.[16] These steps are significant because they go beyond simply prohibiting discrimination on the basis of sexual orientation and affirmatively acknowledge gay and lesbian relationships as legitimate equivalents of traditional heterosexual relationships.

Although the conceptual significance of these two developments is enormous, their practical impact is limited. Most employment and public accommodation laws do not protect families from discrimination, and housing laws often protect only families with children. Moreover San Francisco is politically atypical because of its very substantial and active gay and lesbian constituency. In any case, the impact of a couple's public registration under that city's ordinance on insurance, employment, and other legal benefits is still uncertain.

Further legal progress will depend upon education of the heterosexual majority about its erroneous assumptions about gays and lesbians. Very rarely does anyone suggest that gays are not qualified for most jobs and there is, of course, no data to suggest that. Rather, one common source of prejudice, and probably the one underlying the recent proposal of a gubernatorial candidate that the state not allow gays to be teachers, camp counselors, or foster parents, is the assumption that adult homosexuals are more likely to sexually abuse children under their care than are adult heterosexuals. Such a view ignores the facts. The vast majority of adult homosexuals are attracted to adults of the same sex, just as the vast majority of adult heterosexuals are attracted to adults of the opposite sex. It is a rare and serious aberration for gay persons to seek sexual gratification from children, just as it is for heterosexuals. The available data indicate that most sexual abuse of children is heterosexual.[17]

The major reason that we do not have conclusive statistics or a shared public perception that there is no greater risk to children from homosexuals is that, because of the lack of legal protection discussed here, gay teachers, counselors, babysitters, and coaches are afraid to identify themselves publicly. If all gays were publicly identified and if, as many gays claim, 10 percent of the population is gay, we would quickly see that respected leaders and competent workers in all fields are gay and pose no threat to children. What we do know is that the most prevalent danger to children is from physical, not sexual, abuse, and that the vast majority of physical abusers are parents, custodians, and their partners, who are overwhelmingly heterosexual.[18]

Another significant source of anti-gay discrimination over the years has been the view of many religions that homosexual conduct is sinful and thus that gays are unacceptable role models. Education cannot change religious beliefs, and both our Constitution and our discrimination laws safeguard religious beliefs. But they do not protect those who act on those views in a manner harmful to others and in violation of contrary social policy or criminal laws. Thus, the fact that Mormons did not believe African Americans to be worthy of ordination or that many religions, Christian and Jewish, did not (and some still do not) deem women worthy of ordination does not authorize their adherents to refuse to hire, educate, serve, or transport African Americans and women, or to assault those with whom they come in contact. People may continue to differ on whether homosexual conduct is sinful or unnatural and may choose not to associate with them socially. But in the public domain, the law should permit individuals to act upon those beliefs only if gays objectively threaten harm to others or are objectively unsuited for a particular job or benefit.

Because gays do not pose any objective danger or lack qualifications as a result of their sexual orientation, discrimination against them is not simply unfair—it is bad economic, social, and political policy. It is inefficient and thus economically foolish to reject good workers, including teachers, counselors, and coaches, for reasons unrelated to their qualifications and productivity. It is socially destructive to ostracize, or even worse to penalize, motivated and cooperative members of society. And it is undemocratic and thus politically unsound to ignore, or through stigmatizing actions to prevent the expression of, the views of 10 percent of the body politic.

The law does not and could not compel one to associate privately with those one fears or disdains for personal or moral reasons. But in the public sphere, the law generally does, and in this regard certainly should, limit exclusion to instances of demonstrated individual unsuitability for a particular position or benefit. It is long overdue that the law protect gay as well as straight people from discrimination in all aspects of public life.

Civil Rights Law: If It Ain't Broke, Don't Fix It

A wise jurist out West first introduced me to the legal application of the old adage "if it ain't broke, don't fix it." At the time I was proposing a change in a court rule that no one had complained about. This saying kept coming back to me as I reviewed the Supreme Court's spate of cases in 1989 substantially restructuring civil rights law in this country. Without any evidence that there was a need for change, the Court revised various established understandings of the reach of, and procedures to be used in implementing, the civil rights laws relating to employment discrimination. Both congressional rejection of prior narrowing Court rulings in this area and the near-passage over a presidential veto of a bill in 1990 to countermand the 1989 cases show that the Court is trying to fix what the people think ain't broke. It should stick to the many other areas of the law that are sorely in need of repair.

To understand recent events, some historical perspective is helpful. The Reconstruction Congress of the 1860's adopted the Thirteenth Amendment, which bans slavery, the Fourteenth Amendment, which ensures equal protection of the laws, and the Fifteenth Amendment, which outlaws racial discrimination in voting. Congress in that era also passed a number of statutes to insure that the newly freed slaves would have the same rights in society as whites. These laws, however, lay dormant for nearly a century after the ignominious compromise that gave the 1876 election to the Republicans in exchange for the withdrawal of national authority from the South.

The civil rights movement of the 1950's and 1960's showed that, even when taken seriously, those Reconstruction-era laws were inadequate to the task. The fact that the Supreme Court had to use constitutional analysis to ban segregated public schools is the most obvious example. In 1964, Congress sought to repair this defect by passing a broad-based anti-discrimination law known as the Civil Rights Act of 1964, which bans racial and sexual discrimination in public accommodations (Title II), federally funded programs (Title VI), and most private employment (Title VII). In 1965, Congress passed the Voting Rights Act, which bans any electoral requirement that discriminates on the basis of race. After Martin Luther King, Jr., was assassinated in 1968, the Fair Housing Act, also known as Title VIII, was passed, banning discrimination in housing. In 1972, Title IX was adopted, banning sex discrimination in education, and Title VII was expanded to cover discrimination in public as well as private employment. The basic legal structure to protect civil rights was then in place.

Initially, through the 1960's and early 1970's, the Supreme Court was an equal partner with Congress, providing broad interpretation and rigorous application of both the old and new civil rights laws. In subsequent years, however, the Supreme Court started to slide back from its early commitment to civil rights. On a number of occasions it issued interpretations that restricted the impact or prior reach of those statutes.

On at least five occasions in the past fifteen years, Congress has had to correct judicial misunderstandings of such laws by passing amendments to reaffirm the broader reading.* For example, in 1976 the Court held that a refusal to provide disability benefits to pregnant women, while providing them to men with temporary medical disabilities, was not sex discrimination.[19] In 1978 Congress passed the Pregnancy Discrimination Act, an amendment to Title VII, to show

---

*When Congress disagrees with a Supreme Court decision interpreting the Constitution, it has no power to change it except by proposing a constitutional amendment. But when Congress disagrees with how the Court has interpreted a statute passed by Congress, it can amend the statute or pass a new one in order to implement its original intent. Such a new statute will not change the result in the particular case that the Court previously decided, but only the interpretation of the law that would lead to similar results in future cases.

136

the Court that it was wrong.[20] Similarly, in 1984 the Court ruled that federal funds must be withdrawn only from the specific program found to discriminate, not from the entire college or institution in which the funded program operates.[21] In the aptly named Civil Rights Restoration Act of 1987, Congress expressly rejected that decision and banned federal funding of any part of an institution if one of its programs was found to discriminate.[22] Similar congressional corrections of judicial misreadings have been made in the areas of voting rights and children's rights.[23] It is against this backdrop of repeated congressional rejection of narrow judicial interpretations that we must examine the Court's most recent and massive backsliding.

Many of the 1989 rulings are technical in nature, but they have very profound, practical implications. I will focus on only three of them to show both the breadth of the retrenchment and the fallacious assumptions on which they rest.

In a case called *Patterson v. McLean Credit Union*,[24] the Court dealt with one of the old Reconstruction statutes, known as Section 1981. It provides simply that "all persons within the jurisdiction of the United States shall have the same right in every State and Territory to make and enforce contracts . . . as is enjoyed by white citizens." In a 1976 case, called *Runyon v. McCrary*,[25] the Court had ruled that Section 1981, unlike the Constitution, is not limited to government action and thus applies to private as well as public contracts, in that case a contract to attend private school. Lower courts had applied the statute to all employment claims from hiring and promotion to job conditions and discharges. The *Patterson* case itself involved a claim of ongoing, on-the-job racial harassment brought by an African American woman who was a teller against the private credit union for which she worked.

When it first agreed to hear the *Patterson* case, the Court, on its own, asked the parties to present arguments on whether the Court should reconsider *Runyon* and apply the statute only to government action.[26] This request created an enormous stir and great concern in the civil rights community. A record number of organizations filed friend-of-the-court, or *amicus curiae*, briefs explaining why *Runyon* should be left alone.

In its opinion in *Patterson*, the Court said it should overrule its own interpretation of a statute in only three situations: when there has been an intervening development in the law that undercuts the original ruling; when a risk develops that the ruling might "be a positive detriment to coherence and consistency in the law;" or when the prior interpretation "after being tested by experience, has been found to be inconsistent with the sense of justice or with the social welfare."[27] Applying that standard, the Court said there was no basis to overturn *Runyon*'s application of Section 1981 to private contracts.

But then, remarkably, the Court went on to rule against Ms. Patterson and overturn numerous lower court decisions by ruling that the law bars only racial discrimination in the "making" of a contract—that is, hiring—but not to discrimination in the working conditions and terms of employment after hiring, such as assignments, transfers, on-the-job harassment, and even discharge. This ruling ignores the fact that the statute expressly also protects "enforcement" of a contract. No explanations about intervening developments, inconsistencies, or the social welfare were offered. Thus, while pretending to apply an objective test of when statutory interpretations may be reversed and acknowledging that the test was not met with regard to the main point, the Court substantially reduced the scope of the statute by simply ignoring previous rulings applying the law to all terms and conditions of employment.

Wards Cove Packing Co., Inc. v. Atonio[28] even more dramatically highlights the practical and social impact of the Court's "technical" rulings. In that case, several key issues regarding the modern employment discrimination law, Title VII, were addressed. They concerned lawsuits in which employees did not claim that the company intentionally discriminated on the basis of race or sex but rather showed only that hiring or promotion requirements disproportionately excluded minorities. The questions included: what statistical proof of racial imbalance was sufficient; how specifically applicants must show which of several hiring practices being challenged caused the imbalance; and which party had the burden of proving whether a particular requirement that had already been shown to have a disproportionate impact on minorities was or was not necessary to carry on the business.

The facts of *Wards Cove*, a discrimination suit against five canneries in remote areas of Alaska, are striking. The unskilled cannery workers, who cleaned and canned the salmon, were almost all Eskimos and Filipinos. The workers in the higher-paid jobs, such as dockyard construction gangs, carpenters, cooks, bookkeepers, and on up to machinists and engineers, were almost all white. There were no objective qualifications listed for the latter jobs, openings for them were not posted at the canneries, and the companies did not promote from within. Rather, the better jobs were filled during the off-season at the mainland home offices, typically by word of mouth.[29] Relatives of the management were given preference. "Of 349 nepotistic hires in four upper-level departments during 1970–75, 332 were of whites."[30] Even more striking were the conditions of employment. The companies maintained separate mess halls and residence areas for cannery workers, leading Justices John Paul Stevens and Harry Blackmun to note in dissent the "unsettling resemblance to aspects of a plantation economy."[31]

After fifteen years of litigation, the lower courts had ruled for the Eskimo and Filipino plaintiffs. The Supreme Court reversed, based on three technical rulings. First, the Court said that to show a racial imbalance sufficient to require an explanation from the employer, plaintiffs may not compare the percentage of minorities in different job categories within the company but must compare the workforce whose composition is being challenged to the portion of the general job market qualified for such jobs. The Court insisted on this even though the parties and lower courts found it difficult to define the relevant job market for seasonal work in canneries scattered throughout rural Alaska. Second, the Court insisted that plaintiffs show exactly which challenged practice caused what portion of any racial imbalance proven. This is particularly difficult in cases like *Wards Cove* where the various practices—not posting vacancies, not having job specifications, hiring in off-season, hiring at a distant locale, and nepotism—are closely related and used at the same time for the same jobs.

Third, the Court overruled an unanimous 1971 decision by Chief Justice Warren Burger called *Griggs v. Duke Power Co.*,[32] that required the employer to prove that an employment practice that had a racially disproportionate impact was a "business necessity" or, as later stated, "essential to effective job performance."[33] The Rehnquist Court said that henceforth the complaining employees would have the burden of proving that the challenged practice does not "serve, in a significant way, the legitimate employment goals of the employer."[34] This shift in the burden of proof, despite the employer's greater access to the relevant information, and the lessening of the justification that the employer must have for its practices were again effected without evidence that the overturned interpretation was unworkable, unfair, contrary to a sense of justice, or otherwise needed fixing.

Reflecting on the Court's ruling against the employees in light of the striking facts of the case, Justice Blackmun (who we should remember is an elderly, well-paid, professional, white male appointed by Richard Nixon) remarked:

> One wonders whether the majority still believes that race discrimination—or, more accurately race discrimination against nonwhites—is a problem in our society, or even remembers that it ever was.[35]

The same could be said about the Court's view and memory of sex discrimination in its decision the following week in *Lorance v. AT&T Technologies, Inc.*[36] In that case, three women challenged a new seniority system as sex discrimination. The case revolved around the women's attempt to retain the better-paid position of "tester." Tester positions had traditionally been held almost exclusively by men, while women principally held the non-tester positions. In the 1970's, an increasing number of women took the steps to qualify and then used their seniority in the plant to become testers. After many years of trying, the three plaintiffs in the *Lorance* case were promoted to tester positions between 1978 and 1980.

Until the July 1979 collective bargaining agreement, seniority for layoff purposes was based on the number of years one had worked in the plant. Under the new agreement, a tester's seniority was determined only by the number of years spent as a tester, not overall service at the plant, although a provision allowed one to regain full plantwide seniority after spending five years as a tester. When the 1982 recession hit, the three plaintiffs were demoted from their recently acquired tester positions, although they would not have been had the old seniority system still been in effect.

The women sued within 300 days, the time period set by the law for filing suit in their situation, after their demotion. The Supreme Court ruled, however, that their lawsuit was too late and thus their substantial claims of sex discrimination could never be heard because they should have sued within 300 days of the new seniority system's adoption in July 1979. The Court imposed this rule even though two of the plaintiffs did not even become testers until several months after the seniority system was adopted. Of course, none of them had any way of predicting in 1979 that there would be a recession in 1982 and that it would be bad enough to force demotions so far up the seniority scale as to reach them. By imposing this harsh filing requirement, the Court ignored both human nature, which responds to actual events, not theoretical possibilities, and prior rulings of lower courts. It also insured that most discriminatory seniority systems will be safe from judicial scrutiny.

Literally hundreds of race and sex discrimination lawsuits throughout the country were thrown out in the months following these and related decisions of the Supreme Court.

The insensitivity of the Court to the realities of discrimination in the workplace and the need for continued vigorous enforcement, not technical retrenchments, of the civil rights laws led to yet another congressional reaction. The Civil Rights Act of 1990 was designed to overturn the *Patterson, Wards Cove,* and *Lorance* decisions, as well as three others of similar ilk.

President Bush took the position that the provision in the bill returning the burden of proof on "business necessity" to the employer would force companies to adopt "quotas" for women and minorities. His rationale was that that burden, which had been placed on the employer nineteen years earlier by Chief Justice Burger in the unanimous *Griggs* opinion, could not be met. Thus, the President claimed, to avoid lawsuits based on statistical evidence of racial or sexual imbalance, companies would have to use fixed numerical quotas. This argument, which ignored the fact that companies often had met the *Griggs* burden, led to numerous modifications in the bill, reducing management's obligation from having to prove "compelling reasons" for challenged practices, to showing "substantial reasons," and then only "significant reasons." At the end, the 1990 bill's definition of the employer's burden was weaker than what *Griggs* had originally imposed. After these and other significant amendments to accommodate business interests, the bill passed both the House and Senate by overwhelming majorities.

Notwithstanding these revisions and the lack of major opposition from the main business organizations, the President vetoed the bill, still proclaiming it "a quotas bill." No prior president in the modern civil rights era—not Dwight Eisenhower, Richard Nixon, or Ronald Reagan—had vetoed a major civil rights bill. Sixty-six senators voted to override the veto, leaving the effort only one vote short of the two-thirds majority required by the Constitution. By March 1991, the battle had been renewed in Congress as a new bill was reported out of committee in the House.[37]

The strong congressional reaction shows that the civil rights laws ain't broke and don't need fixing. What is broken is the Supreme Court's promise of the 1950's to minorities in this country that it would protect their right to equal opportunities in all aspects of life. Once again Congress is called upon to do the fixing, this time without the aid of the executive. By now, Congress has had lots of practice. Hopefully its next repair will last and will remind the Court of its historic obligations.

Being Sterile Is Not a Job Qualification

It has been quite a while since this country has seen, and banned, classified newspaper ads listing jobs separately for men and women. It is therefore somewhat startling to see courts taking seriously claims by employers that a policy that bars women capable of bearing children from certain jobs is not sex discrimination. Not only have courts been taking them seriously but three of the four federal appeals courts that have considered this issue have upheld the policies against sex discrimination challenges. The appropriateness of one of those decisions, *International Union, UAW v. Johnson Controls, Inc.*,[38] is before the Supreme Court at this writing. One of the appellate judges in that case predicted that the result could affect twenty million working women. As I will explain, it would also affect the health and safety of millions of working men as well.

The keys facts of the case are undisputed. Johnson Controls makes batteries. The manufacturing process releases lead into the factory air. Everyone, including the company, agrees that airborne lead can have serious adverse health consequences. Among the possible effects, but far from the only one, is deformation of a fetus during the early stages of pregnancy. Less certain is whether exposure to airborne lead could affect a man's sperm and thus injure any fetus conceived thereafter. The federal Occupational Safety and Health Administration (OSHA) has issued standards for reducing airborne lead to protect all workers.

Johnson Controls took another approach. It adopted what is known as a fetal-protection policy. It bars any woman under seventy years old who cannot establish that she is sterile from any job that exposes the employee to lead as well as any other position that could, through future promotions, place one in such a job. Child-labor laws have long

143

prohibited employment of girls before puberty, Social Security and pension incentives induce most employees to retire by seventy, and only a handful of women in any workplace will have had complete hysterectomies or tube-tying operations. As a result, the policy effectively means "women need not apply"—the very same effect as a "classified–men" column in the newspaper.

Judges and lawyers addressing this obvious sex discrimination have gotten twisted up, as usual, in legalistic distinctions. They have debated which of two legal theories is applicable. One approach, called "disparate treatment" analysis, is used to assess claims of intentional discrimination. The other, called "disparate impact" or "adverse impact" analysis, is used when sex- and race-neutral job qualifications, for example, minimum height or written test requirements, tend to exclude a greater proportion of female or minority applicants than of male or white applicants. The reason that this seems to matter so much to lawyers is that the defenses available in each approach differ significantly. To justify disparate treatment, the employer must show that the challenged exclusion is what the law calls a "bona fide occupational qualification" (shortened by lawyers to BFOQ), which means that the characteristic, in this instance sterility, can be shown to be essential to perform the job. For a disparate impact, the company has a "business necessity" defense, which is somewhat broader. Indeed the question of who bears the burden of proof on business necessity and what is a sufficient showing was one of the core disputes in the recent struggle about the Civil Rights Act of 1990, which sought to reverse the numerous misreadings of Title VII that the Supreme Court handed down in 1989. (See "Civil Rights Law: If It Ain't Broke, Don't Fix It," page 135.)

I was pleasantly surprised to see that even President Reagan's director of the Civil Rights Division of the Justice Department, William Bradford Reynolds, agrees with me that a fetal-protection policy is intentional sex discrimination under Title VII, should be analyzed as a disparate treatment case, and was only treated differently by the circuit courts to reach a pro-employer result.[39] But we parted company when he went on to suggest not only that such a policy might be defensible if analyzed under the business necessity defense, but that being sterile might even be a BFOQ. More shockingly, he referred to fetal-protection policies as "benign."

144

It is important to see that such policies are none of those things. They are, first of all, not truly fetal-protection policies but rather management-protection policies. What underlies these policies is not a tender concern for the well-being of unborn fetuses, or for the anguish that women employees would suffer from worrying about or actually delivering a deformed child. Rather, manufacturers worry about their potential civil lawsuit liability for any injury to the fetus, which probably is not covered by the less-expensive workers' compensation system.

A sterility requirement is definitely not a BFOQ. Fertile women, with or without male partners, lesbian women, and sterile women are all fully capable of manufacturing batteries if they have the proper education and training.

Such policies are also not neutral, benign, or a business necessity. They are insidiously anti-worker. They amount to saying, "We know that our manufacturing process produces a chemical that is toxic to all employees. But we know that we will probably only be hit with significant liability if a baby is born deformed. It's a lot cheaper for us to ban women from those jobs than it is to clean up or modify the manufacturing process or shield all our employees from risk." In short, "the workers be damned, let's bring in those who will complain the least"—a policy with an ignoble history in the use of immigrants, illegal aliens, and children in the sweatshops of our textile industry, to cite but one example. The only "business necessity" prompting such a policy is the desire to reduce occupational safety costs by reducing the risks of being sued by the most vulnerable, rather than by improving occupational safety for all. Such a policy is unworthy of a civilized nation.

We Still Need Affirmative Action

Deeply ingrained social problems require persistent and creative solutions. Racial and ethnic prejudice is as old as humankind and particularly virulent in this country because of our slaveholding past. It was thought by some and hoped by many that removal of the formal legal barriers would lead to true racial equality. It didn't happen—either after emancipation or after the civil rights legislation of the 1960's. Much more was needed—in education, housing, and employment. Various forms of so-called "affirmative action" were developed to insure that opportunities were available to minority groups long denied access to higher education and better-paying jobs. Those programs have often provoked strong reactions by those who feel that "better qualified" whites who may themselves have never discriminated have been wrongfully denied positions or promotions in favor of individuals who may never have personally suffered discrimination. Recent events in numerous areas compel us to re-examine the situation and reassess the relative social costs and benefits. I conclude that we should re-affirm the need for continued direct and innovative action to ensure that some day we fulfill the dream that our children will be evaluated not by the color of their skin but by the quality of their characters.

• In January 1989 the United States Supreme Court, in its now famous decision in *Richmond v. J.A. Croson, Co.*,[40] struck down a program in Richmond, Virginia, the former capital of the Confederacy, that required that 30 percent of city construction contracts be awarded to minority-owned businesses. Nine years earlier, the Court had upheld a law passed by Congress requiring that 10 percent of all grants from a federal appropriation of $4 billion for state and local public works

146

projects be awarded to minority-owned businesses.[41] The Court there relied upon the special constitutional powers of Congress, including its power to provide for the general welfare and to enforce the equal protection guarantees of the Fourteenth Amendment. In *Croson*, the Court held that, unlike Congress, states and cities must show in detail the prior discrimination that prompted such "set-aside" programs and establish that no alternative to a racially defined preference would succeed in remedying the situation.

• In the spring of 1990 Professor Derrick Bell of Harvard Law School announced that he would go on unpaid leave from his $120,000 a year job until his school, which has three African American men and five white women out of sixty-two tenured professors, grants tenure to an African American woman.[42]

• In June 1990 the Supreme Court upheld policies of the Federal Communications Commission that give "preference points" to applications by minority-owned businesses for broadcasting licenses and that permit only such businesses to bid at "distress sales" of television or radio stations whose licenses have been called into question.[43]

• In September 1990 a federal judge ruled for the first time that a residency requirement for municipal workers in a nearly all-white community has a racially discriminatory impact and therefore violates Title VII of the 1964 Civil Rights Act.[44]

What do these differing events tell us? First, of course, they tell us that "the problem" is not solved. If the problem is racial prejudice, my knowledge of human nature suggests that we may never find the solution. If, however, we define the task as equalizing opportunities for persons of all origins in all facets of public life, there is hope, though much is yet to be done.

Some background facts from the four cases mentioned highlight the problem. In Richmond in the five years prior to the set-aside program, only 0.67 percent of the $24.6 million in city construction contracts went to minority-owned businesses and there were virtually no minorities in any of the major trade associations in town.[45] Despite admissions and faculty recruitment efforts of many law schools over the past twenty years, minorities still constitute only 8.67 percent of all law faculty.[46] By 1986, despite eighteen years of efforts at that point by the Minority Student Program at my school, Rutgers Law

School in Newark, minority lawyers constituted only 4.7 percent of the New Jersey bar. In 1971, before the various efforts of Congress and the FCC, minorities owned only 10 of the 7,500 radio stations in this country and none of the more than 1,000 television stations. By 1978 minorities owned less than 1 percent of broadcast stations, and by 1986 only 2.1 percent of the by-then more than 11,000 radio and television stations.[47] Perhaps most tragically, twenty-two years after passage of the federal Fair Housing Act barring discrimination in residential housing, the residents of the town of Harrison, New Jersey, whose residency requirement for public employment was just struck down, are still 99.8 percent white and, because of the residency rule, its municipal workforce is 100 percent white.[48]

Second, it is now painfully obvious that removing technical barriers to racial discrimination is not enough. That should not come as a surprise. If one ties up an athlete with ropes throughout the weeks that her colleagues are practicing and then, on the day of the meet, releases her and walks her over to the starting block at the same time as the others, one would hardly expect her to come in first, or even to keep up with her practiced competitors. The same holds true for groups that have been denied adequate education, housing, and employment for decades and are suddenly asked to compete for college or law school seats or skilled job openings.

Third, further efforts are essential. We cannot abandon minority-preference programs that have worked in broadcast ownership or law school admissions contexts because "now everything is equal." Few minorities have an investor base large enough to be serious competitors with CBS or even with other local station applicants. Few have the resources or established track record to compete for municipal contracts in Richmond or elsewhere. And, as the state supreme courts in Texas, Montana, Kentucky, and New Jersey have so poignantly and courageously catalogued in their recent rulings on school finances (see "It's Time to Invest in School Finance Equity," page 234), the educational opportunities for urban minority students in this country are still far less than those for suburban whites, thirty-six years after the Supreme Court mandated integration of schools because separate is inherently unequal.

The hard issue is not whether towns such as Harrison should now have to hire African American or Hispanic clerk-typists, janitors, or firefighters who do not happen to live within the town. There can be

148

little non-racist objection because the residency requirement is clearly not related to qualification for any job; we know that there are many minority candidates from out of town who will be at least as qualified as the persons who have been hired in the past for those positions from the artificially narrowed applicant pool of local residents. Most significantly, removing the residence rule does not create preferential treatment for minority applicants and is thus not affirmative action in the most frequently used sense of that term.

But when it comes to admitting students or picking teachers, many hesitate because they feel it is unfair to give preference to qualified minorities over "more qualified" whites. The sense of injustice is palpable and understandable. But we must consider whether it is justified by asking what we mean by "more qualified." Does an 87 rather than an 82 on a civil service exam, a 600 rather than a 550 on the college Scholastic Aptitude Test, or a 35 rather than a 30 on the Law School Admission Test make one "more qualified" to be trained to be a competent firefighter, teacher, or lawyer? So many of the quantitative tests used to speed decision-making are in fact shortcuts that ignore or distort meaningful measurement of ability or quality. In many cases the pass mark is a meaningful cut-off, and the differences in ability between those who just barely pass and those who score the highest grades are real. But amid the great mass of scores in between, sharp differences in ability are either not measurable or have not been substantiated by evaluations conducted on the job after training.

Even assuming that the measures used reflect actual differences in levels of qualification, the ultimate policy question in any minority preference scheme is whether it is proper to favor those who because of earlier discrimination and inequality have not yet been able to reach the same levels of experience, education, or skill as those not so disfavored. Chief Justice Burger, in approving the federal minority contractor set-aside program mentioned above, explained that "It is not a constitutional defect in this program that it may disappoint the expectations of nonminority firms. When effectuating a limited and properly tailored remedy to cure the effects of prior discrimination, such 'a sharing of the burden' by innocent parties is not impermissible."[49] One of the reasons supporting such a view is that, without the centuries of discrimination, many of the innocent whites who are "victimized" by affirmative action would probably not have ranked higher than the minorities who are admitted or hired under preference programs. That is, had we had all these years an unbiased system of education and employment, minorities would appear at all levels of measurement in the same proportion as they do in the population at large.

What we will need to focus on in the coming years is not whether dismantling affirmative action programs is unreasonable and harmful to the social fabric, for we already know that it is. Rather we will need to analyze closely, among other matters, what kinds of disappointed expectations can reasonably be imposed on innocent bystanders in our search for open opportunity for all. As Justice David Souter warned us in his confirmation hearings in 1990, we will be at this tough question for a lot longer than we had first hoped.

V

POVERTY AND
THE RIGHT TO A HOME

Our society has always included some who are desperately poor. The very poor have become more visible, however, and more irksome to some, as they have become homeless in increasing numbers in the 1980's. Their problems and the reactions to them are not very different from those faced by the poor in the Depression as illuminated by John Steinbeck in *The Grapes of Wrath*. Ironically when I went to see a dramatic rendition of that masterpiece on Broadway in 1990, a poorly dressed man was collecting empty soda cans from the patrons directly in front of the theater. What is striking about the current situation is that we thought we had created a safety net after the Depression to prevent people from falling this far again. Obviously we were not successful.

I am neither an expert on, nor is it appropriate for me to flesh out here, all the possible solutions to this fundamental problem. The question I consider is whether the Constitution has anything to do with the issue. Many people think that neither the body of the original Constitution nor the Bill of Rights addresses economic rights. But they forget our origins. The Revolution, from the Boston Tea Party on, was led and the Constitution was written by the wealthy landed gentry and mercantile class who wanted to preserve their economic status. The most infamous provisions in the Constitution derive from the compromise that guaranteed the perpetuation of slavery: the clause that precluded Congress from interfering with the importation of slaves until 1808; the prohibition on any amendment of that clause until 1808; the provision that a slave be counted as three-fifths of a person for apportionment purposes; and the requirement that fugitive slaves be returned to their owners. But the Constitution has many other significant economic provisions as well: the powers of Congress to collect taxes, borrow and coin money, regulate interstate and foreign commerce, and establish bankruptcy laws; the various provisions limiting head taxes, duties, and preferences among ports of the various states; and the prohibitions on states coining money, imposing duties, impairing contracts, or otherwise interfering with congressional power over commerce.

Nor is the Bill of Rights divorced from economic concerns. The Third Amendment, which prohibits the quartering of soldiers without consent, is in part a protection of property rights. The Fourth Amendment, which bars unreasonable searches, is the outgrowth of the colonial reaction to the general warrants and writs of assistance frequently used by the English to check commercial establishments for customs violations. The Fifth Amendment expressly protects property, as well as life and liberty, against deprivation without due process of law and requires just compensation when the government takes private property for public use. The Seventh Amendment guarantees a jury trial "where the value in controversy shall exceed twenty dollars." The Eighth Amendment prohibits excessive fines.

The main Civil War amendment, the Fourteenth Amendment, although adopted in response to the scourge of slavery, has had a long history of protecting economic interests. The amendment, which prevents deprivation by the states of property as well as life and liberty without due process, was construed by the courts in the late nineteenth and early twentieth centuries to limit the power of states to regulate business. In the most famous case of this type, called *Lochner v. New York*,[1] the Supreme Court struck down in 1905 a New York law prohibiting more than a ten-hour work day or a sixty-hour work week in bakeries because it interfered with the "liberty" of both the employer and the employees to make contracts, in that case for the purchase or sale of labor. This philosophy led to the invalidation of various minimum-wage and price-setting regulations and later to the striking down of several important New Deal initiatives, such as the National

Industrial Recovery Act and its industrial codes. This view gave way only with the great constitutional upheaval of the late 1930's that followed Roosevelt's unsuccessful attempt to "pack" the Court by adding more justices who, he hoped, would support his economic recovery efforts. The modern view of the due process clause is that government may regulate economic behavior whenever the legislation meets a minimal test of being "rationally related to a legitimate state interest." Those attacking wealth-related distinctions have therefore turned recently to the provision for equal protection under law in the Fourteenth Amendment.

Clearly, then, neither the Constitution itself nor the Bill of Rights is solely a political and social compact. What I will explore here is whether the principles of the Constitution have any bearing on the current problem of homelessness. I consider first the application of the First Amendment's free expression protection to begging. I then turn to the broader civil liberties implications of homelessness. Finally, I describe the experience of one state that has construed its state constitution more broadly than the federal constitution and attempted to use it to grapple with the problem of providing housing for the poor.

Homeless Orators: Begging As Free Speech

One notable feature of our legal process is that it permits courts to re-examine established assumptions in light of changed circumstances and, when necessary, re-define the law or at least the debate about what it should be. The 1990 decision of federal Judge Leonard Sand—that begging is constitutionally protected speech that cannot be totally banned in the New York City subways—is such a ruling. The ruling does not entail a drastic leap in established First Amendment law. Yet its conclusion is so unexpected that it makes us all re-think basic premises. The ruling has now been reversed on appeal and the Supreme Court has refused to review it. Thus, its real contribution will not be in expanding the begging opportunities of the down-and-out in New York. Rather it will serve to keep visible, and focus national public attention upon, the people and the problem that our society wants to hide most—the homeless.

Young v. New York City Transit Authority,[2] was a lawsuit brought by two homeless subway beggars and the Legal Action Center for the Homeless. They challenged three restrictions: the Transit Authority's flat ban on panhandling[3] on all Authority property; the Port Authority's refusal to permit such activity in its bus terminal or at the World Trade Center; and a New York State criminal statute penalizing any person who "loiters, remains or wanders about in a public place for the purpose of begging." Judge Sand, who first became famous for holding Yonkers in contempt for ignoring court orders to build low-income housing in white neighborhoods to overcome past segregation, initially determined that the lawsuit could proceed as what is known as a "class action," that is, on behalf of all other people in the same situation. He defined the class as "all needy persons who live in the State of New York, who are or will be asking or soliciting others for

154

charity for their own benefit in the train, bus or subway stations of New York City" and other places under the defendants' control.

The decision first invalidated the state loitering statute because the New York State Constitution permits bans on loitering only when aimed at preventing an independently illegal act, such as theft.[4] Finding no separate prohibition on begging, Judge Sand ruled that the statute preventing loitering for the purpose of begging was unconstitutional.

The Transit Authority insisted, however, that its begging regulations were independent of the state loitering statute. Thus Judge Sand was forced to face directly the key questions: is begging constitutionally protected speech? And if so, are the subways "public forums" where government restrictions on expression are most severely limited?

Judge Sand approached the first issue by considering recent Supreme Court decisions providing First Amendment protection to charitable solicitation. The Court has invalidated various laws that limit the percentage of solicited funds that can be used on administration or paid to professional fundraisers. Its reasoning was that the act of solicitation is "intertwined with informative and perhaps persuasive speech seeking support for particular causes or for particular views on economic, political or social issues."[5] Because the subway regulations expressly permitted solicitation for recognized charities, Judge Sand's primary inquiry was whether there is a meaningful First Amendment difference between raising money for yourself and raising money for others.

His opinion rejected all three distinctions offered by the government. First, Sand noted that beggars also communicate important matters. The plaintiffs in *Young* stated that they frequently answered questions from the people they approached, describing what it is like to be homeless and expressing their views on available public programs. The judge did not rely solely on such interactions but went on to the broader point that even an unadorned request for money "cannot but remind the passer-by that people in the city live in poverty and often lack the essentials for survival. . . . While often disturbing and sometimes alarmingly graphic, begging is unmistakably informative and persuasive speech."[6]

Second, Judge Sand found the differing intentions of the traditional solicitor—to use the money for others, not for personal benefit—

to be irrelevant. The professional fundraiser, after all, is also seeking funds in part for his or her own use. Moreover such a distinction would create the anomaly of banning solicitations by one homeless person for herself but allowing two such persons to solicit donations for each other.

Third, Sand found no clear historical preference for altruistic soliciting. Traditionally, both in England and America, begging was prohibited only for those able to work but permitted, subject to licensing or locational restrictions, for those unable to do so. Panhandling has, thus, been socially acceptable except when seen as violating the Puritan work ethic.

Having concluded that soliciting charity for oneself is constitutionally indistinguishable from begging for others, Judge Sand had little trouble in finding the city's subways and terminals to be "public forums." That is the term used in First Amendment law for those places open to the public and used for public discourse within which limits on communication are subject to the strictest constitutional scrutiny. Because the Transit Authority expressly permits speech-making, music-making, sale of newspapers, including "Street News" which is put out by the homeless, and solicitation by political, religious, and established charitable groups, the subways and terminals are clearly public forums.

Judge Sand then applied traditional First Amendment analysis, which looks to see whether the government's ban is broader than necessary to satisfy its legitimate interests. He appropriately found the state's interest in protecting the public from harassment and intimidation to be very significant. But, he reasoned, the Transit Authority does not need the begging ban to achieve that end, as there are independent prohibitions on obstruction of passageways, harassment, assault, and disorderly conduct, not to mention the various criminal laws, all of which much more directly address that concern. Moreover no attempt was made by the Authority to identify the particular locations within the system, such as on lines near token booths, where passengers are likely to feel as if they are captive audiences to beggars and, therefore, intimidated. The judge concluded that the total begging ban was too broad an instrument to deal with this specific concern, the legal equivalent of using a two-by-four to squash an ant.

Most interesting is the judge's treatment of the state's interest in "preserving the quality of urban life." Although he recognized its legitimacy, he "discounted" that interest when the law's principal effect is "keeping a public problem involving human beings out of sight and therefore out of mind. Indeed, it is the very unsettling appearance and message conveyed by the beggars that gives their conduct its expressive quality."[7]

The opinion concludes by reminding the relevant authorities that only the total ban was invalid under this analysis. Reasonable "time, place and manner restrictions," as they are known in First Amendment law, such as prohibiting begging on moving vehicles, where it is difficult to move away from the beggar or seek police assistance if necessary, would be permissible.

In reversing Judge Sand and reinstating the total ban on begging, the majority of the Second Circuit Court of Appeals, which was divided two to one, avoided the thrust of Judge Sand's First Amendment analysis by concluding that begging is merely conduct, which may constitutionally be regulated more broadly, and not communication. The majority was obviously taken more by "the very unsettling appearance" of beggars than with their very unsettling message in concluding that begging is "nothing less than a menace to the common good."[8]

Despite its reversal as legal precedent, at least until the Supreme Court decides to confront the issue in a future case, Judge Sand's ruling stands as a trenchant civics lesson. His conceptual juxtaposition of the American Heart Association's door-to-door solicitor and a begging homeless AIDS victim or alcoholic forcefully reminds us that it is the messenger or the message, not the medium, that really offends. Just as we will never see a statute banning the bronzing, as compared to the burning, of the flag, we will never see a subway regulation prohibiting the Junior League from "begging" for diabetics or Jerry Lewis from "panhandling" for children with muscular dystrophy. While some charities are "recognized" with the federal tax deduction law's seal of approval, many people want the homeless to be neither seen nor heard.

All of us who are distressed by the increasing number and visibility of beggars in our cities have a way out. We can confront the underlying problem—poverty—and attend to what I suggest in the next essay is the real constitutional interest—the right to shelter. If we eliminate the ugly problem, we can avoid the need for the unpleasant speech.

Why Homelessness Is a Civil Liberties Concern

Whether or not the homeless are permitted to beg, their very presence on the streets or in the bus terminals of our major cities regularly reminds us of this pressing problem. Homelessness is primarily an economic problem, or more precisely a symptom of an economic problem—the failure of our economy, including its housing market, to provide even small housing units affordable to millions of our fellow citizens, some of whom are still employed and willing to spend more than half of their limited incomes on housing. But there are also civil liberties aspects to this tragedy that we need to consider—most prominently the denial of equal protection to the poor and the effective barriers to their exercise of political rights.

The outlines of the problem are easily stated. Estimates vary from three million homeless people upwards nationwide.[9] In some areas, there are simply not enough safe, permanent housing units—most importantly, places to rent—available. The reasons vary: some developers believe there is too much red tape or that rent control is too restrictive; others say the tax deductions have been cut back too far or there is not enough of a market to make it worthwhile for them to build. Where enough units do exist, they are often not affordable to those at the lower end of the economic scale, including the lower-middle class and working poor as well as those on welfare. This is in part because lower-level salaries, minimum wages, and welfare benefits have failed to keep up with the exploding cost of housing over the past fifteen years. Worse yet, we are short of even the shabby alternatives we have created for those who cannot afford permanent housing—namely, the so-called welfare hotels and temporary shelters for the homeless. In New Jersey, for example, with at least 25,000 homeless citizens, there are only about 1,300 non-commercial shelter beds available statewide. Shockingly, this is substantially fewer than the number of almhouse beds available in that state in 1895.[10] The result, quite simply, is that many people sleep every night on park benches, in bus terminals, or on the street.

The problem was vividly described by Ruth Ann Irizarry, a 44-year old widow with a teenage son who was evicted from her apartment when her rent doubled. At the time she was interviewed, she and her son had been living for ten months in a welfare hotel at a cost to the government of $760 per month. Throughout that time she had spent five hours daily looking for an apartment. Then she was told she would have to get out of the hotel. She described her predicament:

> I can't find anything because my welfare check is $322 a month and there's nothing for less than $400. I'd be too embarrassed to ask for more [time]. I know I've got to go. Anyway, they can't pay forever. I've got a daughter with a room, but she'll get in trouble if we stay there. I don't want her to become homeless too.[11]

Perhaps "they" can't pay forever. But we as a society are paying in numerous ways, not the least of which is the absurd expense of putting up families, like the Irizarrys, in run-down motels and hotels for far more than the cost of market-rate apartments. We are also paying the many direct social service expenses, such as increased health care costs, and the indirect social fabric costs, such as increased hostility towards the poor, of having numerous homeless citizens in our midst. Because the government allowed the construction boom of the 1980's to pass without addressing low-income housing needs, we will also be paying more to construct the necessary housing when we finally get around to it.

In addition to the financial and social costs of homelessness, there are serious constitutional implications. The substantial role of government regulation in our modern economy means that the government can no longer escape responsibility for the unequal housing opportunities of rich and poor. Similarly, it cannot ignore the fact that its housing and economic policies have left a significant portion of our body politic effectively unable to exercise its rights of expression, association, and voting.

The plight of the Irizarry family highlights the first civil liberties concern with homelessness: the unequal treatment of rich and poor.

The Fourteenth Amendment prohibits states from denying people "the equal protection of the laws." Terms of such generality are obviously subject to varying interpretations. Because the Fourteenth Amendment was adopted after the Civil War, it is generally agreed that the equal protection clause was primarily intended to guarantee equal legal rights for the newly freed slaves. The provision has, however, been applied to many other forms of discrimination, not only against other racial and ethnic minorities, but also against women, aliens, and the developmentally disabled.[12]

Equal protection has also been used, though sparingly, with regard to inequalities based on wealth and poverty. When certain fundamental rights are at issue, such as the right to counsel or access to the courts, the Supreme Court has ruled that the poor may not be denied the right simply because of their inability to pay. Thus, for example, an indigent criminal defendant must be given a free transcript of his or her trial and appointed a lawyer on appeal as a matter of equal protection.[13] Likewise, a welfare recipient cannot be denied the right to bring a divorce proceeding because she cannot afford the $60 court filing fee,[14] and an indigent sued in a paternity suit must be accorded without charge crucial blood tests that could prove that he was not the father.[15]

However in many comparable instances, the Court has refused to find equal protection violations—for example, when a maximum is imposed on welfare benefits regardless of the size of the family;[16] when the poor are unable to afford abortions[17] or the $25 fee to appeal a reduction in welfare benefits;[18] or when poor school districts have far less to spend per student than wealthier districts.[19] Quite simply, the Supreme Court has refused to subject government programs and laws that have differing effects on the wealthy and the poor to the same "strict scrutiny" employed when race or similarly "suspect" classifications are used to define the beneficiaries of government action, or when "fundamental rights" are directly infringed.[20] Most pertinent here, the Court has refused to find housing to be a fundamental right.[21] Moreover even when such a right is recognized, the government's role has been defined narrowly as an obligation not to infringe directly upon the right, rather than as a duty to insure adequate funds to permit its exercise.[22] The Court's basic rationale is that differences in economic status are the result of the private enterprise system, not of government decisions, and therefore the government has no obligation to compensate for the differing opportunities that flow from those economic disparities.

Recognizing the harshness of those results and the rationale's failure to recognize government's true role, several state courts have taken a different approach to comparable questions under their state constitutions. The courts of ten states have interpreted their state constitutions' provisions for equal protection or free public education to invalidate school financing schemes that are based on local property taxes and thus provide vastly different expenditures per student in different districts. (See "It's Time to Invest in School Finance Equity," page 234.) New Jersey has also ruled that the state constitutional obligation to provide for the "general welfare" requires the state, and the local governments to whom it delegates its zoning power, to make sure that housing is available that is affordable to the poor. The nature and results of that effort are chronicled in the next essay—"*Mount Laurel*: Government Action for Affordable Homes."

We need to understand why the United States Supreme Court's approach is incorrect as a matter of fact and thus grossly unfair as a matter of constitutional law. It is simply no longer true, as it surely was 200 years ago and probably still was 100 years ago, that the private market alone decides when, where, and what kind of housing is built and to whom it will be affordable. Government zoning was introduced in the early part of this century.[23] As the *Mount Laurel* court so forcefully explained: through its zoning power, the government now controls all the land, both public and private. Through zoning laws government decides what kinds of structures (residential or commercial) can be built on each parcel of land, at what size, height, and density they may be built (for example, no more than eight townhouses on a one-acre lot) and with what safety precautions and conveniences (off-street parking, for example) they must be constructed. As a result the government decides how the market can profitably use the land and therefore how likely it is that the land will be developed in a certain way.

Zoning is not the only way that government determines housing output. As Ms. Irizarry's case shows, the government decides the level of welfare benefits and chooses whether to spend funds for renting hotel rooms instead of regular apartments. In most states, like Ms. Irizarry's, welfare levels have lagged far behind the dramatic rise in apartment rents. For example, the New Jersey Commissioner of Human Services certified to the legislature in late 1990 that welfare grants would have to be increased an average of 40 percent to reach the minimal amount needed for a safe and decent standard of living, including housing.[24] The government also decides when and where to build public housing and whether to provide housing subsidies to encourage certain kinds of construction. Government subsidies include lower interest costs through tax-free bonds, tax abatements (relief from taxes for a period of years) for favored projects, faster and greater tax deductions than warranted by actual depreciation, tax deductions for mortgage interest payments (which is the single largest government housing subsidy), direct subsidies to developers, and rent subsidies or vouchers to indigent tenants. Quite plainly, we should require Supreme Court justices to re-take Economics 101 if they truly believe that the Reagan administration's decision to slash almost all housing subsidy programs for the poor was not a significant cause of the dramatic rise in homelessness in the 1980's.

The equal protection analysis is perhaps even more significant if one looks at the broader economic picture. Government at all levels now controls and plans not just the housing market, but other major segments of the economy as well—interest rates, the rate of inflation, minimum wages, price fixing, and taxes, to name the most prominent. All of these economic decisions have a major impact on housing construction costs and the demand for housing. By any realistic assessment, the government simply cannot say now, as it could have when the Constitution was adopted, that the poor cannot afford housing simply because of free enterprise dynamics or private housing or financial market decisions.

Instead the reality is that the government creates and maintains an economic as well as a housing system that operates to deny some individuals the basic necessities of life while substantially benefiting many others. At some point it becomes very hard to say any longer that it operates that way unintentionally. The conclusion is that in a very real sense the government is denying those people equal protection of the laws in the most fundamental sense.

Suggesting that the government is responsible for the net outcome of all its economic regulations and subsidy decisions may seem novel or drastic. But it is, in fact, only a modern application of the basic principles of Hobbes, Locke, Montesquieu, and other political philosophers to whom the Constitution's Framers looked for guidance.

They developed the idea of the social contract—that people left the brutish state of nature and gave up much of their independence in exchange for the security and benefits of organized society. Society, through government, is thus obligated to provide its citizens the most rudimentary of protection—shelter from the harsh natural environment. Whatever the exact contours of the social contract, and thus the precise constitutional obligation, it is certainly the most fundamental breach for society to leave some of its members out in the cold.

There is a second civil liberties aspect of homelessness. When people are homeless and barely able to scratch out a minimal existence, they are simply unable to exercise their constitutional rights of speech, assembly, religion, privacy, education, and political participation. In most jurisdictions in this country, homeless people cannot even register to vote because they do not have a permanent residence. Likewise, some school districts have refused to accept homeless children living in welfare motels. Ironically, some welfare departments also refuse to send checks to the homeless because of their lack of a permanent address. At this writing the Connecticut Supreme Court is considering whether a homeless man has the same Fourth Amendment rights of privacy, with regard to the boxes and sleeping bag stored where he lives under an interstate highway in New Haven, as other citizens have with regard to their more traditional homes.[25]

But even if a person with no home could technically register, how much time, energy, or interest is there to vote? Living on a hot-air grate, one does not have much time to worry about who will be, or what to write to, one's state senator. With a monthly welfare grant of $322 and no apartment costing less than $400 a month, a person could not be very concerned whether Bush or Dukakis became President.

Homelessness, therefore, either formally or effectively deprives the affected individuals of their ability to exercise the most basic civil liberties. Constitutional law has traditionally given the most protection to those who are politically isolated and powerless—referred to as "discrete and insular minorities."[26] Certainly the homeless fit that category and its rationale. Thus, even if one does not accept homelessness as a direct violation of equal protection, one must recognize that it indirectly causes many other constitutional deprivations, which the government should be obligated to alleviate.

163

That effort would not be an entirely selfless one. Broad-scale homelessness deprives the body politic of the input of those with perhaps the most to tell us about how government operates and how to improve public policy, including housing policy. The theory of pluralistic democracy adopted by our Founders—that all interest groups must participate and interact in the political arena to insure effective governance for all—is undermined when a large segment of society is disenfranchised.

Whether or not one is convinced that homelessness involves serious civil liberties violations or believes that it is "just" a social and economic issue, it is clearly a problem affecting all of us, not just those out in the cold. We all pay, in many ways—social, economic and political—when millions of people are homeless. Dostoevsky said that a civilization is judged by the way it treats its prisoners. I would add— and by how we treat our innocent outcasts as well.

Mount Laurel: Government Action for Affordable Homes

To understand the impact that constitutional law could have on the problem of homelessness, it is important to examine the experience of the one state that has actually imposed a constitutional requirement on all towns to provide housing affordable to the poor. The results have been fewer and slower than first hoped and have revealed the limits on judicial ability to force substantial economic redistribution upon an unwilling political majority. Nevertheless the experiment confirms that our constitutions can play a significant role in lessening the disparities in housing opportunities resulting from our heavily regulated housing market.

In 1975, the New Jersey Supreme Court issued a landmark decision in a case called *Southern Burlington County NAACP v. Township of Mt. Laurel*.[27] The local NAACP and various poor individuals had sued a suburb of Camden claiming that its zoning ordinance, which prohibited apartments, townhouses, mobile homes, and small houses on small lots, unconstitutionally excluded the poor. It was notable that the Court even heard the suit, because in federal court and in many states, only a developer denied approval for a specific project could bring a court challenge to a zoning ordinance.[28]

Everyone, including the Court, recognized that the impact, and unfortunately in some cases also the purpose, of apartment bans and large-lot requirements in suburbs was to exclude minorities seeking to move from the center city. But the Court did not rest its decision on either federal or state requirements for equal treatment of racial

165

minorities. Rather, the Court decided the case under the New Jersey Constitution, the very first clause of which states:

> All persons are by nature free and independent, and have certain natural and unalienable rights, among which are those of enjoying and defending life and liberty, of acquiring, possessing and protecting property, and of pursuing and obtaining safety and happiness.[29]

The Court reasoned that, under both the state constitution and the state zoning law, government is responsible for the "general welfare." Because the state controls, through its zoning power, the use of all land, both private and public, it must use that power to provide for the welfare of all, including those at the lower end of the economic spectrum. That burden is particularly heavy when the government deals with matters as fundamental as housing.

If the state transfers its zoning power to local towns, the Court explained, the towns must use it for the benefit of citizens throughout the region. This regional emphasis is very important. Were it otherwise, the state could circumvent its duty to care for the welfare of the entire population by delegating its power to localities, allowing the wealthier ones to zone out the poor. Moreover, the Court recognized that the demand for housing is generally tied to employment: people like and need to live near where they work. As businesses move to the suburbs, it becomes harder for city residents to get to the jobs as public transportation is meager in most suburban settings. Localities that receive the benefit of businesses from elsewhere in the region moving into town and paying local taxes must bear their "fair share," as the Court termed it, of the region's need for housing affordable to all the employees, from janitor to chief executive officer.

The Court concluded that, although government did not have an affirmative duty to build or finance housing, all "developing" towns in New Jersey had an obligation, through their zoning ordinances, to "make realistically possible the opportunity for an appropriate variety and choice of housing for all categories of people who may desire to live there, of course including those of low and moderate income."[30] This meant that towns would have to revise their zoning ordinances by removing provisions, such as minimum acreage and house-size requirements and bans on apartment buildings, townhouses, or mobile homes, that did not affect health and safety but rendered construction expensive or precluded alternatives to traditional single-family homes.

Naturally, many towns resisted this ruling and much litigation ensued about what is a "developing" town, the relevant "region," the nature of the "fair share," and the kinds of zoning changes that were required. Despite the many lawsuits, only a scattering of lower-income units were developed in the eight years following the first *Mount Laurel* decision.

The slow pace of progress led the New Jersey Supreme Court to issue a much more specific and dramatic ruling in 1983, generally known as *Mount Laurel II*.[31] First, the Court abandoned the "developing municipality" limitation and imposed the obligation on all towns. This change flowed from the recognition that some new construction will occur even in fully developed areas and that all localities have some poor residents needing sound, low-priced housing.

Second, the Court went beyond its position in *Mount Laurel I* and clarified that the constitutional obligation is not simply to remove zoning impediments to development of lower-income housing, but rather affirmatively to create incentives for such developments. Incentives are not limited to outright subsidies; they include offering developers the chance to build more units per acre on their land ("a density bonus") if some of them would be affordable to lower-income households ("inclusionary zoning"). Third, the Court adopted the federal housing guidelines that define "low-income households" as those with less than 50 percent of the average household income and "moderate-income households" as those with incomes between 50 and 80 percent of the average.

Fourth, and most dramatically, the Court determined that builders who sue and can show that a town's zoning is unconstitutional are entitled to build a profitable project. The "builder's remedy" is a court order requiring the town to allow the developer to build more units on its land than would be permitted by the existing zoning or, if the land is suitable, to build residential units even though the zoning does not permit such development on that site, on condition that the developer make 20 percent of the units affordable to low- and moderate-income families (known as a "*Mount Laurel* set-aside").

The economics of this remedy are straightforward. If a zoning ordinance allows a maximum of four units per acre but a court, after finding it invalid, were to permit construction of ten units per acre, the developer would still make a substantial profit even though required to sell 20 percent, or two units, at a price below market value.

The large profits from higher-density construction even with the *Mount Laurel* set-aside would, the Court thought, be sufficient to induce developers to bring the costly and time-consuming challenges to local zoning ordinances that the Court realized would be necessary to implement the constitutional obligation. Although the original *Mount Laurel* action was brought by the NAACP, and a suit against twenty-three towns in another county, in which I was later to become co-counsel, was brought by the Urban League, the Court recognized that few community organizations would have the resources to pursue such complex litigation.

The results were dramatic. Within two years, 100 lawsuits affecting seventy towns were filed by developers challenging zoning ordinances on *Mount Laurel* grounds. After wading through numerous, complex planning theories, the three judges specially designated to hear such cases determined in 1984 that there was a need for 240,000 new lower-income housing units in the state of New Jersey by 1990! As a result of the allocation formula the judges adopted, some towns had "fair shares" of more than 2,000 lower-income units. If developments with 20 percent set-asides were employed in such towns, over 10,000 residential units would have to be built. Some of these towns, although in the path of significant development, were still small, often having fewer existing homes than the number of new units projected to meet the *Mount Laurel* obligation!

The resulting firestorm of local opposition prompted the legislature to intervene. In July 1985, it enacted the Fair Housing Act both to implement and restrain *Mount Laurel*.[32] The statute, still unique in the nation, confirms both that every town in the state has a constitutional obligation to provide a realistic opportunity for the development of low- and moderate-income housing and that towns are responsible not only for their resident poor, but also for their fair share of the region's need for lower-income housing. Further, the law retained the Court's approach of defining the obligation as a specific number of lower-income residential units and of measuring low and moderate income in terms of a percentage of the region's median income.

To constrain what many viewed as judicial excesses, however, the statute required that in the future such controversies be heard not by courts but by a new state agency, the Council on Affordable Housing (COAH), whose members were appointed politically under a set formula insuring a predominance of local, county, and state officials. After COAH set the local "fair share" numbers, towns were to submit housing plans to satisfy their obligations. If any person or organization objected to a town's plan, there would be mediation by COAH and, if that proved unsuccessful, a determination by an administrative law judge. The law did not, however, provide a specific remedy for successful developer-objectors. Towns that obtained COAH certification of their plans would be safe from lawsuits for six years. A major innovation was the "regional contribution agreement," a provision allowing a town to "transfer" up to half its obligation by paying another town the money needed to subsidize construction or rehabilitation of the transferred units in the "receiving town."

In its so-called *Mount Laurel III* decision in 1986, which did not actually involve Mount Laurel Township at all,[33] the New Jersey Supreme Court withdrew from the housing arena. It said that the efforts of the legislature appeared adequate—ruling that the statute was constitutional "on its face"—and ordered all pending court cases transferred to COAH, regardless of how close they were to resolution or whether the towns had previously resisted court orders in bad faith. The Court warned, however, that it would monitor COAH's progress to see whether the law was implemented in a constitutional way and would step in again if necessary.

COAH used a narrower definition of need and determined in 1986 that "only" 145,000 new lower-income housing units were needed by 1993. It set 1,000 units as the maximum fair share any town could receive and reduced particular towns' numbers based on shortages of vacant land or of water or sewerage capacity, or for special historical or farmland conservation considerations.

The administrative process has been slow and spotty. After two years, only 161 of the state's 567 towns had filed housing plans with COAH, only 107 of them had petitioned for approval, and only 58 had received final certification. The average number of housing units to be developed in the towns that had come voluntarily before COAH was far below the state's average fair share.[34]

The limited participation reflects a lack of incentives to comply. If someone sues, a town can still ask COAH to certify its previously filed plan. Mediation negotiations have been extended because until ordered by a court, COAH has refused to refer any controversies to administrative law judges for binding decisions. Moreover with one special exception, COAH has refused to provide a builder's remedy to a successful objector. Thus, even if a town has filed a blatantly inadequate plan, it will still get an extended opportunity before COAH to prove its adequacy and if it fails, can simply re-draft its plan, leaving out the developer who had spent all the time and money to prove its deficiencies. Under these circumstances, few developers have thought it worth their while to file objections with COAH.

Despite legislative limitations, judicial withdrawal, and administrative delays, some progress has been made. As of May 1988, 2,830 *Mount Laurel* units had actually been completed in the most active fifty-four towns and an additional 11,133 units were in some stage of development. Seventy-seven percent of all *Mount Laurel* units are for sale, and most of the few rental units are in senior-citizen developments. Surprisingly, 49 percent of the set-aside units are two-bedroom units and 22 percent have three bedrooms, providing real opportunities for larger families. Prices depend on household size and income, unit size, and local taxes, but are generally in the range of $30,000 to 45,000 for low-income units and $50,000 to 70,000 for moderate-income units. Most significantly for present purposes, almost no units have been built that are affordable to families with less than 45 percent of median income. Even the applicants at that income level have had substantial problems qualifying for mortgages. Those who qualify most readily are senior citizens with substantial assets from the sale of their prior home and young couples with entry-level professional salaries subsidized with downpayments contributed by their parents.

The data about the occupants of completed projects are more surprising. Although the mix of family sizes is fairly similar to the general population, *Mount Laurel* households are disproportionately headed by persons under thirty-five (64 percent as compared to the national average of 29 percent), reflecting the generally lower incomes of younger people. Ninety percent are first-time homeowners, having previously rented or lived with their families, indicating that the law is meeting a genuine need in that respect. At least 71 percent of occupants of *Mount Laurel* projects now live within ten miles of their workplace, which was a major goal of the original court decisions. But because of the express priority imposed by most towns for persons living or working in town, typically 70 percent of the *Mount Laurel* buyers previously lived in town or within ten miles of the municipality. Very few people have come from urban or distant areas, as the courts originally had hoped. Also the distribution of occupations—39 percent professional and managerial and 24 percent sales and clerical but only 22 percent blue collar laborers and 15 percent service workers—shows, as do the income and sales price levels, that we are generally not reaching the working poor. Most disappointing is the fact that few units are occupied by racial minorities, and of those that are, very few by African Americans.

What can we conclude from this data? Clearly some progress is being made—several thousand units have been constructed and many more are in the offing. And real needs are being served—people who were renting or living with family are now buying their first homes, senior citizens with fixed incomes are finding safe and reasonable rentals, and some decent, reasonably priced housing is becoming available near work.

But we clearly cannot rest on our *Mount Laurels*. The speed, amount, and nature of the progress is disappointing. *Mount Laurel I* was decided more than fifteen years ago and the Fair Housing Act was enacted more than five years ago. The courts had estimated in 1984 that 240,000 new lower-income units were needed by 1990 and COAH said in 1986 that "only" 145,000 units were needed by 1993. We are light years away from either goal, even if every unit now planned is completed, which is most unlikely as we head into a deep recession. Most units are for sale, not for rent, and then only to persons with over 45 percent of average income. It is clear that the bulk of the working poor are not being served and those who might be are often stymied by mortgage eligibility obstacles. The urban centers and racial minorities are benefited only by the few "transfer" agreements, by which suburbs meet part of their obligation by sending money to the cities to fund some housing units there. Neither economic nor racial desegregation has occurred, although those were express goals of *Mount Laurel*.

Most tellingly, during this intense period of government effort, many of the truly poor became homeless. Estimates in New Jersey alone range from 25,000 people upwards. This should hardly be surprising. The basic welfare grant in New Jersey for a family of four was less than 60 percent of the cost of living and rose by only a third while inflation increased 130 percent from 1975 to 1985.[35] The minimum wage was not increased at all in this country from 1981 to 1989 and then only to a level that assures that even single workers will be poor by government definitions. Thus, the country's most significant attempt to apply constitutional principles of equality to our housing problems failed to address the needs of the neediest.

What lessons can we draw from this constitutional experiment? First, it was not a fair test. Just when real progress was being made, in the few years after the *Mount Laurel II* decision, the legislature and then the courts withdrew the pressure. Moreover, no one ever addressed the really poor—those earning the minimum wage or on welfare—or even the working poor who lack the savings needed for a downpayment.

Second, more importantly, the majority does not want a fair test. Any move toward equality will cost the better-off majority some money. This is why New Jersey's Governor Thomas Kean labelled *Mount Laurel II* "communistic," even though its builder's remedy depended on the entrepreneurial drive of private developers, and why the towns screamed and the legislature responded. In truth, many people really care about constitutional rights only when personally threatened and tolerate their application to others only if doing so will not cost them anything. Because most constitutional rights are intended to protect the minority from the majority and because rights to equal treatment cost money when applied to housing and other tangible benefits, there is little political support for having government take an active role to ensure those rights.

Third, the courts cannot realistically enforce such obligations on their own. Technically speaking they have the power to order compliance and enforce their orders by contempt rulings and fines, as Judge Sand did in the Yonkers housing integration case. But their authority is very limited without the support of a significant segment of society or at least another branch of government. Clearly the integration of Little Rock schools would not have occurred if President Eisenhower had not been willing to enforce the Supreme Court's orders with troops. During the intense period of judicial enforcement after *Mount Laurel II*, local politicians, in a spirit comparable to that of Arkansas Governor Orval Faubus in Little Rock, were threatening to throw themselves before bulldozers to stop projects in their communities. The *Mount Laurel* experience, like the comparable ones with school finance (see "It's Time to Invest in School Finance Equity," page 234), suggests that in highly controversial matters unsettling basic societal expectations, often the best we can expect is see-saw progress. By that I mean that the courts first establish the principle and demand compliance, the political branches respond partially, the courts withdraw to regain credibility, and then in time, when bureaucratic malaise sets in or a partial societal consensus develops, courts can re-enter the fray to move us forward again.

Nevertheless, we cannot abandon the effort. The Constitution is a beacon of light drawing us through our darkened societal tunnel towards a more just community. *Mount Laurel* made the light brighter. We must continue to move forward, seeking to get closer to the light. We will have no trouble figuring out how to do that if we remember that the *Mount Laurel* doctrine, like our constitutions generally, was not designed to make money for developers or lawyers or to help bureaucrats complete checklists. It was created to make this truly a kinder and gentler nation.

VI

THE CRIMINAL PROCESS

Nothing except sex attracts as much public attention as crime, and little about government is as frustrating to most of the public as the way the court system deals with accused criminals. The frustration derives not only from the delays in processing cases, but also from the sense that the "guilty" are too often let go on "technicalities."

Most of these so-called technicalities are found in the Bill of Rights, which addresses the criminal process in more detail than it does any other matter. The Fifth, Sixth, and Eighth Amendments deal with almost nothing else. They address everything from bail before trial and indictment by a grand jury, through a speedy trial by jury with the aid of counsel, to the limits on sentencing and on reprosecution after acquittal or conviction. Almost all of these provisions have been "incorporated" or made applicable to state courts through the Fourteenth Amendment.

What some people find hard to accept is that a person cannot be legally convicted if one of her fundamental rights has been violated in the process. Enforcement of this basic rule is what leads people to think that the "guilty" are let go on "technicalities." That view, however, reflects a misunderstanding of the two basic reasons why criminal defendants are afforded these procedural protections.

First, these rights were created to insure that only those persons who are actually guilty are convicted and sentenced. History is strewn with the sad chronicles of innocent people who were convicted and sometimes executed because public passions, political ambitions, or bureaucratic pressures to clear the docket led to suppression, misinterpretation, or insufficient investigation of the facts. There are also many less famous cases in which simple carelessness, incompetence, or lack of time produced erroneous verdicts. The procedural rights guaranteed to defendants by the Bill of Rights—that one can have the assistance of a legal professional obligated to pursue one's interests vigorously, cross-examine government witnesses as to their motivations, call witnesses in one's behalf, and have all this done in public before an impartial jury of one's peers who must be convinced beyond a reasonable doubt—are designed to overcome the forces that would otherwise frequently lead to unjust results.

This chapter includes accounts of an innocent man ensnared by those forces, of lawyers whose attempts to assert those rights for their clients get them in trouble, and of cities where the caseload is so overwhelming that public defenders cannot begin to undertake the investigations and vigorous advocacy needed to protect the innocent.

Second, the rules were also established to prevent the government from abusing even the truly guilty. We have developed basic standards of decency that we will not allow to be breached even when dealing with those guilty of heinous crimes. For example, police may not beat or torture anyone, not even a fairly convicted murderer or child molester. We fear that once the government is free to cut corners on how it treats any portion of the public, it becomes a threat to all, including those who are guilty of nothing. This concept is capsulized by the phrase: "Power corrupts; absolute power corrupts absolutely." Thus, when the government has broken down doors, lied, or withheld evidence, we do not allow the conviction even of those we are convinced are murderers, because we know, from reading both foreign news and American history, what such a government could do to everyone. The experiences of Nelson Mandela and Eugene Debs remind us that unchecked government will even declare political opposition to be criminal and treat it accordingly.

Concern over the risk of unlimited police power explains why a major outcome of our political revolution against England was a set of rights for criminal defendants. It also underlies my criticism of recent Supreme Court decisions that allow the government to "preventively" imprison before trial people it considers "dangerous" and

176

to impose the death penalty even when the evidence demonstrates that it has been applied in a racially discriminatory fashion. Quite simply, the Framers of the Bill of Rights knew that one cannot safely create a government with unfettered power even over citizens labelled "undesirable."

Preventive Detention: Which Country Is This Anyway?

QUESTION: What government official in which country said the following?

> The Government's regulatory interest in community safety can, in appropriate circumstances, outweigh an individual's liberty interest. For example, in times of war or insurrection, when society's interest is at its peak, the Government may detain individuals whom the government believes to be dangerous . . . Even outside the exigencies of war, . . . sufficiently compelling governmental interests can justify detention of dangerous persons. . . . [These examples confirm] the well-established authority of the government, in special circumstances, to restrain individuals' liberty prior to or even without criminal trial and conviction."

a) The State President of the Union of South Africa
b) The Secretary General of the Communist Party of the Union of Soviet Socialist Republics
c) The Ayatollah of the Islamic Republic of Iran
d) The Chief Justice of the United States Supreme Court

ANSWER: (d)

QUESTION: Where and when was the statement made?

a) In a private diary written during World War II
b) At a political rally during the McCarthy period

178

c) At a cocktail party during street riots in the 1960's when trying to impress the senior partner in his law firm

d) In a majority opinion for the Supreme Court in 1987

ANSWER: (d)

I was first inclined to end this essay here and let these facts speak for themselves, but I feared that some would assume this to be only a paranoid fantasy of an overworked civil libertarian or just plain libel. So I must tell you that this statement can be found at pages 748–49 of volume 481 of the United States Reports in Chief Justice William Rehnquist's May 25, 1987 opinion for the majority of the United States Supreme Court in *United States v. Salerno*. That decision upheld as constitutional the 1984 federal Bail Reform Act's provision for "preventive detention," a procedure for holding a person charged with one crime in jail without bail pending trial because the government suspects that if released he would commit another crime.

Quite apart from the specific decision on preventive detention, the breadth of this and similar statements and the reasoning of the Court in this opinion leave me—and I would hope many others—in a cold sweat. They reveal, once again, the ultimate malleability and barrenness of legal doctrines if not informed by human values. The facts of the case also remind us that, if we wish to retain our system of government, we cannot leave to the executive the decision as to which people may be labelled "dangerous" and locked up for extended periods.

The Court's due process ruling is the best example of technical legal analysis cut loose from constitutional values. The Court reasons as follows: The due process clauses in the Constitution (there is one in the Fifth Amendment that limits the federal government and one in the Fourteenth Amendment that limits state and local governments) ban deprivation of liberty without due process of law. This means the government cannot impose punishment before trial. However, in adopting the Bail Reform Act, Congress did not *intend* preventive detention as punishment. "Congress instead perceived pretrial detention as a potential solution to a pressing societal problem. . . . There is no doubt that preventing danger to the community is a legitimate regulatory goal."[1] Because detention before trial to prevent crime is "regulatory, not penal," it does not violate due process.

No doubt none of the justices has spent sufficient time behind bars to know that jail cells are equally confining and the deprivation of liberty equally painful whether the detention is labelled regulatory or punitive. But it is common knowledge (in part because chronicled in so many judicial opinions) that the conditions in local and county jails in this country, where persons are held awaiting trial because they cannot make bail, are usually far worse (should I say more regulatory?) than in most of the state prisons for dangerous felons who are serving their punitively intended sentences after a full trial meeting due process requirements.

In any case the justices must know that realities do not change because we substitute legal labels. Certainly it is always necessary when developing legal rules to draw lines, and there will always be hard cases at the boundaries. But it is game-playing, not line-drawing, to say that the exact same fourteen-month detention in a jail cell without a trial can be upheld if called regulatory but must be condemned as unconstitutional if the government doing the jailing chooses to call it punitive.

Even the Court majority does not rely solely upon this linguistic distinction. It goes on to say more forthrightly, as quoted at the outset, that the government can justify confinement without trial for compelling reasons, giving as examples cases involving mentally ill patients, enemy aliens, and suspects held overnight for arraignment. But the Court's delayed candor is even more frightening than its technical sleight-of-hand, because it acknowledges the legitimacy of indeterminate incarceration upon government assessment that persons are in some sense "dangerous." Governments throughout the world and throughout history, currently including but certainly not limited to Northern Ireland, Israel, China, and South Africa, and not so long ago every Eastern European government, have used detention without trial against terrorists, government opponents, and other "undesirable" or "dangerous" persons. The Soviet practice of committing political dissidents to mental hospitals hardly leaves me comfortable with the Court's reliance on mental-health commitments as proof of the limited nature of the detention authority it approved in *Salerno*.

But, one might say, it is unfair to take these judicial statements out of context. After all, in the *Salerno* case the government and the Court were only talking about detaining people charged with the most serious crimes after a judge concludes there is a significant risk they will do dangerous things if released pending trial. Also their detention is carefully limited by the time deadlines set by the Speedy Trial Act and the Sixth Amendment. Moreover Anthony Salerno would certainly be seen by most reasonable people as dangerous, not only because government wiretaps in that case showed him to be involved in violent organized crime, but because, during the fourteen-month pretrial detention in dispute there, he was convicted by a jury in a separate case of several serious offenses and sentenced to 100 years in prison.

Though this is true, the facts of that case also show the dangerous capacity for manipulation inherent in government authority to detain people before trial. Salerno's co-defendant, Vincent Cafaro, an alleged "captain" in the Genovese Family, was also "preventively" detained in the same case, after presentation of government evidence indicating he was dangerous. But six months later, with still no "speedy trial" in sight, the government agreed to release Cafaro upon execution of a personal recognizance bond, which is a promise, not secured by any property or money, to pay the amount of the bond if one does not return to court when scheduled. Ostensibly Cafaro's release was "temporarily for medical care and treatment;" in fact, as later revealed to the court, it was because he had become an informant for the government.[2]

I, for one, take little solace in knowing that a danger to the community is working for our government. Knowing the responsiveness of judges to law enforcement requests, I take even less comfort in knowing that prosecutors have nearly open-ended discretion to decide when to request confinement and when to agree to release of dangerous suspected criminals. The fear or reality of indefinite detention may lead the affected person to provide, truthfully or not, precisely the evidence that the government needs against another government target, and such successes will only induce further use of the detention authority. And once secured, that power can as easily be turned on a Sakharov as on a Salerno. For these reasons I hope that the average citizen in our society would agree not with the *Salerno* Court but with a truly conservative Supreme Court majority in 1895 that drew on Roman authority in asking: "If it suffices to accuse, what will become of the innocent?"[3]

Racism at the Gallows

The United States Supreme Court issued another startling decision in the spring of 1987 called *McCleskey v. Kemp*.[4] Despite an unimpeachable statistical study showing that persons prosecuted for killing whites in Georgia are at least four times more likely to receive the death penalty than those accused of murdering African Americans, the Court ruled that the imposition of a death sentence did not violate the constitutional rights of an African American convicted in Georgia of killing a white. One can only gasp at such a decision from the Court that banned racial discrimination in this country almost four decades ago. Apparently the Court considers low visibility, unstructured racism more acceptable than overt, formalized racism.

The challenge in *McCleskey* was not that the death penalty was unconstitutional in all circumstances. The Supreme Court had held in 1972, in another case from Georgia, that the death penalty was unconstitutional as then practiced in this country, because it was applied so arbitrarily and "freakishly" that it amounted to cruel and unusual punishment banned by the Eighth Amendment.[5] Thirty-five states quickly re-enacted the death penalty with various new procedural protections to insure uniform application. In 1976, in yet another Georgia case, the Court ruled that the death penalty was not always cruel and unusual punishment and that the Georgia law in particular was constitutional.[6]

The Court relied, in that and later cases upholding death penalty laws in other states, primarily on two factors. First, the laws narrowed the class of murders to which the penalty was applicable, for example, from all intentional murders to only those committed with extreme cruelty, for pay, or against law enforcement officers. Second, these laws established a separate sentencing proceeding, after the verdict of guilt, at which the jury could hear all kinds of evidence about the defendant and his or her background and then decide whether the "aggravating" factors, such as the heinousness of the murder or a prior record of violent crimes, outweighed the "mitigating" factors, such as the youth or mental condition of the defendant. Also most states required their state supreme courts to review all death sentences to insure that the penalty imposed in any case was "proportional" to the sentences imposed in all other capital homicides, and thus not arbitrary or aberrant.

Because the Georgia death penalty law had already been upheld, *McCleskey* did not pose the question of whether capital punishment was always excessive or whether the procedural protections of the Georgia law were theoretically adequate. Rather it asked the Court to decide whether a system that in reality produced racially discriminatory results was acceptable.

The study in question, known as the Baldus study after the Iowa law professor who conducted it, covered over 2,000 murder cases in Georgia throughout the 1970's. The raw figures showed that prosecutors sought the death penalty in 70 percent of cases in which African Americans were charged with killing whites but only 19 percent of cases in which whites were charged with killing African Americans. Even more strikingly, 22 percent of African American defendants convicted of killing white victims received the death penalty, but only 3 percent of white defendants convicted of killing African Americans were sentenced to death. Most importantly, even after taking into consideration thirty-nine nonracial variables that might have accounted for the sentence, such as the defendant's prior criminal record and the circumstances of the offense, the study found that persons of either race charged with killing white victims were 4.3 times as likely to receive a death sentence as those convicted of killing African Americans.[7] In sum, the study showed that Georgia juries valued white lives far more than others.

The Court did not question the statistical validity of the Baldus study. Rather the Court reasoned that one cannot establish a violation of the constitutional provision assuring equal protection of the laws, which was the section used to eliminate segregation, without proving that the discrimination was *intentional*. Because the study proved nothing about the beliefs or attitudes of the particular jurors who convicted Mr. McCleskey, the Court concluded that he had not established a violation of equal protection and his sentence was lawful.

It is true, of course, that a statistical study tells one nothing about the views of the jurors in any individual case. But in almost all states, it is impermissible for lawyers or courts to question jurors about their deliberations, because the law considers it important that jurors be free from having to account for their decisions. What then is a defendant to do? Wait for a jury to send out a note asking if it is all right to impose a death penalty because of the defendant's or the victim's race? Not a very plausible scenario. Ask for special permission to interview jurors because of the statistical study? Such a request would clearly not be granted, as it would apply to all juries throughout the state and undermine completely the rule against inquiring into jury deliberations. In reality, then, it will be almost impossible to prove that a particular jury chose to impose the death penalty because of the victim's race, even though studies prove and the Supreme Court acknowledged in *McCleskey* that it occurs regularly.

Though the Court recognized that racial prejudices are at work, it discounted that reality because it considered preserving prosecutorial discretion and the secrecy of jury deliberations to be more important. But the Court had ruled in 1880 that exclusion of African Americans from criminal juries violated the then new equal protection clause of the Fourteenth Amendment because: "What is [equal protection but] that all persons, whether colored or white, shall stand equal before the laws of the States, and, in regard to the colored race, for whose protection the amendment was primarily designed, that no discrimination shall be made against them by law because of their color?"[8] What real difference is there between the present Georgia system and the 1861 Georgia Penal Code, which required an automatic death sentence for "coloreds" convicted of murder or of raping a white but permitted others convicted of murder to receive a life sentence on the all-white jury's recommendation and limited the penalty for rape by others to twenty years and for the rape of a "colored" woman to a fine and imprisonment at the court's discretion?[9] The difference is simply that racism was more overt and official then. Views vary as to the wisdom, fairness, or effectiveness of the death penalty generally. But I would hope that all can agree that prejudice is no more acceptable when hidden in the jury deliberation room than it is when incorporated into the state's code of laws.

The House of Representatives adopted that view by passing in 1990 a bill entitled the Racial Justice Act.[10] Reacting to a study by the General Accounting Office that came up with results very similar to those in the Baldus study, the bill would require courts to consider the kind of challenge brought by Mr. McCleskey but rejected by the Court, namely, statistical proof of racial bias in death sentencing. Statistical proof of significant disparities in the imposition of the death penalty based on the race of either the victim or the defendant would establish a prima facie case of discrimination in a particular case and put on the government the burden of showing that pertinent non-racial factors accounted for the verdict in that case. It would not be enough for the government to show that the case fit the statutory criteria for the imposition of the death penalty, because the core of a claim like McCleskey's is that others, who kill those whom some in society view as "less valuable," also fit those criteria but are not sentenced to death. Although the House provision was dropped in the last-minute rush to get agreement on some form of "crime control" bill before Congress adjourned in 1990, the issue will remain as long as the evidence shows that the government is not using its most awesome power in an even-handed manner.

The Court's preference for submerging racial policies is not new. Justice Powell, who wrote for the Court majority in *McCleskey*, also cast the deciding vote in *Bakke*, the famous 1978 case about affirmative action in university admissions. Powell contended in *Bakke* that the so-called "Harvard admission program," in which the admission director gave "points" for race as well as other factors in evaluating admission applications, was better than the University of California at Davis plan before the Court, in which 16 percent of the seats were publicly and explicitly set aside for minorities.[11] Powell claimed that the former system was different because all applicants were able to compete equally for all seats. He ignored the fact that in such a system only minorities receive "points" for their race and that, by quietly adjusting the number of points given for race, the admissions director could easily achieve any preferred percentage of minority admissions. In other words, Powell was then also claiming that considerations of race under the table were better than those made above board.

Affirmative consideration of race to remedy past racial exclusion is constitutional, as Justice Powell confirmed in *Bakke* and later cases.[12] (See "We Still Need Affirmative Action," page 146.) But whatever the specific method used, I submit that it is healthier for our society to be honest about its racial policies. We gain little but heightened suspicions and distrust by condoning hidden racism or obscuring racial preference; we lose much when we recognize racism

185

exists but refuse to address it. The Court's elevation of perception over reality demeans the constitutional promise of equality and fair play. In time, I hope none of us will act on racial grounds. While we still do, however, our courts should at least be honest about what we are up to. And when we are up to no good, they should stop it, especially when people's lives are at stake.

Advocates' Zeal Is Threatened by Court Contempt Power

There is much fuss these days in the legal profession about declining civility among lawyers. One can hardly be against courtesy, just as no one would be caught dead arguing against fairness, equality, or justice. But no policy is cost-free; nor is every goal of equal value. In 1990 the Connecticut and New Jersey Supreme Courts renewed the debate by issuing strong opinions reminding the legal profession of its obligations of courtesy while affirming contempt judgments against attorneys reacting in frustration and anger to trial judges' rulings against criminal defendants they were vigorously representing. The United States Supreme Court, which has not heard a lawyer contempt case in more than twenty years, refused to hear either appeal. I fear that the kinder and gentler profession that the courts seem intent on developing will be less dedicated to its clients, less willing to challenge authority, and hence less true to the Sixth Amendment's promise of effective assistance of counsel to enforce all the other protections in the Bill of Rights.

In re Daniels[13] involved a two-day jail sentence and $500 fine imposed upon a New Jersey public defender. On the day before trial, the attorney had argued several difficult motions seeking to preclude the use of the adverse results of a prosecutor's lie detector test to which his client had consented after his own polygraph examination had definitively cleared him. The lawyer's facial reaction to the last of the judge's rulings that day piqued the judge; Daniels apologized after a short recess. The next day, several more motions were denied. Then right after the jury was selected but before it was sworn in and

187

while it was out of the courtroom, Daniels sought a new jury because the prosecutor had used his peremptory challenges to exclude all black women from the jury. (See "A Civil Liberties Lawyer on Jury Duty," page 25.) The judge ruled that Daniels' motion was made too late.

According to Daniels, and the judge's law clerk and court reporter who later submitted affidavits to the court, upon hearing that ruling, Daniels sat back in his chair, put his head down, and covered his eyes, but did not utter a sound. In contrast, the judge contended that Daniels had laughed, rolled his head, and thrown himself back in his seat. The judge immediately declared a mistrial, found Daniels in contempt—without permitting him to prepare a defense, interview the witnesses in the courtroom, or contact an attorney—and sent him to jail on the spot.

In re Dodson[14] involved a private Connecticut attorney who reacted to what he thought was an unjust sentence imposed on his client. Immediately after the judge pronounced sentence, the transcript reveals the following interchange:

> DODSON: I think it is most unusual. I think that is totally outrageous. The court can do—
> COURT: You may notify the defendant—
> DODSON: Thirty years more on the same set of facts, I think—
> COURT: Notify the defendant of his rights to appeal.
> DODSON: There is no basis—
> COURT: You're out of order.
> DODSON: I know I am, but there is no basis for that sentence.
> COURT: He is held in contempt of this court.
> DODSON: I apologize for my remarks.
> COURT: Notify the defendant of his rights to appeal on the record.[15]

After agreeing to postpone the matter for a few days, the judge convicted Dodson of contempt and imposed a $100 fine.

In both cases, the state supreme courts unanimously agreed that the conduct amounted to criminally punishable contempt and affirmed the convictions. In New Jersey, the Court said that contempt involves any act that "tends to embarrass, hinder, impede, frustrate or obstruct the court . . . or has the effect of lessening its authority or its dignity," while reminding lawyers that they have an obligation to be courteous to "everyone."[16] In Connecticut, the Court condemned conduct which "is directed against the dignity and authority of the court," while reiterating a bar association standard calling for "strict adherence to the rules of decorum and . . . an attitude of professional respect toward [all] in the courtroom."[17] In both cases, the courts noted some procedural defects that should not be repeated in the future, but this led the New Jersey Supreme Court to vacate only the jail sentence, not the conviction or the fine, and led only one judge to dissent in Connecticut. In neither case did the judges address the likely impact of their rulings upon the willingness of criminal defense attorneys to pursue their ethical obligation to represent their clients zealously or upon the Sixth Amendment's guarantee of effective assistance of counsel.

The problem with these decisions is that, out of a desire to make a point about the need for greater attorney courtesy, the courts lowered the boom on lawyers who were vigorously, albeit overexcitedly and perhaps inappropriately, pursuing the interests of their criminal defendant clients. These lawyers did not insult the intelligence, honesty, or education of a witness (though that must often be the impression left on a jury by many entirely permissible cross-examinations). They did not harass a juror or degrade a court clerk. There were no racial epithets or sexist innuendoes. No opposing lawyer was abruptly cut off or put down.

Rather it was the trial judges' rulings, not their authority to make the decisions, that were being challenged. No one likes to see listeners hang their heads in disgust at what he has just said. Similarly, no one likes to hear that his judgment is "totally outrageous." But lawyers are not just encouraged but obligated to challenge judicial rulings adverse to their clients. Consequently, judges, who have enormous power over the persons before them (including lawyers), must, as the United States Supreme Court has previously reminded them, have thick skins and act with great restraint,[18] and then only to prevent disruption of the proceedings, not a challenge to their rulings.[19]

Not only must judges learn to separate their egos from their rulings, but they must recognize that attorneys, too, are human and have unintended emotional reactions. In the heat of hotly contested criminal trials, where the defense is almost by definition fighting an uphill battle, it is nearly inevitable that decorum will sometimes lapse. Lawyers do get frustrated, they do get angry, and at times they express themselves in less than a felicitous manner.

We should not, of course, condone such overreactions. But as Professor Louis Raveson, counsel for Daniels, has so eloquently explained in his definitive articles on "Advocacy and Contempt,"[20] there needs to be some breathing room between the outer limits of advocacy and the inner boundaries of punishable contempt. The analogy comes from First Amendment law. We do not penalize unintentional misstatements by newspapers, but only falsehoods printed intentionally or with "reckless disregard" for the truth, not because we cherish lies but because we are willing to tolerate mistakes in order to insure robust discussion of public issues and thus fulfill the purpose of the First Amendment. Similarly, Raveson argues, we should not penalize all attorney lapses, even behavior that we do not encourage, teach or admire, but only conduct that intentionally and seriously disrupts a court proceeding in a manner that requires immediate response.

Only thus can we insure that lawyers will not be afraid to fulfill their Sixth Amendment obligation to represent criminal defendants vigorously. And only such fearless and single-minded assistance of counsel will assure citizens accused of crimes that they are being afforded all the protections of the Bill of Rights and assure society that the government has acted properly, only the guilty are convicted, and the sentences imposed are just. A slight loss in civility towards judges is a small price to pay for such substantial benefits for all.

Overloaded Public Defenders: The Right to Counsel at Risk

In his wonderful book, *Gideon's Trumpet*, Anthony Lewis chronicled the story of Clarence Gideon, whose case extended to defendants in state courts the constitutional right to have counsel appointed by the court in any serious criminal case if they cannot afford to hire a lawyer. I am still struck by the clarity, strength, and simplicity of Gideon's statement to the Florida court when he was first arraigned on the charge of breaking into a pool room: "The United States Supreme Court says I am entitled to be represented by counsel."[21] That is what the Supreme Court ultimately decided in his case in 1963, although in fact the Court had not said that before. Gideon's trumpet, however, does not sound as clearly today. Indigents are still entitled by law to have legal counsel with them in court, but the value of that right is sharply limited not just by the threat of contempt for vigorous advocacy, as just discussed, but even more by society's unwillingness to commit the necessary funds to assure meaningful representation.

Two recent studies, in Atlanta and New York, highlight the problem. From 1985 to 1989, the number of persons indicted in Atlanta for felony charges more than doubled—from 6,604 to 13,325. Up to 80 percent of defendants cannot afford a lawyer. At any time, as many as 1,500 defendants who are unable to make bail and do not yet have a lawyer, wait in jail for three or four months just for their arraignment, the first formal court appearance at which time one enters a plea to the charge. Most indigent defendants first meet their lawyer at arraignment and consult for only five or ten minutes before having to decide on a plea. The lawyer assigned to represent the defendant at later appearances may not be the one who was at arraignment.

Public defenders in Atlanta are forced to handle caseloads of more than 500 clients a year, although a national commission had recommended a standard for public defenders of no more than 150 cases per year. (This recommendation is itself staggering. With fewer than 250 working days in a year, the recommended standard would leave a public defender with less than two days for each case.) In October 1990, one Atlanta public defender took the unprecedented step of asking the court to limit the number of cases it gave her. By that point, she had already completed 476 cases in 1990 and had 116 pending. She asked that she not be assigned more than six new cases a week—double the national recommended standard. The court refused and she was later transferred to juvenile court duty for having made the request. A report on the Atlanta situation, prepared by a consultant who has studied defender systems for indigents in forty states for the American Bar Association, indicates that the problems in Atlanta are typical of, although clearly worse in degree than, those in almost every other major city. For example, full-time public defenders throughout the country average 200 to 250 cases a year.[22]

Poor defendants and their lawyers in New York City fare little better. A right to counsel in criminal cases was recognized by the New York State Constitution in 1777. In 1881, the Criminal Procedure Law was amended to provide that indicted defendants must be asked if they want a lawyer and one must be appointed if requested, although there was no provision to compensate the lawyer. In 1893, compensation was provided for appointed counsel in homicide cases. In 1917, the Legal Aid Society, prosecutors, police, and private philanthropists joined to form the Voluntary Defenders' Committee with staff attorneys to represent indigent defendants. The committee, which ultimately became the Criminal Division of the Legal Aid Society, handled 500 cases in its first year, but was up to 35,000 cases by 1959.

In 1966, three years after the decision in Gideon's case, the City of New York chose to meet its newly defined constitutional obligation primarily through an annual contract with the Legal Aid Society, supplemented by appointment of private attorneys in homicide cases and when the society had a conflict of interest, as in multiple-defendant cases. The caseload grew further when the United States Supreme Court ruled in 1972 that counsel must also be provided to indigents in state misdemeanor cases if they will be imprisoned upon conviction.[23] By 1984 the Legal Aid Society had a staff of 502 lawyers— smaller than in 1973 although the society's assignments had increased by 27 percent since 1973. In 1983 it was handling 150,000 assignments in Criminal Court alone, which is the lower court that handles all misdemeanors and first appearances in felonies.

Most strikingly, of the $2 billion spent by New York State and New York City in 1984 on the criminal justice process—police, prosecutors, defenders, courts, and prisons—only $55 million, or 2.7 percent, was spent on criminal defense for the indigent.[24]

The outcome of this arrangement is predictable. In New York, as is true in other major cities, judges typically have calendars of as many as 100 cases per day. When a case is called, the prosecutor describes the state's version in about thirty seconds and then announces to which charge a guilty plea would be accepted and what an acceptable sentence would be. The judge then usually indicates what sentence would be imposed, often adding that if the offer is not accepted then, it would be stiffer at the next court appearance; for example, "The offer is two to four years but next time it will be three to six" or "That is the offer for today only." Not surprisingly, therefore, in 1984 guilty pleas accounted for 63 percent of all Criminal Court dispositions. Prosecutors dismissed 36 percent of cases, leaving only 0.6 percent of cases to be tried. In the separate trial court that heard felony cases, about 76 percent of dispositions were guilty pleas, 12 percent were dismissals, and only 10 percent went to trial.[25] The latter percentages are typical of criminal dispositions throughout the country.[26]

The overwhelming caseload and the pressure to plead guilty and do so promptly leave little room or incentive for preparation of cases. In 74 percent of homicide cases, 82 percent of other felony cases, and 90 percent of misdemeanor cases, private counsel in New York City who were assigned to represent the defendant did not claim compensation for an interview with the defendant. Attorney investigation was claimed in only 27 percent of homicide cases, witness interviews in only 21 percent, and visits to the crime scene in only 12 percent of such cases. Experts were consulted in only 17 percent of homicides and less than 2 percent of all other felonies.[27] In one New York homicide case in which I handled a subsequent challenge in federal court, the private lawyer assigned to do the trial had sought compensation for a total of only six hours of preparation during the fourteen months he had been assigned to the case, including just one hour in the two weeks before trial.[28] These statistics support the complaints of indigent defendants that they go through the court system effectively unrepresented.

What can we draw from this dismal picture? Not much hope, I am afraid. Atlanta and New York are typical of court systems nationwide. The New York study reveals that the system was even more overloaded in 1984 than it was 1973. And the caseload per lawyer in Atlanta in 1990 was even higher than in New York at its worst. The system simply does not work as required by the Bill of Rights because society is unwilling to pay for it to work. Too many people think that because so many defendants plead guilty under these circumstances, they must be guilty and thus unworthy of more extensive representation. But if 36 percent of charges are dismissed by the prosecutor outright without insisting on a plea, how many of the other 64 percent of the cases are also weak? How often do the police or prosecutors overcharge, for example, charging aggravated assault instead of simple assault, robbery instead of theft, or grand larceny instead of petit larceny, or adding conspiracy and other multiple charges for a single incident? Studies show that overcharging and multiple charges are common, particularly for less serious offenses, and are often used to pressure defendants to plead guilty to a lesser charge.[29] In addition, one must ask, how often is there a factual defense, such as an alibi, self-defense, or mental incapacity, that goes undiscovered because of the lack of interviews and investigation? More importantly, from society's perspective, how many are sent to jail or subjected to unsupervised probation who could benefit from an educational, vocational training, or drug treatment program?

The right to counsel is not designed to help the guilty get off. It is meant to insure that persons are tried fairly, convicted only of that which they have done and for which the law holds them responsible, and are then sentenced justly, balancing longer-term rehabilitation and the immediate protection of society. Like other rights explored before, this one costs money to implement. But we must recognize that when we do not enforce it, we are still paying for it in many other, often far less pleasant ways. It is time to re-tune Gideon's trumpet—for everyone's sake.

Law v. Justice: A Twisted Case

In the powerful recent movie on racial injustice in South Africa called "A Dry White Season," Marlon Brando plays an experienced civil rights attorney. In explaining to Donald Sutherland, the white employer of a black gardener who died in police custody, why a formal inquest into the death would be worthless, Brando drawls: "Law and justice are at best distant cousins. But here they are not even related."

In America we sometimes hear complaints that the two are not related because courts are letting guilty people off on "technicalities," a term occasionally used when courts enforce constitutional rights that are designed to assure a fair and accurate procedure for determining guilt. To remember why we need these rights, it is important to hear also about the many cases, like the one in the movie, in which the innocent are unjustly charged and convicted. This can happen, not only because of carelessness and incompetence, but also because the heinous nature of a crime, the political or career ambitions of the prosecutor or police, or the persistence of a heavy backlog of unsolved crimes creates pressures to find and convict a perpetrator and to do so quickly. Such pressures lead police and prosecutors to cut corners—to ignore inconsistent leads, omit confirming lab tests, or fail to tell the defense about witnesses who name someone else as the perpetrator. They also sometimes lead judges to ignore or twist the law to avoid dismissing charges or overturning convictions. It is precisely because the participants in the criminal process are human and prone to err—for innocent as well as malevolent or corrupt reasons—that we have strict rules and need to enforce them rigorously.

This is the story of an innocent man, who at this writing is still not free after more than fourteen years, despite innumerable revelations that the government withheld evidence showing his innocence and the guilt of another, because the pressures to convict a cop killer and save that conviction have overpowered considerations of justice.*

Vincent James Landano was convicted of murder in 1977 for shooting an off-duty police officer in the midst of a robbery of a check-cashing operation in Kearny, New Jersey in August 1976. The facts of the crime are clear. Two men, one dark-haired and one red-headed, came to the site mid-morning. One went inside the trailer to rob the place while the other stayed outside in the parking lot. When police officer Snow, who was delivering cash to the facility, drove up, the man outside went up to his car and fired at him point blank, instantly killing him. The two criminals then drove off with the loot from the trailer, with the killer driving the getaway car.

At the trial the state's primary witnesses were Joseph Pascuiti, who was working nearby and observed the shooting; Allen Roller, the red-headed participant and passenger in the getaway car, who pled no contest to felony murder and received a thirty-year sentence, of which he served eight years, in exchange for his testimony; Jacob Roth, owner of the robbed check-cashing service; and Raymond Portas, a truck driver who observed the getaway car maneuvering in traffic.

Pascuiti said the killer was a dark-haired man with short curly hair and no moustache. He could not identify Landano at trial. Roller, a member of a motorcycle gang called the Breed, admitted that he planned the robbery with Victor Forni, another member of that gang, whose gun was the murder weapon. However, he insisted that Landano, who was not a member of the gang, rather than Forni, was the other participant who shot the officer. He acknowledged that the Breed had a strict code forbidding members from "ratting" on each other. Roller also denied that he had ever committed any other crimes with Forni. In contradiction to Roller, Roth claimed that Landano was the hold-up man at the window, not the one in the parking lot who shot the officer. Portas, the truck driver, had picked out a picture of Lan-

---

*The facts recounted here are found in the state and federal court opinions noted and in other court documents. The reader should know, however, that I have been assisting the defense in this case since 1987, first as Legal Director of the American Civil Liberties Union of New Jersey, because the case raises many significant civil liberties issues, and then on my own, because I became convinced of the injustice perpetrated.

dano as the driver of the getaway car from a photo display in the prosecutor's office eight months after the crime and identified him at trial.

Landano testified that he was innocent and had not even been in New Jersey on the day of the crime. He established, by his signature on the register, that he had gone to a methadone clinic in Staten Island, where he lived, at about 6:30 that morning. (Landano had a drug problem and had been previously convicted of drug-related, but non-violent, crimes.) He also introduced a picture taken of him at about 12:50 p.m. that day when he cashed his unemployment check in Staten Island. The picture showed him to have straight, long hair and a bushy moustache. His girlfriend and a friend of hers testified that he was with them from 9:00 to 11:00 that morning. The prosecutor also had notes of an interview with a man who confirmed that Landano had played cards with him that morning, but the man was not available at trial. Landano tried on for the jury the killer's jacket, which had a streak of blood across it establishing that it was zipped at the time of the crime. Landano, who is six-foot-one, could not even zip up the jacket, which was also about six inches too short for him in the sleeves.

In his summation to the jury, the prosecutor stressed that "throughout this case there is no suggestion of police malpractice or coercion of these [photographic] selections."

The jury deliberated for two days and then informed the judge that "we honestly feel we cannot get a twelve vote count on guilty or not guilty" on any of the counts. The judge then gave the jury additional instructions, in what is known as a "supplemental charge," informing them that "we are in the fifth week of this trial and I think you realize what is invested as far as time, money and everything else." He said that "this case at a future time must be decided" and "there's no reason to suppose that the case will ever be submitted to 12 persons more intelligent, more impartial or more competent to decide it." Fifty-three minutes later, the jury came back with unanimous guilty verdicts on all counts. Landano was sentenced to life imprisonment.

Subsequently, Forni, who had been able to fight extradition from New York for eighteen months, was tried for all the crimes, including felony murder, but convicted only of conspiracy to commit armed robbery, primarily because of Roller's testimony that he had planned the crime but had not been there during its commission. Forni received a three-year sentence, of which he served only eight months in jail.

The prosecution's version began to unravel almost immediately. Soon after the trial Landano learned of fingerprint and ballistic evidence showing that, contrary to Roller's testimony, Forni and Roller had committed several other armed robberies together and that the prosecutor's office in Landano's case knew this before his trial. Two inmates came forward and said that Roller had admitted to them in prison that he had falsely accused Landano because he needed to name someone outside the Breed gang. The trial judge denied a new trial because he disbelieved the inmates and thought that the evidence of Roller's involvement with Forni in other crimes, although contradicting what Roller had said at trial, would not have been enough to change the jury's mind. There is a longstanding constitutional obligation on the state to provide the defense with any evidence favorable to the defendant, known as "exculpatory evidence."[30] But if the defense does not learn about it until after trial, the defense must show not only that it would have been helpful, but that, by itself, it probably would have changed the verdict.[31] The problem is that it is very hard for a judge, who did not hear the jury's deliberations, to know what additional evidence would have raised a reasonable doubt in at least one juror's mind. On appeal, the Appellate Division affirmed Landano's conviction and the denial of a new trial, and the New Jersey Supreme Court refused to hear the case.

In 1981, the trial prosecutor gave a speech at a state college, at the invitation of a professor who had become interested in the case. The prosecutor stated that Jacob Roth, the owner of the robbed check-cashing facility, had been under investigation at the time of the crime for organized crime connections and payoffs to Officer Snow. He described Roth as an uncooperative witness: "we had to like coerce him" to testify against Landano. He also explained the intense career pressures he felt at the time: in essence, a prosecutor who fails to get a conviction in a cop killing is going nowhere.

Soon thereafter the professor wrote about the case in a magazine. (Landano had gained some public notice because while in prison he established the "Scared Straight" program, nationally reputed for trying to educate youth as to the dangers of a criminal life.) Shortly after reading the article, which showed that all the evidence was weak except for the truck driver's identification of Landano, Portas, the truck driver, came forward to reveal problems with the identification of Landano he had made at trial.

At a state court hearing in 1982, Portas explained that, at the prosecutor's office, he had first picked out of a group of pictures a photo of someone other than Landano, which was removed and never seen again. After further discussion, Portas said "If this man [pointing to Landano's picture] wasn't so fat, I would have picked him." The prosecutor said "That's the man we want" and asked Portas to initial the photo. Portas testified that he would not have initialed the photo if the prosecutor had not said that Landano was the man they wanted.

Portas also testified that, while he was waiting in the court hallway on the day of trial, two well-dressed men had passed by him. When he went into the bathroom, a person whom he assumed was a detective asked him: "Do you know who the two were that just went in? You know, that's our man." In fact, Portas had not recognized Landano in the hall and was not even sure when he got in the courtroom which of the two men the detective was referring to, until one of them said he was the lawyer.

Portas stated that he had been so disturbed after his trial testimony that he wanted to talk to the judge but first went to see a priest who told him not to worry because the police knew what they were doing. After reading the magazine article, he had gone first to the prosecutor's office, but they also told him not to worry about it; only then did he approach the defense.

The hearing judge, who had not presided at the trial, refused to vacate the conviction. He treated Portas as a "recanting witness"—one who says that he lied previously but is now telling the truth—and discounted his testimony based on New Jersey's nearly insurmountable presumption against believing such a witness. Portas, of course, was not recanting but merely explaining the police pressures that led to his trial testimony. Second, this judge concluded that the new evidence about the investigation and coercion of Roth, although helpful to the defense, was not likely to have changed the jury's mind.

Finally, the judge refused to apply to Landano's case a ruling of the New Jersey Supreme Court that had been issued just a few weeks after Landano's first appeal had been denied. That decision said that the kind of supplementary instructions given in Landano's case when the jury announced that it was deadlocked, known as a "dynamite

199

charge," was too coercive and was no longer to be used, as many other state and federal courts before and since have also concluded. The judge hearing Landano's case concluded that that ruling only applied to cases still on appeal when it was issued. Because Landano's appeal to the Appellate Division had been concluded before the ruling but his appeal to the state supreme court had not been filed until a few weeks later (in accordance with the court rules), the judge concluded he was "in a no court land" when the new ruling had been issued and thus could not benefit from it![32]

Again, in 1984 the Appellate Division refused to disturb the conviction, though using a different reason for not applying the ruling on dynamite charges. Again the state supreme court refused to hear the case.

Landano's outstanding and tireless attorney, Neil Mullin, who had not handled the trial but had become involved in the case in 1980 and had not been paid for any of his work up to that point, then filed a habeas corpus petition in federal court in 1985.

"Habeas corpus" is Latin for "let us have the body." It is an ancient English legal writ, first mentioned in English court papers in 1220, by which the sheriff is ordered to bring the prisoner to court to allow inquiry into whether the confinement is lawful. It was one of the first and most significant judicial limits upon executive discretion in arresting and holding citizens. Habeas corpus was seen as such an important guarantee of liberty by 1787 that the Framers inserted into the body of our Constitution a provision that: "The privilege of the Writ of Habeas Corpus shall not be suspended, unless when in Cases of Rebellion or Invasion the public Safety may require it." It has only been suspended once in our history—during the Civil War. In 1867, the federal courts were given the power to inquire through the writ of habeas corpus whether a person was confined in violation of the Constitution. In the 1960's a series of decisions in which Justice Brennan figured prominently established that the federal courts can review imprisonment resulting from a criminal conviction in state court to determine whether it was obtained in violation of any of the rights of the Fifth, Sixth, and Eighth Amendments that had been "incorporated" into the due process clause of the Fourteenth Amendment. (See "Embodying the Spirit—Justice William Brennan," page 8.) If a federal habeas corpus court concludes that constitutional error occurred at a trial, it may, like a state appeals court, vacate the conviction. However, the state may then still re-try the defendant, because double jeopardy does not apply when a conviction is overturned following a challenge brought by the defendant.

The federal judge, H. Lee Sarokin, gave Mullin an opportunity to review some of the prosecutor's files. Mullin discovered a police report revealing that two photos of Victor Forni as well as several photo displays had been removed from the police vault on the day that Portas, the truck driver, had testified he had examined photos and picked out one that was removed. Mullin also found a manila folder with an eight-picture display, including a photo of Forni, which a detective said had been shown to "a truck driver" during the investigation. Forni's photo shows him to have short, dark curly hair and no moustache, matching Pascuiti's description of the killer and the police drawing shown to witnesses. Judge Sarokin held a hearing so he could personally hear and observe Portas.

In his opinion in September 1987, Judge Sarokin found Portas fully believable. He concluded that Portas had probably initially identified a photo of Forni, which was removed, and that his subsequent identifications of Landano, both in and out of court, were the product of improper police suggestion and hence were constitutionally inadmissible.[33] In a shocking and bizarre twist, however, the judge, well known for his courageous enforcement of constitutional rights, declared himself unable to grant relief. He explained that the habeas corpus statute requires a federal court to "defer" to the state court's findings of fact—in this case the determination that Portas was not credible—even when the federal judge disagrees with that finding, unless he concludes that the state court hearing was not fair or did not fully develop the facts. He found no exception applicable, even though the defense had been denied access in state court to the report and the folder with Forni's photos. Sarokin therefore felt compelled to deny relief, but expressed his concern that "a great injustice has occurred" and, in a most unusual move, expressly invited a higher court to reverse him. He also ruled that the exculpatory evidence about Roller and Roth discovered after trial would not have changed the jury's mind without Portas' new testimony and that the supplemental charge to the jury was not sufficiently coercive to be a constitutional violation.

The federal Court of Appeals for the Third Circuit affirmed the denial of habeas corpus relief, relying on the federal obligation to defer to state courts, without even mentioning the possible injustice that had caused Judge Sarokin such "anguish." The United States Supreme Court refused to hear the challenge to the deference rule in February 1989.[34]

The case appeared to be at an end when yet another crucial piece of evidence was discovered. In the files of Forni's defense lawyer, James McCloskey, founder of Centurion Ministries, which investigates cases of convicted persons it believes are innocent, found a police report stating that one Joseph Basapas had picked Victor Forni's photo out of a seventeen-photo array shown to him in January 1977, "as the man who drove the car away from the scene of the holdup," whom all agreed was the killer. No one had ever before mentioned such a witness; indeed, on an earlier appeal in state court, the government had told the court: "No one chose Forni's photograph as depicting the murderer."[35]

Based on this discovery, Judge Sarokin issued an extraordinary order—that the federal marshal seize without notice to the state all the files concerning the Landano case in the hands of the prosecutor and the various police departments involved. He then allowed Mullin to go through every document in the files in the presence of an attorney for the state. Among other evidence discovered were: a handwritten note indicating Joseph Basapas had identified Forni; a document labelled "ID on Landano" in which Pascuiti, the eyewitness who said the killer was a curly-haired man without a moustache, said "hair not right—suspect had curly hair;" a handwritten document labelled "Civilian Witnesses" which said "Jacob Roth . . . Biggest Problem in the Case—8/26—*Tentative* id of Landano," and a police report showing that Roth was questioned by the Internal Affairs Division of the Newark Police Department about possible payoffs to Newark Officer Snow on the morning of Roth's August 31 positive identification of Landano; and an empty brown envelope with the prosecutor's name and address imprinted on it with the following handwritten note: "Forni looks like guy who was driving down street; Det. Rose; Pictures of (3) three suspects."

Based on this newly discovered evidence of Landano's innocence and Forni's guilt, Judge Sarokin finally issued the writ of habeas corpus and vacated Landano's conviction in July 1989.[36] He concluded that the state had repeatedly withheld or suppressed crucial exculpatory evidence in violation of the longstanding constitutional obligation, finding the police report of the Basapas identification of Forni and the Pascuiti "hair not right" statement to be the most telling. He released Landano, after thirteen years in jail, on an unsecured bond, pending appeal or a new trial. The federal appeals court required that Landano wear an electronic bracelet that could monitor his whereabouts.

Around this time one of the original trial jurors told the press that she had been the hold-out juror and that she felt coerced by the judge's "dynamite charge" to vote with the others despite her doubts.[37] Under both state and federal court rules, however, a juror's testimony about jury deliberations will not be considered unless it shows improper influence, such as bribes or threats, by persons not on the jury. Thus, this disclosure was not presented in the court record.

The ultimate legal technicality was to be applied on the state's next appeal. The federal Court of Appeals, by a vote of two to one, refused in 1990 to consider Landano's claim that evidence was unconstitutionally withheld. The court noted that the federal habeas corpus law requires that all claims be presented first to the state courts; this is known in the law as "exhaustion of state remedies." Landano had repeatedly claimed in all his many state court proceedings that the prosecutor had withheld exculpatory evidence and had presented all the evidence he had obtained by then to the state courts. And, of course, the Basapas and Pascuiti reports had been in the state's files the entire time. But the federal appeals court said that Landano still must start all over again because the state court had never seen those two documents! In October 1990, the United States Supreme Court again refused to hear the case.[38]

In state court, Landano was again before the judge who had originally tried the case. (He has been temporarily off the bench during the 1982 state proceeding.) He first denied bail, although it was undisputed that Landano had been employed and had faithfully abided by all conditions in the fifteen months since his release. Within a week the New Jersey Supreme Court reversed him and ordered Landano released pending the hearing in state court. In March 1991, the trial judge denied Landano a hearing because, contrary to what the federal appeals court had said, the state rules do not allow a defendant to have an issue reconsidered—in this case, prosecutorial misconduct in withholding evidence—even though new evidence relevant to that issue is later discovered! He also concluded that in any case the new evidence would not have changed the jury's mind. Landano will either appeal in state court or head back to federal court. It is important to remember that even if a state court or ultimately the federal court finds for Landano again, the state would still be free to try him again with whatever evidence it thinks is still worth presenting to a jury.

What lessons can we derive from this ordeal? The most significant is that, despite all the constitutional protections that we so highly value and sometimes complain about when they seem to shield those thought to be guilty, the system has not protected one who is innocent or, in the view most generous to the state, "only" received a grossly unfair trial, from serving thirteen years in prison. Indeed, had Landano been charged with this crime before 1971 or after 1982, when the death penalty was in effect in New Jersey, he would have been executed soon after the United States Supreme Court refused to hear what then looked like his final appeal in February 1989. No doubt the fact that Landano had a prior criminal record made it easier for all involved to presume that he was guilty, whatever the evidence kept showing, or to be less concerned about whether a mistake had been made. The extensive documented history of mistaken identifications as well as scientific evidence of the unreliability of identification evidence[39] confirm that Landano's case is, unfortunately, not an isolated incident.

It is also vital to see the practical difficulties in vindicating constitutional rights. Every judge from the outset has recognized that the prosecution had a constitutional obligation to disclose to the defense before trial any exculpatory evidence. The only reason that Landano was not released earlier, and is still not free of the charge, is that if a prosecutor manages to keep evidence secret until after the trial, the defense must convince a judge that the withheld evidence was so strong that it would probably have changed the jury's mind. It is nearly impossible to meet that burden and vindicate the undisputed constitutional right to receive all exculpatory evidence without the assistance of an attorney. Yet the Constitution has been interpreted not to require that a poor inmate be given a free lawyer for any proceeding after the first appeal and most states and the federal courts do not provide one.[40] Landano was just plain lucky that he got a first-rate lawyer like Mullin interested enough to pursue his case for ten years and enforce his undisputed constitutional rights. Yet even when Mullin finally convinced a court that so much evidence had been withheld that it certainly would have changed the jury's mind, he was told that the state court must get a chance to review the evidence, even though that chance had been denied only because the prosecution had violated the Constitution and improperly withheld the evidence and denied its existence for years!

The dogged evasion by the prosecutors, the hesitance of the courts to intervene, and the persistence of the government even after the dirty linen has been aired are probably attributable to the nature of the crime—a cop killing—and the state's inability to prosecute the killer now because he has already been tried and acquitted of related charges for this crime. But it is precisely when the stakes are highest that the need for enforcement of the rules is the greatest, for it is then that the authorities are most tempted to cut corners.

When we next hear charges that courts are coddling criminals by enforcing "technicalities," we should think about Jimmy Landano and recall why criminal defendants need all the safeguards in the Bill of Rights.

VII

FREEDOM OF RELIGION

This country has a deep and historically grounded commitment to freedom of religion. Many of the colonies were founded by religious minorities, such as the Puritans, fleeing persecution by the Church of England. Once in command of their own territory, however, these colonists saw little problem with having the government that they installed both levy taxes to support their churches and legislate their view of Christian morality and practice, to the detriment of other denominations.

To deal with the growing abhorrence of these practices as well as the longstanding colonial sensitivity to religious persecution, the Framers placed two provisions about religion in the First Amendment. The very beginning of the Bill of Rights reads: "Congress shall make no law respecting an establishment of religion, or prohibiting the free-exercise thereof." These are known as the establishment and free exercise clauses.

The current interpretation of the establishment clause reflects changes in our religious practices and concerns. It was drafted primarily to prevent the government from designating one Christian denomination as the official religion and imposing taxes to pay its ministers' salaries and build and maintain its churches. But over time the problems became more complex as the country grew to include not only a great variety of Christian denominations but also Jews, Muslims, Buddhists, and adherents of various newer religions. Moreover, with the overall decline of religion, agnostics and atheists as well as a variety of ethically based cultures asserted themselves. No longer was there a single holy book, a common name for the All-Powerful, or universally shared holidays.

Accordingly, the focus of attention under the establishment clause has shifted to preventing government from favoring or endorsing any religious practices. The Supreme Court now asks whether the government action has the purpose or primary effect of advancing religion or entangles the state in the administration of religious institutions. As a result, prayers, however nondenominational, are now banned in schools, and moments of silence are suspect. Creches on city property are subject to careful scrutiny. School concerts of both Christmas carols and Chanukah songs are criticized. Even laws limiting abortions have been challenged because they conform to, and thus are said to "establish," the views of the Catholic Church.

Modern rulings on the separation of church and state have provoked dismay among many. The rejection of Bible readings and prayer in schools has prompted complaints that our children are not being given moral guidance. Challenges to displaying the symbols or singing the songs of different religions have been seen as narrow-minded, reducing rather than enhancing understanding and tolerance. These are serious concerns. I address in the first two essays of this chapter the debates about placing religious symbols on public property and holding moments of silence in public schools.

The current controversies about the free exercise clause, addressed in the third essay, are no less complex. Because all religious people are wary of government encroachment, there is broad social consensus about the need to preserve the right to practice one's religion as one sees fit. But religious beliefs sometimes dictate certain behaviors: for example, not working on the sabbath, ingesting certain substances at communion, wearing certain symbols or headgear, or refusing to join the military, attend school, or pay taxes. When acting in such ways, believers often come into conflict with various neutral regulations of government that are otherwise unobjectionable. Important questions then arise: when, how often, and in what ways must we create exceptions for sincere religious objectors to uniform state rules in order to satisfy the free exercise clause? And how can we do so without creating the kind of special treatment for religion that is prohibited by the establishment clause?

Of Carols, Creches, and Menorahs

At the end of every year, we have a special season. I do not mean the period of meaningful religious devotion, nor am I referring to the weeks of commercial exploitation of religious holidays. Rather I mean the time when government is called upon—by both public officials and private groups—to display religious symbols on public property and to sing religious songs in public schools.

Many feel that it is of no great moment whether a creche is placed on the city hall lawn or "Silent Night" is sung in the school assembly. On one level, they are right. Each individual incident is quite minor and no permanent religious role in government is established. The cumulative effects, however, are insidious. For many, these practices cheapen religion; hence the opposition of clergy from many denominations to such displays and performances. More importantly from a civil liberties point of view, they undermine our confidence that government is free of religious influence and that all citizens will be treated equally regardless of their religion.

A little history helps us to gain perspective on current church-state controversies. The Holy Days and Fasting Days Act of 1551, never revoked in England, makes it illegal to skip church on Christmas Day and assigns penalties for those who have "no lawful or reasonable excuse to be absent." The Lawful Games Act of 1541 forbade all sports on that day except archery, leaping, and vaulting, and an Act of 1625 limited such activities to one's backyard, as "there shall be no meetings, assemblings or concourses of people out of their own parishes for any sport or pastime whatsoever."

In contrast, under the Puritan Commonwealth established by Oliver Cromwell in the 1640's, any celebration of Christmas was discouraged. The Puritans rejected the holiday as rooted in the pagan worship of ancient Britons who celebrated December 25 as the Birthday of the Unconquered Sun, marking the end of the old year and the beginning of the new one. Accordingly, a 1644 law made it illegal to bake and eat mince pies and Christmas pudding on Christmas Day, declaring them "abominable and idolatrous confections to be avoided by Christians." Parliament sat on Christmas Day, soldiers tried to keep shops open, and evergreen decorations were prohibited.[1]

This split view of Christmas was carried over to this country. Episcopalians, Catholics, Lutherans, and members of the Reformed Church kept the holiday while Quakers, Methodists, Baptists, Amish, Puritans, Congregationalists, and Presbyterians rejected it. In 1659, the holiday was banned in Boston; anyone caught feasting could be fined five shillings. The ban was lifted twenty-two years later, but the Puritan leaders Increase Mather and Cotton Mather tried for years to discourage the practice, arguing that: "Christmas savors of superstition. It can never be proved that Christ was born on December 25. It is most probable that the Nativity was in September." Christmas suffered another setback during the Revolutionary War, when it was associated with the Anglican English troops and their American Tory sympathizers. Only when Thomas Jefferson championed separation of church and state did Christmas become again a commonly celebrated American Christian holiday.[2]

Consistent with the Framers' rejection of the historical entanglement of the state with certain Christian practices, the Supreme Court ruled in the early 1960's that the First Amendment prohibits Bible reading and the saying of prayers in public schools.[3] The Court ruled that no specific showing of coercion is necessary to prove a violation of the establishment clause, because "when the power, prestige and financial support of government is placed behind a particular religious belief, the indirect coercive pressure upon religious minorities to conform to the prevailing officially approved religion is plain." As the Court explained, that constitutional provision rests "on the belief that a union of government and religion tends to destroy government and to degrade religion."[4]

By 1984, however, the Court seemed to have forgotten both the historical backdrop and the constitutional rule that government cannot sponsor or determine religious practices when it upheld the public display of a creche. Its ruling also muddied the law because it relied on the fact that the creche was part of a holiday exhibit consisting otherwise of entirely secular objects, such as Santa's house, reindeer, sleigh bells, and a wishing well.[5] Lower courts have struggled since then to determine what is a mixed and hence permissible display and what is a purely religious display, such as an unadorned cross or creche.[6]

In 1989, the Court tried to clarify its earlier distinction in a case from Pittsburgh. First, it held that a creche placed on a county courthouse's grand staircase surrounded only by a fence, a small evergreen tree, some flowers, and a sign noting its donation by the Holy Name Society violated the First Amendment. But then it went on to find that a display one block away of an eighteen-foot menorah in front of city hall was fine, because it stood next to a forty-five-foot Christmas tree (which the Court considers a secular object!) and a sign saluting liberty.[7] Needless to say, these rulings left officials and lawyers even more confused.

The Supreme Court's approach is unfortunate for several reasons, quite apart from its failure to provide clear guidelines. First, it encourages the juxtaposition of reindeer and creches, doing a disservice to the religious symbols and the religions that revere them.

Second, in its apparent effort to authorize more public displays while sticking to its doctrine barring religious symbols, the Court has chosen to downgrade, and in my view demean, the religious significance of several figures and objects. For example, the Court seems to have conveniently forgotten that Santa Claus is Saint Nicholas, not just a jolly bearer of gifts, and that the Christmas tree, though derived from pagan practices, was developed by German Christians as a religious object, with hanging wafers symbolizing the host and candles representing Christ.[8] Justice Blackmun's statement in the latest case that the government may celebrate both Christmas and Chanukah as secular winter holidays hardly reveals respect for our country's religious traditions.

Third, the Court's new approach of allowing government to mix secular and religious displays makes it easier, not harder, for government to become enmeshed with religion. This is the very opposite of what the First Amendment was designed to achieve.

As unfortunate as the Court's retreat has been the reaction of some Jewish groups which, instead of urging an end to public displays of all religious symbols, have sought equal time—a menorah of equal size for each creche displayed, one Chanukah song for each Christmas carol sung. Two wrongs, or in this case two songs, never did make a right. It is true that this approach would provide more equal treatment of two current major religions, but it would undermine the constitutional structure while creating practical problems of administration. Cognizant of the insidious effects of government involvement and of the historical differences about even basic Christian matters such as Christmas, the Framers chose not to have government embrace all religions equally, but rather to preclude government from establishing any religion. The proposed alternative would force the state to decide which religions are important or legitimate enough to recognize and how much room to afford them in public displays. Our government has enough trouble figuring out which regimes to recognize overseas and which social needs to address domestically. We should not overtax our bureaucrats by forcing them to determine what is a legitimate religion, an appropriate display, or a typical musical offering. Even assuming government could undertake such a delicate task, minority religions should remember that most likely the bureaucrats applying such rules would not share their theological persuasion.

Yet another disheartening development has been the growing number of requests by private groups, Christian and Jewish alike, for permission to put up their own religious symbols on public land. Clearly the Constitution guarantees the right of all religious people to express their views, of whatever nature, in a public forum open to all other forms of expression. But there is a big difference between Martin Luther King invoking religious images during a civil rights rally or a preacher on a soap box predicting doom, on the one hand, and placing a private creche on a city hall lawn, on the other.

First, it is most unusual for the city hall lawn, town green, or village park to be an open forum for four-week exhibitions of any group's physical displays. Does anyone really believe that the mayor who allows the church men's club to place a creche on the city hall lawn from Thanksgiving to Christmas would also allow the Socialist Workers Party to put up a May Day display on the same spot, the Black Muslims to exhibit the Koran during Ramadan, or the Hare Krishnas to erect a display during four weeks of their choosing?

Moreover, the privately placed religious symbol sits there alone, without explanation or attribution. Simply by being on public land, it appears to be a government-sponsored display and thus suggests government endorsement, which is clearly not permissible. One inge-

212

nious court tried to resolve the apparent endorsement problem by requiring the private group to place next to its creche a waterproof sign of sufficient size and content to announce its sole sponsorship of the display and to pay the costs of any electricity used.[9] On a practical level, I wonder: do such plastic or neon signs really improve the beauty of the religious symbol or the park? On a policy level I ask: is this the best use of government accountants? From the constitutional perspective, I think we should inquire: must we make every public park into a display case for private religions and if so, can we realistically accommodate all religions fairly and equally?

Next December, or whenever next celebrating a religious holiday, consider whether religion is more devoutly practiced, government more respected, and liberty more protected when we ask the state to sing our religious songs and display our holy symbols. I pray that our people will once again agree with our Framers that in the long run "a union of government and religion tends to destroy government and to degrade religion."[10]

Do Children Need a Moment of Silence in School?

As explained in the last essay, the Supreme Court held unequivocally in the 1960's that the reading of the Bible and the saying of prayers in public schools violate the First Amendment's separation of church and state. Legislators throughout the country have sought to evade these clear but controversial rulings in several ways. The most common approach during the 1980's was the enactment of laws allowing or requiring a "moment of silence" in every classroom at the beginning of each school day.

The Supreme Court invalidated Alabama's attempt because it was clear from the wording of the statute—a moment of silence "for meditation or voluntary prayer" —and from the statements of the legislative sponsor that the law's purpose was to bring prayer back into public schools.[11] This conclusion rendered the bill unconstitutional under the Supreme Court's three-pronged test for judging whether a law violates the First Amendment's establishment clause: a) was the enactment passed with the purpose of advancing religion or religious practices; b) is that in any case its primary effect; or c) does the law entangle government in religious issues or in the administration of religious entities?[12] However, Justice Sandra Day O'Connor indicated in the Alabama decision, and several other members of the Court agreed with her, that a moment of silence law not passed for such a purpose might be constitutional.

The Court was to face that harder case—a moment of silence law that did not expressly refer to prayer and for which a secular purpose was asserted—when it agreed in 1987 to hear the ACLU's challenge to the New Jersey moment of silence law, in which I was co-counsel for the citizens. That law required that all public schools hold a moment of silence at the beginning of each school day. However, the Court avoided the sensitive constitutional issue by ruling that the individual legislators who sought to appeal on their own the lower courts' ruling, which invalidated the law, did not have legal authority or "standing" to do so.[13] Examination of the four rationales for such laws offered in the New Jersey case and others is, however, instructive in answering a fundamental question posed by such statutes, which is relevant to the constitutional inquiry: namely, what is it that our public school children need but are not getting without such a moment of silence? If it is religion, such laws are unconstitutional.

In the New Jersey case, the lower courts agreed with the teachers, parents, and students on whose behalf the ACLU brought the challenge, that the purpose was in fact the constitutionally impermissible one of trying to circumvent the Supreme Court rulings of the 1960's and bring prayer back to the public schools. Unlike the Alabama law, the New Jersey statute did not have the word "prayer" in its text. Nevertheless, the intent was quite clear. Not only was this law the eighteenth bill introduced over fourteen years to achieve that purpose, despite three gubernatorial vetoes, but the chief Assembly sponsor said at the time of its adoption: "It is important that our society get back to religious values." When asked why the bill was necessary, as students already had opportunities to pray at quiet moments during the school day, the sponsor replied: "They publicly won't do it [pray] unless they are directed." The state senator who led the fight for passage said the bill was designed to "bring prayers back into the school through the front door. This bill will not harm any school-age child. Rather it will restore his faith in his Creator."[14]

After the law was challenged in court, the legislature for the first time came up with a second and secular justification—to provide a transition between the hustle and bustle of the schoolyard and the serious work of the school day. This idea had not even been raised during the legislative consideration of the bill. Indeed, all the educational groups that had appeared before the legislature—the New Jersey Education Association, a union representing 84,000 teachers, the New Jersey School Boards Association, representing 611 school boards, and the New Jersey School Administrators' Association—had testified that the law was unnecessary as an educational matter and opposed it because it would reintroduce prayer into the schools. The transitional period idea did not surface even when the legislature voted to override the governor's veto, which was expressly based upon constitutional concerns.

Nor was the transitional period concept sound when finally proposed. "Quiet time" and other calming techniques, such as short writing or quiet reading assignments, to still an overactive or overheated student body have been used in schools for a long time. No legislation is needed to authorize teachers to use them. Moreover, mandated uniformity denies teachers the flexibility required by particular circumstances. The first minute of the school day may not always be the time when a moment of silence is most needed, nor is one minute always enough time. Quite simply, the proposal made no educational sense, which is why the trial court rejected it as "an after-the-fact rationalization" designed to cover up the real purpose—namely, to permit prayer in school.[15]

Following the suggestion of Justice O'Connor in the Alabama case, various organizations that appeared as "friends of the court" or *amici curiae* in the New Jersey case and others offered a third rationale. They suggested that the real purpose—again not stated in the legislative history—was to "accommodate" the desire of religious students who wished to pray during the school day.

In First Amendment law, "accommodations" of religion are steps taken by government to undo impositions upon religious adherents effected by general government requirements. For example, Congress wrote into the Social Security law an exemption from the tax on the self-employed for those people who are religiously opposed to government pensions. Although this law was expressly adopted to aid religious communities, such as the Amish, who have strict theological views about such programs, it does not violate the establishment clause. The reason is that the exemption does not create a preference for a particular religion but seeks only to restore to those people the ability to practice their religion that had been infringed in the first place by the adoption of the general tax obligation. Likewise, regulations that allow Muslim prisoners to leave their work assignments mid-day on Fridays to attend services or exempt Jewish prisoners from work on Saturdays are accommodations to religious views that were imposed upon by the original neutral work assignments. (See "The Free Exercise of Religion: When and How Far?" page 219.)

In schools, we have no such imposition requiring an accommodation. True, everyone under sixteen must by law attend school. But there is no obstacle to prayer during school hours. Children can pray in the yard, hallways, or classrooms either before, between, or after classes. They can also pray during lunch and in study hall. Nor are they prohibited from praying in class if they finish their assigned work early. Similarly, prayer is not prohibited should the teacher choose, in the exercise of pedagogical discretion, to have a quiet moment to allow students to settle down and compose themselves. In any case no religion requires prayer precisely at the start of a day of secular studies.

As there is no imposition requiring an accommodation, what would be the primary effect on students, to use the language of the second part of the constitutional test, if a mandatory, daily moment of silence law were implemented? What would they think if they saw students and teachers standing quietly with bowed heads and perhaps with hands held together? Would it not look and feel like the prayers they see in church, synagogue, or mosque? Would they not assume that they are supposed to pray as well? Would they not expect teachers to lead them or suggest prayers for them? Would they not consider it embarrassing or "uncool" to ask to be excused from the room during that time? In short, unless the school makes clear that the exercise is designed only to accommodate the religious obligations of a few, most students would conclude that the school expects everyone to pray.

Some have suggested a fourth purpose—that moments of silence will help bring moral standards back to schools. There has, in fact, been a growing movement to teach "values" directly in school. But what values will students learn from one minute in which everyone stands silently? Will they really think better of school or take it more seriously? Or will they think that the whole thing is silly or that school is really a place to pray? If we want to teach important civic values, such as tolerance for differences, respect for all people regardless of background or viewpoint, use of non-violent means for resolving disputes, and willingness to help others in need—and I for one think that we certainly should try—how can we do that during an undirected moment of enforced silence at a set time? And if the teacher tries to provide direction by telling students what they should think about, will the moment not inevitably appear to be a religious one?

217

As co-counsel for the New Jersey plaintiffs challenging the moment of silence law, my own answers to these questions would hardly be a surprise. But I ask the reader to consider not only whether such a statute violates the formal three-pronged test used by the Supreme Court to gauge establishment clause cases, but also whether a mandatory moment of silence at the beginning of each school day makes sense. Is it good public policy? More importantly, is it something that our kids really need, are not already getting, and cannot get better elsewhere, for example, at home or in church? I suggest that we could better use all the time, money, and energy spent on enacting, challenging, and defending the constitutionality of moment of silence laws to develop intelligent and meaningful curricula for teaching civic values that we can all agree are important and that will help all students, regardless of their religious backgrounds.

The Free Exercise of Religion: When and How Far?

• A Seventh-Day Adventist, discharged because she would not work on Saturday, her sabbath, is denied unemployment compensation benefits for "failing to accept suitable work without good cause."

• An Orthodox Jewish psychologist at an Air Force base clinic is reprimanded and threatened with a court martial for violating an Air Force rule against wearing headgear indoors by wearing a yarmulke, a religious skullcap, while on duty.

• An Amish father, who believes that sending his children to high school would conflict with a religious obligation to live in a church community separate from the world, is fined for violating a law that requires school attendance until age sixteen.

• A woman is denied a driver's license because she refuses to have her photograph on the license, believing it would violate the biblical injunction against graven images.

• An Amish farmer refuses to pay the Social Security tax for his Amish employees, believing it is sinful for a family not to provide for its elders.

• Muslim minimum-security prison inmates assigned to work outside the main building are not allowed to return to the building at midday Friday to attend Jumu'ah, their required weekly congregational service.

• A conscientious objector to a particular war and one opposed to all wars based on ethical but not theological beliefs are prosecuted for draft refusal.

• A Native American is fired from his drug rehabilitation job and denied unemployment compensation because he ingests peyote, an illegal drug, in accordance with his religion, in which the peyote plant embodies the deity and eating it is an act of worship and communion.

These are real cases, all but one of them decided by the United States Supreme Court. In each, the individual claimed that the clause in the First Amendment that prevents the government from "prohibiting the free exercise" of religion requires that he or she be allowed to undertake the religiously inspired action without penalty or loss of the relevant benefit. These cases force us to consider when, and to what degree, the government must modify general legal obligations to "accommodate" conflicting religious beliefs.

These are hard cases for several reasons. First, these are not situations in which the government is improperly questioning, banning, or penalizing religious beliefs. The drug laws did not outlaw the Native American Church and the prison did not ban Muslim services. Nor was the government questioning the sincerity of the individuals' adherence to their respective religious tenets. Rather the government was focusing upon the actions or refusals to act that were prompted by those religious beliefs.

Second, no one is suggesting that the state cannot regulate the conduct at issue. These cases do not present general constitutional objections to the government outlawing peyote, enforcing school attendance, requiring payment of taxes, or demanding that prisoners work.

The matter is further complicated by the First Amendment's establishment clause, which prevents government favoring one religion over another. In general, it would be improper to treat Muslims, Orthodox Jews, or Amish more leniently than the rest of society. Thus, when faced with claims for religious exemption from the draft, taxes, work, or school, the government often responds that such an exemption would amount to impermissible establishment of religion. The most common answer to this last point is: if the free exercise clause compels an exemption, then the establishment clause cannot prohibit it. The problem thus boils down to determining when the obligation to protect the free exercise of religion requires that an exemption from a valid general regulation be granted.

In this, as in many other areas of civil liberties where the government has sound reasons for its rules but the individual is asserting reasonable, good-faith objections, there rarely is a simple, clear-cut answer. The competing values must be weighed and hard choices made. The core question here is how much weight to give to the government's interest in uniformity of regulation.

Until recently, the Supreme Court has dealt with this problem by requiring that the government bear a heavy burden of justifying its rejection of a religious claim. The government had to "demonstrate that unbending application of its regulation to the religious objector 'is essential to accomplish an overriding governmental interest,' or represents 'the least restrictive means of achieving some compelling state interest.' "[16] As a consequence, for example, the Court required that the Seventh-Day Adventist get unemployment benefits[17] and the Amish father not be compelled to send his children to high school.[18] The Court determined that the important government interests in denying unemployment benefits to able-bodied employees when work is available and in having all children receive a basic, common education would not be significantly undermined, because the Seventh-Day Adventist was willing to accept any job that did not require work on Saturday and the Amish are a tight-knit, law-abiding community intent on providing adequate training of their young people.

Many have questioned the Court's rejection of most of the other claims under this test. For example, the Court refused to allow the psychologist to wear his skullcap in the Air Force clinic, out of deference to the military's judgment as to the need to "foster instinctive obedience, unity, commitment, and esprit de corps," even though he had previously done so with no problem for many years and the rule was first enforced against him after he had testified for the defense in a court martial.[19] Congress reacted by adopting a statute that addressed the religious concerns but created a problem of its own. The law provides that: "A member of the armed forces may wear an item of religious apparel while wearing the uniform . . . [unless] the wearing of the item would interfere with the performance of the member's military duties; or . . . the item of apparel is not neat and conservative."[20] The first half correctly limits religious practices only when they undermine the government's overwhelming interest in assuring performance of military functions. Congress did little better than the Court, however, in giving equal weight to the military's concern with neatness and in using such an imprecise and politically laden standard as "conservative."

Whatever their differences about the earlier cases, there was an overwhelming and nearly unanimous uproar from the religious community when the Court indicated in the 1990 peyote case that it was abandoning the "compelling state interest" test described above for judging most free exercise of religion claims.[21] Justice Scalia, for the majority, said that the test had only been used in the past in unemployment compensation cases (ignoring the fact that the peyote case involved a denial of unemployment benefits) or when, as in the Amish school case, the government's rule also implicated another right, in that instance the right of parents to direct the education of their children. Scalia said that courts should not go about deciding what practices are central to a person's religion and that the test would create an administrative nightmare in dealing with claimed exemptions from every civic obligation from taxes to vaccinations.

Justice O'Connor wrote a strong opinion criticizing the Court for needlessly abandoning a sound test that has effectively protected both public need and religious liberty, even though she agreed with the majority on the result in that case, after undertaking the strict scrutiny and careful weighing demanded by that test. The three justices in dissent noted that the Native American Church has strict internal restrictions on the use of peyote, that there was no evidence of injury to anyone from religious use of the plant, and that twenty-four states, including Oregon where the case arose, had created exemptions from their criminal laws for the religious use of peyote.[22] In an extraordinary step, a large, very diverse group of religious, community, and civil liberties groups asked the Court to reconsider its decision. Although the Court refused to do so, one can hope that the breadth and depth of the reaction will give it pause in future cases.

What the Court ignored is that religion touches the deepest, most intense, and personal bases. People care more about their religion than they do about almost anything else, as it defines their very sense of self. The tragedies of religious warfare in India, Northern Ireland, and the Middle East remind us that people will often give even their lives for their religion. It should be no surprise, therefore, that otherwise entirely law-abiding citizens will defy the law and the established order on religious grounds when they would never do so for any other reason. In light of the intensity of such feelings and to avoid infecting politics with the venom of religious division, which was one of the primary concerns of the Framers of the religion clauses of the First Amendment, we should allow religious exemptions from civic obligations whenever possible—that is, whenever strict enforcement of the law is not "essential to accomplish an overriding government interest." The slight loss of uniformity in the law that we will suffer is far outweighed by the assurance that the descendants of the Puritans, Quakers, and other oppressed religious minorities that fled to these colonies will never feel persecuted again.

VIII

OF WAR, SCHOOLS, YOUTH, AND LOVE

Not all civil liberties questions fall neatly into general categories or under particular provisions of the Bill of Rights. This chapter looks at four such issues.

The division of war-making powers between Congress and the President, which is set forth in the body of the Constitution, is a striking example of how the Framers protected individual liberty by carefully structuring the distribution of governmental authority as well as by directly imposing limits on that power in the Bill of Rights.

The controversy about how public school education should be financed is primarily a dispute about how far society should go to equalize the treatment of citizens of differing economic status. Like housing, the school finance issue also touches upon three other central civil liberties questions: When can state constitutional law provide more protection for individuals than the federal constitution? What is the interrelationship between the judiciary and the other branches of government in implementing constitutional mandates? When must state government supplant local control to insure uniform compliance with constitutional obligations?

Curfews limit the freedom to go about one's lawful business in public at certain hours. This right is not mentioned in any constitution but is so fundamental to the very concept of liberty that it has been treated as inherent in our system. The questions, as always, are what societal interests justify overriding that freedom and whether alternative regulations would minimize the loss of liberty? I address those questions in the context of the current trend towards imposing nighttime curfews upon young people. Such curfews raise the additional question of the degree to which government may regulate children more extensively than adults.

The right to marry is also not mentioned in the Bill of Rights. Yet even the most conservative justices have concurred in the view that the Constitution protects family matters against unwarranted intrusions. The story of the difficulties encountered by a court clerk who marries a police officer in her town highlights both the contours of that right and the broader question of what limits the government may fairly place upon those citizens who work for it.

Declaring War on Undeclared Wars

The Persian Gulf War, like the invasion of Panama in the prior year, the bombing of Libya and the invasion of Grenada earlier in the 1980's, and, of course, the Vietnam and Korean Wars before that, requires us once again to examine the question of who has the power under our Constitution to commit American military forces to combat. The Constitution is quite clear about situations like the one confronting the country in the last few months of 1990. The issue was temporarily clouded, however, by Congress acting as if its copies of the Constitution were missing Article I, by the President asserting increasingly breathtaking conceptions of his military authority, and by the unprecedented unanimity of the United Nations. It is, therefore, helpful to review the basics before exploring the latest wrinkles.

Why is the distribution of war-making powers a civil liberties concern? First, as former Attorney General Ramsey Clark recently said: "Throughout history war has been the greatest single cause of human rights violations."[1] We need only remember the internment of more than 120,000 Japanese Americans during World War II and the now discredited 1944 Supreme Court decision in *Korematsu v. United States*[2] validating that action to confirm the soundness of that statement. Constitutional provisions that ensure careful deliberation and broad-based consensus for military engagement help prevent hysterical or jingoistic reactions and limit the civil liberties intrusions that inevitably attend war.

Second, the freedom to go about one's life without being shipped overseas and ordered to shoot and be shot at is about as fundamental a right as any I can conceive of. The decision to go to war directly and vitally affects the lives of more people than almost any other government action. There is, of course, no provision in the Bill of

227

Rights that permits a member of the armed forces to refuse a direct order of a superior to kill, except perhaps when the objection is religiously grounded, and the Constitution has been construed not to protect citizens against a military draft. The people's constitutional protection against unjustified use of government authority to pledge their lives rests, therefore, precisely in the separation of powers and the obligation of their elected representatives to debate, to consider public opinion, and then to decide what is in the nation's best interest. As the Framers indicated, dividing up military power was "calculated to guard against" a hurried decision to endanger the lives of people.[3]

It is important to review how they divided up that power. Article I of the Constitution gives Congress the power "to declare War," "to provide for the common Defense," "to make Rules concerning Captures on Land and Water," "to raise and support Armies," "to provide and maintain a Navy," "to make rules for the Government and Regulation of the land and naval Forces," "to provide for organizing, arming and disciplining the Militia, and for governing such Part of them as may be employed in the Service of the United States," and the catch-all authority "to make all Laws which shall be necessary and proper for carrying into Execution the foregoing Powers, and all other Powers vested by this Constitution in the Government of the United States."

Article II vests in the President "the executive Power," makes him or her "the Commander in Chief of the Army and Navy of the United States, and of the militia of the several States, when called into the actual Service of the United States" and gives the President the "Power, by and with the Advice and Consent of the Senate to make Treaties . . . and . . . appoint Ambassadors, other public Ministers and Consuls" and the obligation "to receive Ambassadors and other public Ministers."

It is clear from these rather extensive specifications that it was intended that foreign affairs and military decisions be shared by the President and Congress. Some of the sharing or, more accurately, division of power is precisely defined. The President can receive and send ambassadors, presumably implying the authority to negotiate with foreign governments, but cannot appoint an ambassador or make a treaty without Senate concurrence. Likewise, the President commands the army but Congress decides how much and what kind of an army to raise and support and creates the rules for its governance.

It is somewhat less clear how the President's power as com-mander-in-chief is circumscribed by the mandate that Congress de-clare war. During the Constitutional Convention, the Framers amended the clause on congressional authority to provide not a power to "make" war but one to "declare" war.[4] It is generally understood that this change was meant only to clarify the President's authority to repel sudden attacks against the country without a formal decla-ration of war.[5] In light of the intent of that amendment, it is interesting to note that on one of the rare occasions when the territory of this country was attacked, namely the bombing of Pearl Harbor in 1941, the President asked Congress the very next day for a formal decla-ration of war.

There is nothing in the Constitution or its making, however, to tell us when a military engagement is a "war" requiring congressional action. Such points of ambiguity even on important matters are to be expected in a document such as the Constitution, which is the product of intense political struggle and is meant to set up a broad structure designed to last indefinitely and to apply to varied and often unfo-reseeable events. But what we do know is the basic intent: "This system will not hurry us into war; it is calculated to guard against it. It will not be in the power of a single man, or a single body of men, to involve us in such distress; for the important power of declaring war is vested in the legislature at large."[6]

Textual gaps are often filled in by practice. Throughout our history presidents have placed troops in hostilities without congressional ap-proval more than 130 times, yet on only six occasions, counting the Persian Gulf resolution, has Congress declared war. In the nineteenth century most of those incidents were not combat with foreign states but police actions to protect Americans from pirates or conflicts with Native American tribes. Even then there was controversy. In 1801, President Jefferson apologized to Congress for sending naval forces to repel pirates from the Barbary States without prior congressional authorization. Only since 1945 has the presidential practice been extended to more typical international military actions. American troops were sent to Lebanon in 1958 and to the Dominican Republic in 1965, and the Navy blockaded Cuba in 1962 under presidential orders. Grenada and Panama were invaded in the 1980's on presi-dential directive. Most strikingly, Congress did not declare either the three-year war in Korea or the eight-year war in Vietnam, each of which involved hundreds of thousands of troops.

Advocates of greater war-making power for the President make three basic types of claims. The first—that the constitutional distribution of powers needs updating in an age of nuclear weapons that require split-second decision-making—is questionable. As already noted, the Framers understood that the President must have authority to repel a physical attack on the country without consulting Congress, even in the days when such an attack and the response took weeks, not minutes, to prepare. The offensive initiation of a nuclear attack would, however, not be very different from, and would generally afford no less lead time than, the launching of any other military offensive, which is a "war" for constitutional purposes. Moreover, none of the military actions proposed or undertaken by presidents since the opening of the nuclear age in 1945 have involved nuclear weapons! In any case, if there is a genuine need for change, as the Framers anticipated there might be in some areas, the Constitution can be amended using the procedures set forth in Article V.

The second major executive claim—that the power to defend the country against sudden attack necessarily includes the power to defend American troops, wherever located, against attack—ignores the difficult question of who can send troops overseas in the first place. For example, prior to the congressional authorization for force in the Persian Gulf, President Bush asserted the power, as commander-in-chief, to defend the hundreds of thousands of troops and many ships in the Persian Gulf against any "unanticipated provocations" by Iraq. On its face that seems like a reasonable position. Those forces, however, were initially sent to the region on the President's command ostensibly in response to a request of the government of Saudi Arabia, not by order of Congress or in accordance with a treaty with that country that the Senate had approved. The difficult constitutional question, usually overlooked by politicians and scholars alike, is whether the undisputed presidential powers to carry on diplomacy and to command the armed forces include the power to place any number of troops at any time in any foreign country, especially when armed conflict in that location appears likely and no treaty creates an obligation to send troops.

Recently added to the contention that the commander-in-chief can direct troops anywhere and then defend them against any threats, is a third executive claim: that the Senate's ratification of the United Nations Charter constitutes authority for the executive to commit troops to combat whenever the Security Council authorizes the use of force to enforce its resolutions. It is true that the charter generally commits member-states to support actions of the Security Council and General Assembly. It was the clear understanding of the drafters of the charter, however, that the Security Council does not have authority to commit the military forces of member-nations to action without regard to their respective constitutional requirements for such a commitment.[7] This reflects one of the weaknesses of the United Nations—its dependence on the concurrence of its members to undertake any particular action. Although many, including myself, would welcome the creation of a permanent peacekeeping force under exclusive United Nations command, that simply is not the current legal structure.

After the Vietnam War, Congress, disturbed by the increasing assertion of presidential military authority, sought to address the ambiguities in the Constitution by adopting the War Powers Resolution in 1974 over President Nixon's veto. This legislation deals not only with the power to commit troops to armed conflict but also with "situations where imminent involvement in hostilities is clearly indicated by the circumstances."[8] It requires that "in the absence of a declaration of war, in any case in which United States Armed Forces are introduced (1) into hostilities" or into such "situations," (2) into the territory of a foreign nation, "while equipped for combat," or "(3) in numbers which substantially enlarge United States Armed Forces equipped for combat already located in a foreign nation, the President shall submit within forty-eight hours" a report to Congress on the necessity and authority for the action taken.[9] The next section provides that, within sixty days after a report is submitted "or is required to be submitted, . . . the President shall terminate any use of United States Armed Forces" covered by the report, unless Congress "has declared war or has enacted a specific authorization for such use of" troops or "has extended by law such sixty-day period."[10] Finally, reflecting concerns about presidential claims concerning the impact of senatorial approval of treaties on the division of the war-making powers, the resolution clearly states that authority to introduce troops into hostilities "shall not be inferred from any treaty heretofore or hereafter ratified unless such treaty is implemented by legislation specifically authorizing the introduction" of troops.[11]

Although Congress was very assertive in adopting the War Powers Resolution, it has utterly failed to enforce it. Presidents since 1974 have railed against the resolution, claiming it infringes upon the executive's constitutional prerogatives, and have generally refused to file the mandated reports. Congress has failed to assert its prerogatives and has never adopted a resolution either refusing to authorize the use of troops, terminating appropriations for such military actions, or simply declaring the President to be in violation of the resolution and ordering the troops home. Indeed, quite apart from the War Powers Resolution, it seems obvious that the power to declare war must include the power not to declare war. That is, whenever Congress disagrees with the President's military moves, it could nullify them by adopting a resolution not to go to war. The War Powers Resolution simply clarifies what should be the obvious consequences of such a negative vote.

The Persian Gulf situation is a classic example of the increasingly grandiose claims of presidential authority and the prolonged failure of Congress to perform its constitutional duties. Placing 240,000 troops with guns, tanks, and planes near the border of a recently invaded country while insisting that the invader withdraw, and imposing a naval blockade on all trade with that nation enforced by gun salvos and the boarding of ships that appear to violate the embargo are plainly forms of military engagement. Indeed international law has long treated a forcible naval blockade as an act of war. In any case, it would certainly seem to constitute a "situation where imminent involvement in hostilities is clearly indicated by the circumstances," and thus where congressional approval is required by the War Powers Resolution.

If there were any doubt about the latter proposition, it was dispelled both by the President's commitment in November 1990 of an additional 200,000 troops to develop, in his words, "an adequate offensive military option," and by his reliance on the United Nations authorization to use "all available means" if Iraq did not withdraw by a specified date. Yet in response to a lawsuit by fifty-four members of Congress filed that month, the President claimed that as commander-in-chief he could authorize some "offensive military attacks" that are not "war."[12] Meanwhile, Congress had adjourned in October, rather than simply recessing, without taking any action. Only in January 1990, five months after the dispatch of troops and initiation of the blockade and just a few days before the deadline for action set by the President, did the new Congress finally debate the issues. They voted on three resolutions: one asserting Congress' own constitutional power, one refusing to authorize force until economic sanctions had been given more time to take effect, and one authorizing the use of force.[13] By that point, many representatives felt compelled to vote for the resolution authorizing force simply to avoid undercutting the President and the troops already placed there at his command. We will never know what the course of events would have been if Congress had voted on the matter at the outset, or at least when the commitment to offensive action was made, as the Framers of both the Constitution and the War Powers Resolution intended.

What is clear now, as it was when the Constitution was written, is that 535 civilians voting in two separate groups are less likely to engage us in military combat, with its horrible toll on human life and inevitable restriction on established liberties, than is a single individual who directly commands the troops. This is why the Framers deemed it vital that those whom the people elect to represent them undertake in a timely and meaningful fashion to share the burden and pain of making the most important decision affecting the liberties of Americans.

It's Time to Invest in School Finance Equity

Everyone agrees that education is vital to the future of this country. It is generally seen as the most important function of local government and by many also as a vital mission of state government. Commission after commission, on both national and state levels, however, has decried the failures of our educational system, particularly in the poor and urban areas, to prepare children for their roles in the marketplace and the political system. Yet taxpayers often revolt and refuse to raise taxes for education.

This inconsistency reflects not only the general hesitance to pay more taxes but also the widespread insistence on local control of education, the ability of property-rich districts to pay for a good education with a low tax rate, and the unwillingness of the better-off to support the poor. In an attempt to resolve this dilemma, lawsuits have been brought across the country over the past twenty years seeking to equalize the funding of rich and poor school districts. These suits rely upon the equal protection provisions of both federal and state constitutions and the common state constitutional mandates for free universal public education. Quite apart from the technical legal responses, court decisions in this area have provoked outcries of judicial encroachment upon legislative prerogatives.

It is important to examine not only the underlying educational problem but also the constitutional issues: the scope of government's obligation to educate all citizens equally regardless of wealth, the degree to which state constitutions may impose greater duties on the state than the Bill of Rights does, whether financing disparities can be justified by the preference for local over state control of education, and whether the judiciary can enforce constitutional mandates for legislative action on education.

Schools in this country have for a long time been financed primarily through the municipal tax on real property. This reflects the strong demand for local control over education. The result of this local financing system, however, is that far more money is available for, and is spent on, education for children who live in wealthier school districts. In Texas, for example, the wealthiest school district in the state has more than $14 million of taxable property *per student* while the poorest has only $20,000 per student, a ratio of 700 to 1![14] The disparity is gross even when one moves away from the very ends of the spectrum: the 300,000 students (10 percent of the state's total three million school children) in the poorest schools are supported by less than 3 percent of the state's property, while the 300,000 in the wealthiest schools are backed by more than 25 percent of the state's total property.

Because of the higher value of the property available, the richer districts can tax at a much lower rate and still spend substantially more on education. The 100 poorest districts in Texas had an average tax rate of 74.5 cents per $100 valuation in 1985-86 and spent an average of $2,978 per student, while the wealthiest 100 districts had an average tax rate of only 47 cents yet spent an average of $7,233 per student.

Although all experts agree that money is not the cure-all, there can be little dispute that wide disparities in funding make for substantial inequalities in educational opportunities. One-third of Texas school districts could not even meet the state-mandated standards for maximum class size. More specifically, districts such as San Elizario, one of the poor Hispanic districts in Texas, are unable to offer foreign language, chemistry, physics, calculus, and college preparatory or honors classes, not to mention extracurricular activities such as band, debate, or football. Nearby high-wealth districts not only provide all those courses and activities but also have modern technological equipment, lower student-teacher ratios, and more experienced teachers and administrators.

The results are predictable. In New Jersey, for example, where comparable disparities in funding and offerings exist, only 54 percent of the ninth graders in the poorest tenth of the school districts passed the statewide high school proficiency test in reading, only 42 percent received a passing grade on the math portion, and only 43 percent passed the writing section. In the top tenth of the school districts, in contrast, the pass rates were 97, 93 and 95 percent, respectively.[15] Although social and other forces account for some of these differences, school funding limitations are regularly acknowledged to play a significant role.

Poor school districts cannot extricate themselves from these circumstances on their own. Because of the inadequate tax base, they must tax at significantly higher rates in order to meet minimum accreditation requirements, such as maximum class size, yet their educational programs remain inferior. It is almost impossible to raise school taxes much because the many other demands on local government—police, fire, sanitation, and the like—combined with the limited tax base have already pushed the total local tax burden to the limit. The location of new industrial and residential development is, however, strongly influenced by local tax rates and the quality of local schools. Poor districts are therefore hard put to attract new businesses or luxury residences that would increase their tax base. For this reason, poor districts and their parents and students have looked to state government, with its broader tax base, to overcome the financing disparities. The lack of response by state government has led to court challenges.

The United States Supreme Court reviewed the Texas system in 1973 in a case called *San Antonio Independent School District v. Rodriguez.*[16] After reviewing the then current data on district wealth and school finance disparities, the Court concluded that these differences did not violate the equal protection clause of the Fourteenth Amendment. It noted first that the system was not discriminatory against the poor in the classic sense because not only poor people lived in the districts with less property wealth per student and because children were not denied all education because of the relative poverty of their districts. It therefore refused to apply the strict constitutional scrutiny that is used by courts when they review governmental actions or programs that employ "suspect classifications," such as race or ethnicity. The Court also concluded that strict review was not necessary because education was not one of the "fundamental rights" either explicitly or implicitly protected by the federal Constitution. As a consequence, the Court applied the kind of superficial review that courts give purely economic regulations: whether the state's school finance system bears "some rational relationship to legitimate state purposes." The goal of not "sacrificing the benefits of local participation" in education was sufficient to find the system rational and hence constitutional[17]

Advocates of the poor meanwhile had turned to state courts. Unlike the federal constitution, which does not contain the word "education," all but two state constitutions have, in addition to equal protection clauses, provisions on public education similar to the one in Texas, which makes it "the duty of the Legislature of the State to establish and make suitable provision for the support and maintenance of an efficient system of public free schools." State courts are free to interpret such state constitutional provisions to ensure greater equality of funding than is mandated by the Fourteenth Amendment to the United States Constitution. The federal Bill of Rights thus sets a floor, not a ceiling, on individual rights. Recognizing this, California led the way by striking down its school finance system in 1971 under its state constitution.[18] There followed a flurry of litigation and some similar rulings in other states in the first part of the 1970's.

Whether as a product of litigation or otherwise, many legislatures throughout the country increased state aid to local school districts in the ensuing years, often directing more aid to poorer districts. From 1970 to 1990, the states' share of educational expenses nationwide rose from 40 to 50 percent.[19] Yet the financial and educational disparities between rich and poor school districts stubbornly persisted, indeed grew, in time producing a new round of state court litigation in the late 1980's. In 1989 and 1990 alone, the state supreme courts of Kentucky, Montana, New Jersey, and Texas ruled that their state school finance systems were invalid and ordered their state legislatures to find new ways of financing education that would diminish the vast inequalities created by the existing tax structure.[20] Indeed in Texas in 1991, the supreme court rejected as inadequate the legislature's first attempt to respond to the initial ruling of unconstitutionality—an increase in the state sales tax producing $528 million more for education and bringing the state's share of school expenditures to 50 percent—and ordered even greater funding for poorer districts.[21] In all, twenty-four state constitutional challenges have been decided over the past two decades, with ten state courts having found some aspect of their state's educational financing system to be a violation of either the education or equal protection clauses of their state constitutions.

237

The state courts have had difficulty defining the constitutional obligation with precision. The clearest, simplest, and thus most attractive judicial standard is equality in spending. There is, however, tremendous political resistance to strict state-enforced equality, because local constituencies that can afford it see no reason why they should not be able to spend more than the state-equalized average. Yet if better-off districts are allowed to spend above a set level, as they are so far everywhere except in Hawaii, which has state funding, they invariably spend substantially more, thereby reintroducing great disparities in per-pupil expenditures.

Because equality in spending is so difficult to enforce, courts have, in the alternative, tried to define a minimal level necessary for an adequate education and assure that the poorer districts receive at least that amount. It is relatively easy to state the ultimate goal: an "educational opportunity . . . needed in the contemporary setting to equip a child for his [sic] role as a citizen and as a competitor in the labor market."[22] It is a lot harder, however, to specify exactly how many teachers and administrators, and what kinds of programs, equipment, and supplies are needed to achieve that goal. The most obvious guide is what school districts that can afford it—and have been successful in educating their children—have been spending. But that brings the courts full-circle back to trying to equalize spending, this time at the level of the most successful districts. Although phrasing the standard in different ways, the state courts have generally talked about equalizing educational opportunities but issued commands to *substantially* equalize the amounts of money available to all school districts in the state, even while acknowledging that absolute parity cannot occur while local districts are allowed to exceed the state-set level.

Politicians and their taxpaying constituencies have reacted in outrage at what they view as judicial encroachments upon the legislative job of financing government and the executive job of administering the schools. They correctly see only two basic choices in response to the court decrees, neither of which is very palatable: raising taxes so more money can be given to the poorer districts, or equalizing the allocation of current tax monies, thereby risking a decline in the quality of education in the richer districts. The public reactions are similar to that encountered when the courts in New Jersey mandated statewide efforts to insure housing for the poor. (See "*Mount Laurel:* Government Action for Affordable Homes," page 165.)

I will not repeat here the justifications for judicial intervention to secure equality. It is important to note, however, that the case for judicial involvement is even stronger in education than in housing. Public schools are directly and exclusively created, financed, and operated by the government, and almost all state constitutions make education a state responsibility. Perhaps for these reasons, state courts have been more willing to act in the education field and, despite some footdragging and complaining, state legislatures have more often responded by raising taxes and improving the spending formulas to equalize financing. The results have not been fully satisfactory, and they never will be, because education finance equality, like housing equality, costs money and the better-off majority is only willing to go so far to help pay for the less fortunate. For that reason the courts must continue to play the role of limiting the unfortunate impact on the powerless of the fiscal and political majority's self-interested choice of school financing arrangements.

The major justification offered for retaining substantial reliance on the local property tax is the need to maintain local control of education. This is at least partially a smokescreen. The provision of education has been for over a century in most states a constitutional requirement of *state* government. States have long had school attendance laws and have increasingly established curricular and administrative requirements for local districts, with some form of state oversight or monitoring. States have increased their share of the expenses to almost half. Even so, local school boards retain substantial control over education in their communities—deciding whom to hire, when and where to build what kinds of school buildings, what equipment to buy, what disciplinary procedures to follow, what curriculum to use, and what extracurricular activities to offer.

In contrast, there is no local control over poverty and inadequate tax bases. Municipalities, as noted, cannot simply choose to bring in valuable new offices and homes that would enhance their tax bases. And surely no local citizenry would choose to keep using dilapidated eighty-year-old school buildings or reject foreign language and calculus courses or new computers if the necessary funds were available. If the state were to provide full financing at adequate levels through state-generated revenues, all local school boards and parents would have some real alternatives over which they could exercise local control. In sum, local participation in education will actually be enhanced for many by state-equalized financing.

There is no debate about the need to improve our education to meet the demands of the future. Increasingly complex technology demands enhanced skills from workers. Growing global interdependence requires greater awareness of other cultures and heightened political sophistication. We cannot run an economy or operate a democracy with only the most fortunate tenth of the population being fully educated. School finance equity is, therefore, not a question of charity for the poor; it is a matter of survival for all.

Rethinking Juvenile Curfews: Whom Are We Protecting?

There are fads in government regulation as in all human affairs. For a while loyalty oaths were the big thing. In another period conspiracy charges abounded. Catch-all, street-clearing ordinances are always popular with police and local authorities, although they take on different forms: disorderly conduct and breach of the peace were "in" during the civil rights movement, followed by loitering and identification ordinances in later years. Recently juvenile curfews have been experiencing a boomlet, primarily because of the rise in crime, most importantly drug-related crime, committed by younger people. Small towns from Panora, Iowa, to Bordentown, New Jersey, and cities from Pueblo, Colorado, to Washington, D.C., enacted or began to enforce curfews in the late 1980's.[23] In November 1990, Atlanta adopted a juvenile curfew and Boston's mayor announced that he was considering one.[24] Although such curfews seek to respond to serious and legitimate concerns, they constitute overkill, needlessly infringing on basic liberties without accomplishing their goals.

Typically a juvenile curfew specifies a specific time in the evening (Atlanta and Washington set it at 11:00 p.m. during the week and midnight on weekends, Pueblo and Panora at 10:00 p.m., and Bordentown at 9:00 p.m. on all nights) after which young people (Atlanta said those under seventeen, while Bordentown and Washington applied it to all under eighteen) may not be out in public (sometimes meaning not even outside their own residence). During riots and similar emergencies, some cities have temporarily imposed similar curfews on citizens of all ages in the affected areas. Juvenile curfews usually contain several exemptions: for travel to and from a job, school, or church; if accompanied by a parent or other adult (Bordentown also allowed being out with a police department pass issued upon a parent's application); and during an emergency. Penalties vary from simply being ordered or taken home to being arrested and charged for violating the ordinance and held until picked up by a parent. Increasingly, ordinances (those in Panora and Bordentown are examples) have tried to hold parents responsible, by fines or even imprisonment, for curfew violations by their children.

Before turning to the constitutional issues, it is worth recalling the origin and history of curfews. The term comes from the French phrase "couvre feu" and refers to medieval rules requiring that everyone cover, and thus put out, their fires at a certain time each night, to eliminate the risk of accidental nighttime disasters.[25] We have come far from that neutral, uniform public safety regulation. The modern curfew is a special rule applied to a distinct population or area that bans mere presence, not inherently dangerous conduct like setting fires, on the theory that some people might commit dangerous or unlawful acts if allowed to remain outdoors.

Curfews have had an ugly history in America. Before the Civil War they were used in the South to restrict when slaves could be on the streets. During the great immigration wave of the late 1800's, curfews became popular again because of fears that immigrants would not or could not control their children. During World War II, curfews were imposed upon American citizens of Japanese ancestry living on the West Coast.[26] In sum, curfews have generally been imposed upon the despised, distrusted, or powerless in our society. This fact alone should ring constitutional bells.

There are two major constitutional challenges to juvenile curfew ordinances. The first attacks the vagueness of the terms used. Protection against vague laws comes from the due process clause, which has been interpreted to require that laws generally give citizens clear notice of what is prohibited. The Supreme Court has required the greatest specificity in laws affecting fundamental rights, such as the right to travel or speak, to avoid arbitrary or discriminatory use of police discretion in arresting and detaining, for example, those whose views are unpopular or who are considered to be the "wrong" color for a particular neighborhood.

Vagueness challenges to curfews have primarily questioned the imprecision of the terms used to define the exceptions, as in these examples from the Panora and Bordentown cases: What is an "approved" place of work? Does "traveling" include walking as well as driving? Who are the "other responsible persons" with whom youth may travel? What is "legitimate business" and what is an "emergent condition?" Some of these questions may seem petty, as we all have a sense of what was generally intended. The Constitution, however, does not permit the city council to leave the answers up to the officer on patrol when stopping a young person on a deserted street at midnight.

The second problem with any curfew and the main focus of constitutional analysis is the broad interference with peaceful and proper behavior. That is, in trying to curb the minority of delinquents who might, if allowed out in public, commit acts that are already against the law, curfews inevitably restrict everyone's rights. The freedom to go about one's business peacefully in public without police interference is not mentioned in any constitution, because it need not be. It is the quintessential difference between a constitutional democracy and a police state. Curfews, therefore, rub against our constitutional grain.

As noted, some ordinances seek to limit this problem by creating exceptions for work or school travel. By definition, however, they do not exempt all non-criminal behavior in public. Attendance at school basketball games, job training programs, community meetings, or political rallies, socializing on a neighbor's lawn, or as occurred in the Bordentown case, going out for a late Chinese dinner or taking an evening stroll, are often banned, even though rioting, vandalism, and selling drugs, the real objects of the law, are already illegal. Most curfews also fail to take into account emancipated or married minors, or trips in the company of responsible adult friends. Moreover, those curfew laws that seek to hold parents responsible often fail to differentiate between parents who have custody and those with only occasional visiting privileges, and between parents who know of their children's intentions and those who set entirely appropriate guidelines that are violated without their knowledge. Significantly, although normally not part of the constitutional equation, it is important to note that many police departments oppose curfews because, like roadblocks, they inefficiently draw limited police resources away from investigation and prosecution of observed crime to unproductive, broad-based prophylactic measures.

Why the overkill, then? Is it because most of us think that children are different and need more protection and guidance? If so, we need to scrutinize those differences carefully and ensure that any variation in constitutional rules is directly tied to such justifications.

The Supreme Court has identified only three reasons why the law may treat minors differently from adults: because children are particularly vulnerable, because they are unable to make critical decisions in an informed, mature manner, and because parents are assured of the guiding role in childrearing. All three justifications are inapplicable in the situations covered by a curfew.

First, there is no special vulnerability involved in going to church, a basketball game, dinner, or any other bona fide nighttime activity. Moreover, as one court noted, if vulnerability to injury were the true justification for the law, why couldn't a city ban the handicapped or elderly as well from the streets at night?

Second, the associational choices and related travel for the activities outlined generally do not involve the kind of critical, life- or career-threatening decisions that require special maturity. Ironically, most curfew ordinances have express exceptions for young people to travel in health emergencies that might involve such decisions, and clearly employment and educational activities, which are exempted from most curfews, require more mature decision-making than hanging out on the street corner, which is banned.

Third, and most importantly, these ordinances actually undermine parental discretion in childrearing by displacing parental limits with legal limits and by requiring that a parent accompany the child outdoors, apply for a special permit, or put his or her consent in writing, regardless of the circumstances, the age of the child, or the relationship between parent and child.

Let us stop pretending to protect children by arresting them for being in public peacefully and to help parents by charging them criminally for giving their children leeway. If government really wants to help kids in trouble or parents who cannot control their children, why not offer a supervised, nighttime teen center, professional family counselling services, or free municipal bus service to and from key points in town? If we are genuinely concerned about drug abuse, we

244

should increase police patrols, offer free and effective treatment, and provide meaningful drug education for all. I side with the medievals— let us put out the fires and arrest the firemakers. We should, however, leave the rest alone or really offer to help them.

Why Can't Love and Justice Coexist?

Love knows no rules. Courts, alas, know of little but rules. This is a tale of love ensnared in court rules.

In 1977 the New Jersey Supreme Court issued a directive that one could not become a clerk of the municipal court, the local court where traffic offenses, ordinance violations, and minor criminal charges are heard, if a spouse, parent, or child is a police officer in the same town. A grandparent clause permitted clerks who were already in office when the rule went into effect and already so related to law enforcement personnel to remain in office. Such clerks were simply required to disqualify themselves from (not participate in) a case if a relative were involved. In 1988, the state supreme court amended the rule to make it apply also to those "co-habitation situations that appear to be substantially similar to that of a marital relationship." No exception was made this time for those who had been "co-habiting" prior to the rule's extension.

Two court clerks are challenging the constitutionality of this rule in federal court. In the summer of 1988, Marie Williams, the municipal court clerk in North Arlington, New Jersey since 1981, married Joseph Hughes, a police officer in the same town since 1971 and now a detective. They did so only after being advised by the municipal court judge in their town that the rule did not apply to clerks already in office. The state Administrative Office of the Courts saw it differently and demanded the termination of Marie Hughes unless her husband left the police force. The couple sued, with the assistance of the ACLU. The town and the administrative office agreed to let Ms. Hughes stay in office until the case is resolved but insisted that she disqualify herself should her husband appear on any matter in her court.

Jeannie DuBois, the municipal court clerk in Millville, New Jersey, has had a personal relationship since 1985 with a police officer in that town. Knowing of the court rule, she and her companion did not marry. She even bore their child out of wedlock to protect her job. In July of 1988, she was informed of the Court's extension of the rule to co-habitors and the lack of a grandparent clause. Threatened with application of the rule upon her return from maternity leave, she also sued. Others threatened by the rule who have not yet gone to court include a court clerk in another town whose son has recently decided to become a police officer.

The rule is intended to prevent even the appearance of a conflict of interest by court officials. A criminal defendant would be appropriately suspicious if the clerk signing an arrest or search warrant, granting an adjournment, or making a scheduling change to accommodate the arresting officer were the officer's spouse or child. No one questions those fears. The concept of conflict of interest, and the even more refined concern with the appearance of conflict, are well embedded in the law and for good reasons. But so, too, is the remedy: disqualification of the court official from any particular case in which there is the potential for a conflict. Certainly if a judge, a court official with far greater authority and discretion than a clerk, does not have to give up the bench entirely because of marriage to a police officer but would only have to avoid deciding particular cases in which the spouse is involved, a clerk should not have to forfeit her or his job simply for marrying an officer.

Quite apart from the fact that the rule treats clerks far more harshly than the more visible and powerful judges, the rule suffers from two other defects that we do not tolerate when government regulates fundamental rights like the right to marry. It is at the same time too broad (or what we call in constitutional law overinclusive or overbroad) in that it covers situations that do not affect the state's interest in avoiding conflicts, and too narrow (or underinclusive) in that it does not apply to other situations where the state has the same interest.

Looking first at its overbreadth, we find many examples where the rule applies but there would be no conflict of interest. For example, Detective Hughes is assigned to investigation and other tasks at the county-court level, known in New Jersey as the superior court, and thus almost never appears in the municipal court where his wife works. Why should his wife lose her job merely because he works for the police force in the same town if his work never intersects with hers? The rule also would force the discharge of a clerk who has been separated from his or her spouse for a long time or is even in the midst of a divorce proceeding when the spouse joins the local police force. Also, why must all pre-rule co-habitors, like Dubois, be fired, but not all pre-rule spouses?

Strikingly, the rule is at the same time too narrow because it fails to address many relationships that would appear to pose the same danger of conflicting allegiances as those covered by the rule. If the state truly believes that close personal relationships undermine professional objectivity or the public appearance thereof in all matters, not only the specific cases in which the other person is legally involved, then why shouldn't a clerk be fired if a brother, sister, aunt, uncle, cousin, niece, nephew, fiancee, or just plain boyfriend or girlfriend with whom they do not live becomes an officer in the same town? What about friends of the same sex who share an apartment? What about lifelong best friends who have lived in the same neighborhood for thirty years?

Some would ask: why nitpick about a rule that obviously has a kernel of sense to it, addresses important interests in the fair administration of justice, and affects so few people? The first answer is that we are dealing with fundamental rights—in this case, the right to marry, the right of intimate association, and the right to choose with whom to live. These are rights of importance to everyone, not just court clerks. To preserve fundamental constitutional rights in all settings, we rightfully demand that the government draw very careful lines whenever it intrudes upon these rights and use the least drastic means of achieving only the most compelling government goals. Second, although this particular personnel rule directly affects only a few people, governments in this country employ millions of people. If we were to allow the government free rein in establishing rules for its employees, we would not only endanger fundamental rights in other settings but directly impact a significant group in our society and seriously diminish the attractiveness of government service. Illustrative of this concern are the repeated court challenges and recent legislative attempts to modify the various so-called Hatch Acts that limit the political activity of millions of federal, state, and local civil servants.[27]

Some might respond: we should protect the fundamental rights of public employees, but how can you say that the right to marry or co-habit is a fundamental *constitutional* right when it is not even mentioned in the Bill of Rights? Both conservative and liberal members of the Supreme Court, those characterized as restrained and free-wheeling alike, have long agreed that some rights, although not explicitly mentioned in the Bill of Rights, are inherent in our Constitution and are subject to the strictest judicial protection. We have already considered this point in the privacy area, where the Court has developed protection for decisions to terminate a pregnancy and refuse medical treatment, using both the catch-all provision of the Ninth Amendment and the expansive concept of "liberty" in the due process clauses of the Fifth and Fourteenth Amendments. Similarly, the Court has recognized a right to travel, which is implicated in both the roadblock and curfew settings, even though not expressly mentioned in the Constitution. The other major development concerns matters relating to family life.

Most noteworthy is Justice Powell's opinion in a 1977 case called *Moore v. East Cleveland*,[28] ruling unconstitutional a city ordinance that barred a grandmother from living with her two grandsons because they were first cousins (children of two different sons) rather than brothers. The Court recognized a fundamental liberty under the due process clause to choose the family members with whom one wishes to live. Justice Powell, generally viewed as a conservative justice, explained, in writing for a four-justice plurality, that judges can extend protection to rights not expressly enumerated in the Bill of Rights without fear of degenerating into subjective preferences if they show "respect for the teachings of history [and] solid recognition of the basic values that underlie our society." Noting that both the nuclear and extended family are "deeply rooted in this Nation's history and tradition," Powell concluded that "[w]hen a city undertakes such intrusive regulation of the family . . . the usual judicial deference to the legislature is inappropriate."[29]

Using a similar approach, the Supreme Court struck down the next year a Wisconsin law that prohibited non-custodial parents with child support obligations from re-marrying without court approval. Such approval was to be granted only if applicants could show that any children they were obliged to support were "not then and are not likely thereafter to become public charges."[30] The Court found that the rule needlessly infringed on the fundamental right to marry and that the state's interests could have been more narrowly satisfied. In a similar vein, some state courts, including New Jersey's, have struck down, under their state constitutions, local zoning ordinances that bar from single-family dwellings persons not related by blood or marriage, such as two-family co-ops, college roommates, or residents of group homes.[31]

Applying the strict scrutiny test to the fundamental right to marry, a federal judge ruled that the New Jersey Supreme Court had failed to draft its rule on clerk-officer relations precisely enough and, therefore, found it unconstitutional.[32] On appeal, the federal circuit court refused to decide whether the rule was constitutional, because it thought, as the municipal court judge in Hughes's town had thought, that the rule could be interpreted not to apply at all to clerks who were appointed prior to their marriage to an officer. The appeals court came to this conclusion even though the only reason that the case was in court was that the state Administrative Office of the Courts and Attorney General's Office both had insisted that the rule applied to Hughes. The appeals court, therefore, held off deciding the constitutional issue until the New Jersey Supreme Court has had a chance to provide a definitive interpretation of exactly to whom its rule applies.[33]

It is, I believe, time to rescind the rule and apply only the longstanding remedy of disqualification to clerks as well as judges, to newlywed and long-cohabiting as well as long-married clerks. It is important to accord full recognition to the fundamental rights of government employees while taking steps to ensure that litigants and others who seek action from government feel confident that the decision-maker is truly impartial and fair. It is time, in short, to declare that love and justice can coexist.

Conclusion

The struggle to keep the Bill of Rights alive and healthy never ends. As illustrated by the wide variety of topics in the foregoing essays, almost all public issues implicate constitutional rights. I have touched on many of the most prominent current or recurrent of those issues but do not claim to have been exhaustive. Even an entirely comprehensive survey could not, however, have a true conclusion. As times, temperaments, and technologies change, we or the next generation must re-visit each question to determine the evolving meaning of each provision. Ten years ago this book would not have included essays on AIDS, drug testing, or homelessness. Almost every week the news media herald new situations requiring civil liberties analysis. We must repeatedly recapture the spirit.

Rather than being comprehensive or definitive, I have tried to introduce the reader to basic questions and to provoke thought about current problems and possible solutions. I hope this book also has provided an overall perspective on the Bill of Rights.

First, I hope the book evokes an appreciation for the splendor of the work of our Framers. For people who did not even imagine cars, computers, telephones, and airplanes, not to mention a nation this size or a world so interrelated, they provided us with a remarkably sound and flexible blueprint for governance. The fact that we have adopted only sixteen amendments in the 200 years since the Bill of Rights is a testament to both the universality of the questions they considered and their foresight.

Second, I hope readers will recognize that all public policy questions, including civil liberties issues, involve basic value choices and a weighing of relative risks and benefits. The Fourth Amendment, for example, does not protect privacy absolutely nor was it designed to preclude effective law enforcement. It recognizes the importance of both but strikes a balance by requiring a warrant and probable cause

251

for an arrest or search. No question worth thinking about will have an absolute or an easy answer.

Third, we need to remember that the basic balance was struck by the Framers and may not be fundamentally restructured without a constitutional amendment. Yet we must apply those value judgments to current problems. We must, for example, consider how the Framers' basic understanding of the scope of individual liberty affects whether and when to disconnect a respirator from an unconscious car accident victim with no hope of recovery. The Framers' language and their discussion of their purpose help. So does history. But we need to plumb deeper and understand the basic value choices and then implement those choices in the current setting.

Finally, we need to be pragmatic and creative in these endeavors. Not surprisingly, the Constitution does not say whether door-to-door canvassing must stop at 5:00 p.m. or 9:00 p.m., whether public defenders should handle 150 or 250 cases per year, or whether court clerks may marry police officers in their town. In approaching those issues, we not only must understand the underlying value choices but also should consider carefully the practical consequences of each decision and the alternatives that might exist. The most basic value choice the Bill of Rights made was to require the government to justify any intrusion on our fundamental rights by showing that no other approach would do the job yet intrude less on citizens' freedom.

This seems a heavy burden, especially when there is a pressing need for action and for efficient implementation. At bottom, however, the Bill of Rights was meant to slow government down. The Framers, still smarting from King George's oppression, were wary of governmental power and valued people's rights above mere efficiency. It is every citizen's job to insure that government observes that priority at all times, for our liberty is at stake. Therefore, my parting reminder to all who care about the Bill of Rights is the same one used since the eighteenth century—the price of liberty is eternal vigilance.

The Bill of Rights

Amendment I

Congress shall make no law respecting an establishment of religion, or prohibiting the free exercise thereof; or abridging the freedom of speech, or of the press; or the right of the people peaceably to assemble, and to petition the Government for a redress of grievances.

Amendment II

A well regulated Militia, being necessary to the security of a free State, the right of the people to keep and bear Arms, shall not be infringed.

Amendment III

No Soldier shall, in time of peace be quartered in any house, without the consent of the Owner, nor in time of war, but in a manner to be prescribed by law.

Amendment IV

The right of the people to be secure in their persons, houses, papers, and effects, against unreasonable searches and seizures, shall not be violated, and no Warrants shall issue, but upon probable cause, supported by Oath or affirmation, and particularly describing the place to be searched, and the persons or things to be seized.

Amendment V

No person shall be held to answer for a capital, or otherwise infamous crime, unless on a presentment or indictment of a Grand Jury, except in cases arising in the land or naval forces, or in the Militia, when in actual service in time of War or public danger; nor shall any person be subject for the same offence to be twice put in jeopardy of life or limb; nor shall be compelled in any criminal case to be a witness against himself, nor be deprived of life, liberty, or property, without due process of law; nor shall private property be taken for public use, without just compensation.

Amendment VI

In all criminal prosecutions, the accused shall enjoy the right to a speedy and public trial, by an impartial jury of the State and district wherein the crime shall have been committed, which district shall have been previously ascertained by law, and to be informed of the nature and cause of the accusation; to be confronted with the witnesses against him; to have compulsory process for obtaining witnesses in his favor, and to have the Assistance of Counsel for his defence.

Amendment VII

In Suits at common law, where the value in controversy shall exceed twenty dollars, the right of trial by jury shall be preserved, and no fact tried by a jury, shall be otherwise re-examined in any Court of the United States, than according to the rules of the common law.

Amendment VIII

Excessive bail shall not be required, nor excessive fines imposed, nor cruel and unusual punishments inflicted.

Amendment IX

The enumeration in the Constitution, of certain rights, shall not be construed to deny or disparage others retained by the people.

Amendment X

The powers not delegated to the United States by the Constitution, nor prohibited by it to the States, are reserved to the States respectively, or to the people.

Notes

Embodying the Spirit—Justice William Brennan

1. Barron v. Baltimore, 32 U.S. (7 Pet.) 243 (1833).
2. Gitlow v. New York, 268 U.S. 653 (1925).
3. Mapp v. Ohio, 367 U.S. 643 (1961).
4. Duncan v. Louisiana, 391 U.S. 145 (1968).
5. Adamson v. California, 332 U.S. 46, 68 (1947) (Black, J., dissenting).
6. Baker v. Carr, 369 U.S. 186 (1962).

When Will the Government Ever Learn?

7. New Jersey Citizen Action v. Edison Twp., 797 F.2d 1250 (3rd Cir. 1986).
8. 479 U.S. 1103 (1987).
9. State v. Baker, 81 N.J. 99, 405 A.2d 368 (1979).
10. Borough of Glassboro v. Vallorosi, 221 N.J. Super. 610, 535 A.2d 544 (Ch. Div. 1987). That ruling has since been affirmed by the state supreme court. 117 N.J. 421, 568 A.2d 888 (1990).
11. Allen v. Bordentown, 216 N.J.Super. 557, 524 A.2d 478 (Law Div. 1987).
12. Hague v. CIO, 307 U.S. 496 (1939).
13. United States v. Grace, 461 U.S. 171 (1983).
14. Crandall v. Nevada, 73 U.S. (6 Wall.) 35 (1867).
15. See, e.g., Memorial Hospital v. Maricopa County, 415 U.S. 250 (1974) (holding unconstitutional one-year residence rule for indigents to qualify for nonemergency medical care at county expense); Doe v. Bolton, 410 U.S. 179 (1973) (striking down residence requirement for abortion); Dunn v. Blumstein, 405 U.S. 330 (1972) (invalidating requirement that one live a year in the state and three months in the county to register as a voter); Shapiro v. Thompson, 394 U.S. 618 (1969) (striking down three state statutes denying welfare until one has resided a year in the state).
16. Civil Rights Attorney's Fees Award Act, Public Law No. 94–559, codified as 42 U.S.C. Section 1988.

Can We Risk a Constitutional Convention?

17. Letter of James Madison to George Lee Turberville, November 2, 1788, in Paul J. Weber and Barbara A. Perry, *Unfounded Fears: Myths and Realities of a Constitutional Convention*, 31–32 (Greenwood Press 1989).

18. *New York Times*, July 17, 1990, A20.

A Civil Liberties Lawyer on Jury Duty

19. Two excellent and very readable books about the entire jury process from selection through verdict are Mary Timothy, *Jury Woman* (Emty Press 1974), written by an actual juror in the famous murder trial of Angela Davis in California in 1972, and Seymour Wishman, *Anatomy of a Jury* (Penguin Books 1986), written by an attorney describing, with fictitious names, an actual murder case in New Jersey.

20. Rodwan, "Bias in the Jury Selection Process: Michigan Responds to One Impediment to the Search for Truth," 4 *Cooley Law Rev.* 559 (1987).

21. Cal. Code of Civ. Proc. Sec. 198.

22. *New York Times*, October 4, 1990, B6.

23. Martin, "Men and Women on the Bench: Vive La Difference?" 73 *Judicature* 204 (1990).

24. *Wall Street Journal*, March 21, 1990, B1.

25. Brooks, "One-Day, One-Trial: Are Jurors Inventing Excuses?", 120 *N.J. Law Journal* 389 (1987).

26. Williams v. Florida, 399 U.S. 78 (1970).

27. Ballew v. Georgia, 435 U.S. 223 (1978).

28. John Profatt, *Trial by Jury*, sec. 147 (S. Whitney & Co. 1986).

29. Batson v. Kentucky, 476 U.S. 79 (1986).

30. Harry Kalven, Jr., and Hans Zeisel, *The American Jury* (Little Brown 1966).

31. See, e.g., Fed. R. Evid. 606(b).

A Civil Liberties Agenda for the 1990's

32. Samuel Warren and Louis Brandeis, "The Right to Privacy," 4 *Harvard Law Rev.* 193 (1890).

33. 389 U.S. 347 (1967).

34. Tyler v. Bervat, 877 F.2d 705 (8th Cir. 1989), cert. den., 110 S.Ct. 723 (1990).

35. Rendell-Baker v. Kohn, 457 U.S. 830 (1982).

36. State v. Schmid, 84 N.J. 535, 423 A.2d 615 (1980).

37. Robins v. Pruneyard Shopping Center, 23 Cal.3d 899, 153 Cal. Rptr. 854, 592 P.2d 341 (1979).

38. Webter v. Reproductive Health Services, 492 U.S. 490 (1989).

39. DeShaney v. Winnebago County Dept. of Social Services, 488 U.S. 189 (1989).

40. *New York Times*, January 18, 1991, B16; October 9, 1990, A8.

41. *New York Times*, January 7, 1991, A14.

42. *New York Times*, January 18, 1991, B16.

II. FREE EXPRESSION

Mother England's Not-So-Free Press

1. Attorney General v. Guardian Newspapers, Ltd. (No.2), 3 All Eng. Rpt. 545, 553 (1988). Many of the events surrounding *Spycatcher* that are described in the text are detailed in this opinion.

NOTES

2. *Id.* at 555–56.

3. *Id.* at 642.

4. 444 U.S. 507 (1980).

5. Official Secrets Act of 1989, Sections 1(4), 3(2).

6. 844 F.2d 1057 (4th Cir.), cert. den., 488 U.S. 908 (1988).

7. *New York Times*, August 4, 1989, A10; August 24, 1989, A21.

Flagging the Burning Issues: Disrespect and Offense

8. 135 Cong. Record S8862 (101st Cong., 1st Sess. July 26, 1989), and S12987 (October 7, 1989).

9. *New York Times*, Aug, 4, 1989, A11.

10. *New York Times*, August 11, 1989, A27.

11. *Star-Ledger*, Newark, New Jersey, August 8, 1989, 8.

12. *Star-Ledger*, August 27, 1990, 17.

13. *New York Times*, August 8, 1989, Op-Ed page.

Writing Letters May be Hazardous to Your Rights

14. Patterson v. Federal Bureau of Investigation, 705 F. Supp. 1033, 1046 (D.N.J. 1989).

15. 5 U.S.C. Section 552a(e)(7).

16. 705 F. Supp. at 1045–46.

17. *Id.* at 1041.

18. 893 F.2d 595 (3d Cir. 1990).

19. 111 S.Ct. 48 (1990).

Charging for Free Speech

20. I have personally handled or consulted on at least a dozen such matters in recent years in California and New Jersey. For a much longer and more legalistic article on the subject, with citations to all the relevant cases and much more extensive elaboration of the analysis summarized here, see my article "Charging for Free Speech: User Fees and Insurance in the Marketplace of Ideas," 74 *Georgetown Law Journal* 257 (1985).

21. 458 U.S. 886 (1982).

Talking Politics Door-to-Door

22. 797 F.2d 1250 (3rd Cir. 1986), cert. denied, 479 U.S. 1103 (1987).

23. *Id.*, Brief of Appellants at 12–13 (testimony of Dr. James Finckenauer).

24. *Id.* at 17.

25. *Id.*

26. *Id.* at 14.

It's Scandalous What Some Think is Slanderous

27. 376 U.S. 254 (1964).

28. See, e.g., Cochran and Vairo, "Rule 11: An Eventful Year," 4 *Civil Rights Litigation and Attorneys' Fee Annual Handbook* 343, 344 (1988) (the percentage of plaintiffs sanctioned in civil rights and employment discrimination cases is 17.3 percent greater than the average for plaintiffs in all other cases).

Racial Slurs: Free Speech or Discrimination?

29. Collin v. Smith, 578 F.2d 1197, 1199 (7th Cir. 1978). Another ordinance passed at the same time required marchers to post $300,000 insurance for bodily injury and $50,000 for property damage. This requirement was held unconstitutional as applied to the Nazis because they could show that no one would write them an insurance policy. *Id.* at 1207–08. (See "Charging for Free Speech," page 000.)

30. This policy as well as the guidebook and incidents described below are all set forth in the opinion of the federal court that invalidated the policy as unconstitutional. Doe v. University of Michigan, 721 F. Supp. 852 (E.D. Mich. 1989).

31. Chaplinsky v. New Hampshire, 315 U.S. 568, 572 (1942).

32. See, e.g., Lewis v. City of New Orleans, 415 U.S. 130, 131 (1974) (reversing conviction for saying "you god damn m.f. police" to an officer); Gooding v. Wilson, 405 U.S. 518, 520 (1972) (reversing conviction for saying "white son of a bitch, I'll kill you" to a police officer).

33. See, e.g., Houston v. Hill, 482 U.S. 451 (1987).

How Can You Petition When the Doors Are Closed?.

34. John E. Nowak, Ronald D. Rotunda and J. Nelson Young, *Constitutional Law* 1003 (3d. ed. West Publ. 1986).

35. Edwards v. South Carolina, 372 U.S. 229, 233 (1963).

36. In re Petitions for Rulemaking N.J.A.C. 10:82–1.2 and 10:85–4.1, 223 N.J. Super. 453, 538 A.2d 1302 (App. Div. 1988). This ruling was later affirmed by the New Jersey Supreme Court. 117 N.J. 311, 566 A.2d 1154 (1989).

Students Learn From Free Expression and Due Process

37. Tinker v. Des Moines School District, 393 U.S. 503 (1969).

38. Goss v. Lopez, 419 U.S. 565 (1975).

39. Board of Educ., Island Trees Union Free School District v. Pico, 457 U.S. 853 (1982).

40. New Jersey v. T.L.O., 469 U.S. 325 (1984).

41. Hazelwood School District v. Kuhlmeier, 484 U.S. 260 (1988).

III. PRIVACY

Legal Roadblocks to Traffic Roadblocks

1. James B. Jacobs and Nadine Strossen, "Mass Investigations Without Individualized Suspicion: A Constitutional and Policy Critique of Drunk Driving Roadblocks," 18 *Univ. of Cal. Davis Law Rev.* 595, 640 n. 200 (1985).

2. Michigan Dep't of State Police v. Sitz, 110 S.Ct. 2481 (1990), rev'ing 429 N.W. 2d 180, 184 (Mich. Ct. App. 1988). Some major programs show an even lower rate. For example, in New York City between 1983 and 1985, 1,107,945 people were stopped at roadblocks, but only 4,823 or .4% were arrested for drunk driving. Jacobs and Strossen, *supra* note 1, at 645.

3. Jacobs and Strossen, *supra* note 1, at 638–45; Hugh L. Ross, *Deterring The Drinking Driver: Legal Policy and Social Control* (Lexington Books 1982).

NOTES

4. See, e.g., Seattle v. Meslani, 110 Wash. 2d 475, 755 P.2d 775 (1988); State v. Henderson, 114 Idaho 293, 756 P.2d 1057 (1988); State v. Olgaard, 248 N.W.2d 392 (S.D. 1976).

5. See, e.g., State v. Jones, 482 So. 2d 433 (Fla. 1986); State v. Martin, 145 Vt. 562, 496 A.2d 442 (1985); State v. Deskins, 234 Kan. 529, 673 P.2d 1174 (1983).

6. State v. Barcia, 228 N.J. Super. 267, 271, 272, 277, 283, 549 A.2d 491, 492, 493, 495, 498 (Law Div. 1988), affirmed, 235 N.J. Super. 311, 562 A.2d 246 (App. Div. 1989).

7. 228 N.J. Super. at 273, 281, 549 A.2d at 493, 497.

8. State v. Encarnacion, No. A-99-88T6 (N.J. App. Div. July 27, 1989).

9. *San Diego Tribune*, July 3, 1990, B1.

10. 440 U.S. 648 (1979).

Going Too Far: Police Strip Searches

11. Roderique v. Kovac, No. 85-5778 (D.N.J. Sept. 14, 1987).

12. Weber v. Bell, 804 F.2d 796 (2d Cir. 1986), cert. denied sub nom. County of Monroe v. Weber, 483 U.S. 1020 (1987); Jones v. Edwards, 770 F.2d 739 (8th Cir. 1985); Stewart v. County of Lubbock, 767 F.2d 153 (5th Cir. 1985), cert. denied, 475 U.S. 1066 (1986); Giles v. Ackerman, 746 F.2d 614 (9th Cir. 1984), cert. denied, 471 U.S. 1053 (1985); Hill v. Bogans, 735 F.2d 391 (10th Cir. 1984); Mary Beth G. v. City of Chicago, 723 F.2d 1263 (7th Cir. 1983); Logan v. Shealy, 660 F.2d 1007 (4th Cir. 1981), cert. denied, 455 U.S. 942 (1982).

13. N.J. Statutes Annotated 2A:161A-1 *et seq.*

Do We Expect Our Garbage to be Inspected by Police?

14. 486 U.S. 35 (1988).

15. *Id.* at 46.

16. State v. Hempele, 120 N.J. 182, 576 A.2d 793 (1990); State v. Tanaka, 67 Hawaii 658, 701 P.2d 1274 (1985).

17. 486 U.S. at 39.

18. *Id.*

19. *Id.* at 41.

20. Smith v. Maryland, 442 U.S. 735 (1979) (pen register); California v. Ciraolo, 476 U.S. 207 (1986) (airplane overflight).

21. 126 *N.J. Law Journal* 1045 (Oct. 18, 1990).

Should We Tolerate "Zero Tolerance?"

22. Calero-Toledo v. Pearson Yacht Leasing Co., 416 U.S. 663, 689-90 (1974).

Job Tests, Not Urine Tests

23. Capua v. City of Plainfield, 643 F. Supp. 1507, 1517 (D.N.J. 1986).

24. For excellent summaries of the current scientific literature and understanding, see David J. Greenblatt, "Urine Drug Testing: What Does It Test?" 23 *New England Law Rev.* 651 (1988-89), and Kurt M. Dubowski, "Drug-Use Testing: Scientific Perspectives," 11 *Nova Law Rev.* 415 (1987). I will not provide individual citations for each scientific assertion from these sources that is presented in this essay.

25. Hugh J. Hansen, Samuel P. Caudill, and Joe Boone, "Crisis in Drug Testing: Results of CDC Blind Study," 253 *Journal of the American Medical Association* 2382 (1985).

26. "Failing the Test: Proficiency Standards Are Needed for Drug Testing Laboratories," House Report No. 100–527, House Committee on Government Operations, 100th Congress, 2d Session (March 28, 1988).

27. There is some evidence that a person can also test positive after simply having been, and hence breathed, in a relatively small, contained area in which marijuana smoke was prevalent. Greenblatt, *supra*, 23 *New England Law Rev.* at 659.

28. Steven W. Gust and J. Michael Walsh, eds., "Drugs in the Workplace: Research and Evaluation Data," National Institute on Drug Abuse, Research Monograph 91 (1989).

29. Maine Commission to Examine Chemical Testing of Employees, Report (1986). This excellent report, prepared by a statewide panel of public, management, and labor representatives, surveyed the strengths and weaknesses of all chemical tests, including urine drug tests and breathalyzers. The majority recommended a ban on all tests except breathalyzers.

30. *New York Times*, March 6, 1990, C1.

What Ever Happened to Probable Cause?

31. See, e.g., Transportation Institute v. United States Coast Guard, 727 F. Supp. 648 (D.D.C. 1989) (invalidating random testing of nearly all crew members on commercial vessels, because relationship to safe operation of ships is too attenuated).

32. National Treasury Employees Union v. Von Raab, 649 F. Supp. 380 (E.D. La. 1986).

33. 392 U.S. 1 (1968).

34. Florida v. Royer, 460 U.S. 491 (1983) (investigative stop of airport passenger based on "drug courier profile"); Pennsylvania v. Mimms, 434 U.S. 106 (1977)(driver ordered out of car after stop for expired plates and frisked when "bulge" in pocket observed).

35. New Jersey v. TLO, 469 U.S. 325, 342 (1985).

36. O'Connor v. Ortega, 480 U.S. 709 (1987).

37. Skinner v. Railway Labor Executives Ass'n, 489 U.S. 602 (1989).

38. National Treasury Employees Union v. Von Raab, 489 U.S. 656, 673 (1989) (only 5 of 3,600 employees tested positive).

39. *Id.* at 670.

Constitutional Rights Should Apply at Work

40. Rendell-Baker v. Kohn, 457 U.S. 830 (1982).

41. Robins v. Pruneyard Shopping Center, 23 Cal.3d 899, 153 Cal. Rptr. 854, 592 P.2d 341 (1979); Batchelder v. Allied Stores Int'l, Inc., 338 Mass. 83, 445 N.E. 2d 590 (1983); Viar v. Alstores, Inc., No. C4919–83E (Ch. Div. Bergen Cty., N.J. 1984); Alderwood Associates v. Washington Environ. Council, 96 Wash. 2d 230, 635 P.2d 108 (1981).

42. State v. Schmid, 84 N.J. 535, 423 A.2d 615 (1980).

43. Peper v. Princeton Univ. Bd. of Trustees, 77 N.J. 55, 389 A.2d 465 (1978).

44. See, e.g., Hill v. National Collegiate Athletic Ass'n, 223 Cal. App.3d 1642, 273 Cal. Rptr. 402 (Cal. App. 6 Dist. 1990), review granted; Luck v. Southern Pacific

NOTES

Transp. Co., 218 Cal. App.3d 1, 267 Cal. Rptr. 618 (Cal. App. 1 Dist.), cert. denied, 111 S.Ct. 344 (1990); Wilkinson v. Times Mirror Corp., 215 Cal. App.3d 1034, 264 Cal. Rptr. 194 (Cal. App. 3 Dist. 1989).

45. Hennessey v. Coastal Eagle Point Oil Co., 6 IER Cases 113 (N.J. Law Div. April 28, 1989), appeal argued December 18, 1990.

46. Novosel v. Nationwide Ins. Co., 721 F.2d 894 (3rd Cir. 1983).

47. See, e.g., the Employee Polygraph Protection Act of 1988, 29 U.S.C. Section 2001.

48. Restatement (Second) of Torts, Chapter 28A (1976) (common law tort of invasion of privacy).

The Abortion Debate is Unresolvable and Avoidable

49. *New York Times*, November 8, 1990, A28.

50. *Id.*

51. Philip J. Hills, "The Birth Control Backlash," *New York Times Magazine*, December 16, 1990, 41.

The Right to Die: New Laws Are Needed

52. 110 S. Ct. 2841 (1990).

53. *New York Times*, February 6, 1991, A13.

54. 110 S.Ct. at 2869, n.11.

55. *Id.* at 2869 n.11 and 2875 n.21.

56. *Christian Science Monitor*, October 23, 1990, Home Forum, 17.

IV. CIVIL RIGHTS AND DISCRIMINATION

Fight AIDS, Not the People We Fear Have AIDS

1. Poff v. Caro, 228 N.J. Super. 370, 549 A. 2d 900 (Law Div. 1987).

2. Ill. Public Act 85–935; Ill. Public Act 86–884.

3. *Boston Globe*, December 1, 1990, 1.

4. Public Law No. 100–430, amending 42 U.S.C. Section 3601 *et seq.*

5. Public Law No. 101–336.

6. See ABA Commission on the Mentally Disabled and Center on Children and the Law, *AIDS and Persons with Developmental Disabilities: The Legal Perspective* (1989).

7. *New York Times*, December 5, 1990, A24.

Men-Only Clubs: Illegal Discrimination or Protected Association?

8. Board of Directors of Rotary International v. Rotary Club of Duarte, 481 U.S. 537 (1987); Roberts v. United States Jaycees, 468 U.S. 609 (1984); Kiwanis International v. Ridgewood Kiwanis Club, 627 F.Supp. 1381 (D.N.J.), rev'd, 806 F.2d 468 (3d Cir. 1986), reh'g denied, 811 F.2d 247 (3d Cir. 1987).

9. See, e.g., New York State Club Association, Inc. v. City of New York, 487 U.S. 1 (1988) (organization representing 125 private clubs challenged New York City law banning discrimination by clubs with over 400 members that serve meals and regularly produce income from the use of facilities by non-members).

10. Frank v. Ivy Club, 117 N.J. 627, 569 A.2d 1331 (1990), cert. denied sub nom. Tiger Inn v. Frank, 59 U.S.L.W. 3502 (Jan. 22, 1991).

11. 42 U.S.C. Section 3604.

12. Moore v. City of East Cleveland, 431 U.S. 494 (1977).

Anti-Gay Prejudice Should Not Be Public Policy

13. 478 U.S. 186 (1986).

14. *New York Times*, November 5, 1990, A14.

15. Braschi v. Stahl Associates Co., 74 N.Y. 2d 201, 543 N.E. 2d 49 (1989).

16. *New York Times*, February 15, 1991, A16.

17. V. Van Hasselt, R. Morrison, A. Bellack, and M. Hersen, *Handbook of Family Violence* 159–61 (1988) (one of the most widely recognized studies shows that 19.2 percent of women but only 8.6 percent of men reported being sexually victimized by someone within or outside of the family before the age of seventeen, and studies of both male and female victims show that between 92 and 98 percent of adult perpetrators of sexual abuse are male).

18. *Id.* at 124, 159 (3.5 percent of parents admit physical violence that could cause injury against one of their children in the year prior to the survey, as against the highest estimate of sexual abuse of 1.4 victims per 1,000 children).

Civil Rights Law: If It Ain't Broke, Don't Fix It

19. General Electric Co. v. Gilbert, 429 U.S. 125 (1976).

20. Public Law No. 95–555, now codified as 42 U.S.C. Section 2000e(k).

21. Grove City College v. Bell, 465 U.S. 555 (1984).

22. Public Law No. 100–259, now codified as 42 U.S.C. 2000d; see note following 20 U.S.C. Section 1687.

23. Voting Rights Act Amendments, Public Law No. 97–205 (1982), now codified as 42 U.S.C. Section 1973, overturning the decision in City of Mobile v. Bolden, 446 U.S. 55 (1980), which had limited Act by requiring proof of intent to discriminate; Handicapped Children's Protection Act, Public Law No. 99–372 (1986), now codified as 20 U.S.C. Sections 1415(e)(4)(B)–(G), overturning the decision in Smith v. Robinson, 468 U.S. 992 (1984), which had denied attorney's fees to parents who prove that the school placement of their handicapped children is improper. See also Civil Rights Attorney's Fees Awards Act, Public Law No. 94–559 (1976), now codified as 42 U.S.C. Section 1988, overturning the decision in Alyeska Pipeline Services Co. v. Wilderness Society, 421 U.S. 240 (1975), which had denied attorney's fees to any civil rights litigant unless expressly provided by statute.

24. 109 S.Ct. 2363 (1989).

25. 427 U.S. 160 (1976).

26. 485 U.S. 617 (1988).

27. 109 S.Ct. at 2370–71.

28. 490 U.S. 642 (1989).

29. Atonio v. Wards Cove Packing Co., Inc., 768 F.2d 1120, 1122–24 (9th Cir. 1985).

30. *Id.*, 827 F.2d 439, 445 (9th Cir. 1987).

31. 490 U.S. at 662, 664 n.4.

32. 401 U.S. 424 (1971).

33. Dothard v. Rawlinson, 433 U.S. 321, 331 (1977).

34. 490 U.S. at 659.
35. *Id.* at 662.
36. 490 U.S. 900 (1989).
37. *New York Times*, March 13, 1991, A22.

Being Sterile Is Not a Job Qualification

38. 886 F.2d 871 (7th Cir. 1989).
39. Bruce Fein and William B. Reynolds, "Employer Fetal Protection Policies Skirt Title VII, 126 *N.J. Law Journal* 978 (Oct. 11, 1990).

We Still Need Affirmative Action

40. 488 U.S. 469 (1989).
41. Fullilove v. Klutznick, 448 U.S. 448 (1980).
42. *New York Times*, November 21, 1990, B11.
43. Metro Broadcasting, Inc. v. Federal Communications Commission, 110 S.Ct. 2997 (1990).
44. NAACP v. Harrison, 749 F. Supp. 1327 (D.N.J. 1990), appeal pending.
45. Richmond v. J.A. Croson, Co., 488 U.S. at 534.
46. American Bar Association, *1989–90 Annual Report of The Consultant on Legal Education to the American Bar Association* 7.
47. Metro Broadcasting, Inc. v. F.C.C., 110 S.Ct. at 3003.
48. NAACP v. Harrison, 749 F. Supp. at 1328.
49. Fullilove v. Klutznick, 448 U.S. at 484.

V. Poverty and the Right to a Home

1. 198 U.S. 45 (1905)

Homeless Orators: Begging as Free Speech

2. 729 F. Supp. 341 (S.D.N.Y.), rev'd, 903 F.2d 146 (2d Cir.), cert. denied, 111 S.Ct. 516 (1990).
3. The term "panhandling" derives from the early practice of American beggars of using tin pans to solicit funds. William Morris and Mary Morris, *Morris Dictionary of Word and Phrase Origins* 432 (Harper & Row 1977).
4. People v. Bright, 71 N.Y.2d 376, 526 N.Y.S.2d 66, 520 N.E. 2d 1355 (1988), interpreting N.Y. State Const. Art. I, Section 6.
5. Village of Schaumburg v. Citizens for a Better Environment, 444 U.S. 620, 632 (1980).
6. 729 F. Supp. at 352.
7. *Id.* at 358.
8. 903 F.2d at 156.

Why Homelessness is a Civil Liberties Concern

9. House Report No. 100–10(I), 2 *U.S. Cong. and Admin. News* 362, 363 (100th Cong. 1st Sess. 1987).

10. Brief of Public Advocate for Appellants in McCurdy v. New Jersey Dep't of Human Services, reported sub nom. Franklin v. New Jersey Dep't of Human Services, 111 N.J. 1 (1988), at 71, n.

11. *The Record*, Hackensack, New Jersey, January 19, 1988, A13.

12. See, e.g., City of Cleburne v. Cleburne Living Center, 473 U.S. 432 (1985) (denial of a permit for operation of a group home for the mentally retarded violated the equal protection clause).

13. Griffin v. Illinois, 351 U.S. 12 (1956) (free transcript); Douglas v. California, 372 U.S. 353 (1963) (appointed attorney).

14. Boddie v. Connecticut, 401 U.S. 371 (1971).

15. Little v. Streater, 452 U.S. 1 (1981) (although prompted by concerns about the unequal position of poor paternity defendants, the Court relied in this case primarily on the due process clause, which guarantees "a meaningful opportunity to be heard" when threatened with significant liability).

16. Dandrige v. Williams, 397 U.S. 471 (1970).

17. Harris v. McRae, 448 U.S. 297 (1980).

18. Ortwein v. Schwab, 410 U.S. 656 (1973).

19. San Antonio Independent School District v. Rodriguez, 411 U.S. 1 (1973).

20. See, e.g., Kadrmas v. Dickinson Public Schools, 487 U.S. 450, 457–58 (1988).

21. Lindsey v. Normet, 405 U.S. 56 (1972).

22. See, e.g., Harris v. McRae, 448 U.S. 297 (1980) (government need not provide Medicaid payment for abortions, even though the right to choose an abortion is a fundamental right and Medicaid pays childbirth costs).

23. Euclid v. Ambler Realty Co., 272 U.S. 365 (1926), is the first major Supreme Court case on zoning.

24. *Star-Ledger*, December 8, 1990, 1.

25. 126 *N.J. Law Journal* 1045 (October 18, 1990).

26. United States v. Carolene Products, 304 U.S. 144, 153 n.4 (1938) (assuring strict judicial review of laws significantly restricting political participation or resulting from prejudice against "discrete and insular minorities").

Mount Laurel: *Government Action for Affordable Homes*

27. 67 N.J. 151, 336 A.2d 713 (1975).

28. See, e.g., Warth v. Seldin, 422 U.S. 490 (1975).

29. N.J. Const. Article I, paragraph 1.

30. 67 N.J. at 187, 336 A.2d at 731.

31. Southern Burlington County NAACP v. Township of Mount Laurel, 92 N.J. 158, 456 A.2d 390 (1983). That ruling actually decided five other lawsuits involving many other towns in addition to the case against Mount Laurel.

32. N.J. Statutes Annotated 52:27D–301 *et seq.* (West 1986).

33. Hills Development Co. v. Township of Bernards, 103 N.J. 1, 510 A.2d 621 (1986).

34. Lamar, Mallach, and Payne, "*Mount Laurel* at Work: Affordable Housing in New Jersey, 1983–88," 41 *Rutgers Law Rev.* 1197 (1989). At points, I have also relied on public reports by COAH.

35. In the Matter of Petitions for Rulemaking N.J.A.C. 10:82–1.2 and 10:85–4.1, 117 N.J. 311, 316–17, 566 A.2d 1154, 1156–57 (1989).

NOTES

VI. THE CRIMINAL PROCESS

Preventive Detention: Which Country Is This Anyway?

1. 481 U.S. at 747.
2. 481 U.S. at 757–58.
3. Coffin v. United States, 156 U.S. 432, 455 (1895) (quoting a Roman authority from 359 A.D.).

Racism at the Gallows

4. 481 U.S. 279 (1987).
5. Furman v. Georgia, 408 U.S. 238 (1972).
6. Gregg v. Georgia, 428 U.S. 153 (1976).
7. 481 U.S. at 286–87.
8. Strauder v. West Virginia, 100 U.S. 303, 307 (1880).
9. 481 U.S. at 329–30.
10. Title 18 of H.R. 5269 (101st Cong.).
11. Regents of the University of California v. Bakke, 438 U.S. 265, 316–19 (1978).
12. See, e.g., Fullilove v. Klutznick, 448 U.S. 448 (1980) (federal contracting law's 10 percent set-aside for minority contractors held constitutional); Wygant v. Jackson Bd. of Educ., 476 U.S. 267, 280–84 (1986) (although striking down a school board's plan protecting newly hired minorities against layoffs in order of least seniority, Powell recognized the legitimacy of affirmative action in hiring).

Advocates' Zeal Is Threatened by Court Contempt Power

13. 118 N.J. 51, 570 A.2d 416, cert. denied, 111 S.Ct. 371 (1990).
14. 214 Conn. 344, 572 A.2d 328, cert. denied, 111 S.Ct. 247 (1990).
15. *Id.* at 347–48, 572 A.2d at 330–31.
16. 118 N.J. at 68, 74, 570 A.2d at 425, 428.
17. 214 Conn. at 352, 358, 572 A.2d at 333, 336.
18. Craig v. Harney, 331 U.S. 367, 376 (1947) ("The law of contempt is not made for the protection of judges who may be sensitive . . . Judges are supposed to be men of fortitude, able to thrive in a hardy climate").
19. In re McConnell, 370 U.S. 230, 236 (1962) ("The arguments of a lawyer in presenting his client's case strenuously and persistently cannot amount to a contempt of court so long as the lawyer does not in some way create an obstruction which blocks the judge in the performance of his judicial duty").
20. 65 *Univ. of Washington Law Rev.* 477 and 743 (1990).

Overloaded Public Defenders: The Right to Counsel at Risk

21. Gideon v. Wainwright, 372 U.S. 335, 337 (1963).
22. *New York Times*, November 30, 1990, B5.
23. Argersinger v. Hamlin, 407 U.S. 25 (1972).
24. Michael McConville and Chester L. Mirsky, "Criminal Defense of the Poor in New York City," 15 *N.Y.U. Rev. of Law & Social Change* 581, 584, 610, 618, 627, 646, 690, 692 (1986–87).
25. *Id.* at 584, 587.

26. See William F. McDonald, *Plea Bargaining: Critical Issues and Common Practices* (Nat'l Institute of Justice 1985).

27. McConville and Mirsky, *supra* note 24, at 759–64.

28. Johnson v. LeFevre, 615 F.2d 1351 (2d Cir. 1979), cert. denied, 445 U.S. 931 (1980).

29. McDonald, *supra* note 26, ch. 2.

Law v. Justice: *A Twisted Case*

30. Brady v. Maryland, 373 U.S. 83 (1963).

31. United States v. Agurs, 427 U.S. 97 (1976).

32. State v. Landano, No. 73–76, letter-opinion, 2 (Law Div., Hudson Cty., July 13, 1982).

33. Landano v. Rafferty, 670 F. Supp. 570 (D.N.J. 1987).

34. Landano v. Rafferty, 856 F.2d 569 (3rd Cir. 1988), cert. denied, 489 U.S. 1014 (1989).

35. State's Brief on Appeal from Denial of Defendant's Motion for New Trial and Petition for Post-Conviction Relief, State v. Landano, A–2649–82T4, at 12.

36. Landano v. Rafferty, 126 F.R.D. 627 (D.N.J. 1989).

37. *Star-Ledger*, June 27, 1989, 25.

38. 897 F.2d 661 (3rd Cir.), cert. denied, 111 S.Ct. 46 (1990).

39. Stephen A. Saltzburg, *American Criminal Procedure* 544–57 (3rd ed. West Publishing 1988).

40. Murray v. Giarratano, 109 S.Ct. 2765 (1989).

VII. FREEDOM OF RELIGION

Of Carols, Creches, and Menorahs

1. J. Golby and A. Purdue, *The Making of the Modern Christmas* (Univ. of Georgia Press 1986); *Star-Ledger*, December 23, 1990, 3.

2. Philip Rulon, *Keeping Christmas: The Celebration of an American Holiday* (Archon Books, 1990); *Star-Ledger*, December 25, 1990, 3.

3. Engel v. Vitale, 370 U.S. 421 (1962) (prayers); Abington School District v. Schempp, 374 U.S. 203 (1963) (bible reading and Lord's Prayer).

4. Engel v. Vitale, 370 U.S. at 431.

5. Lynch v. Donnelly, 465 U.S. 668 (1984).

6. See, e.g., ACLU v. City of St. Charles, 794 F.2d 265 (7th Cir. 1986) (unadorned cross).

7. County of Allegheny v. ACLU, 109 S.Ct. 3086 (1989).

8. 2 *Encyclopedia Britannica* 904 (1980).

9. Huddleston v. Borough of Haworth, No. L-021280-82 (Law Div. Bergen Cty., N.J., Dec. 14, 1984).

10. Engel v. Vitale, 370 U.S. at 431.

Do Children Need a Moment of Silence in School?

11. Wallace v. Jaffree, 472 U.S. 38 (1985).

12. Lemon v. Kurtzman, 403 U.S. 602, 612–13 (1971).

13. Karcher v. May, 484 U.S. 72 (1987).

NOTES

14. May v. Cooperman, 572 F. Supp. 1561, 1564 (D.N.J. 1983); Brief of Appellees in Karcher v. May, 484 U.S. 72 (1987), at 18–19.

15. 572 F. Supp. at 1571.

The Free Exercise of Religion: When and How Far?

16. Employment Division, Department of Human Resources v. Smith, 110 S.Ct. 1595, 1611 (1990) (concurring opinion of Justice O'Connor).

17. Sherbert v. Verner, 374 U.S. 398 (1963).

18. Wisconsin v. Yoder, 406 U.S. 205 (1972).

19. Goldman v. Weinberger, 475 U.S. 503, 507 (1986).

20. Public Law No. 100–180, amending 10 U.S.C. Section 774 (1987).

21. Employment Division, Department of Human Resources v. Smith, 110 S.Ct. 1595 (1990).

22. *Id.* at 1618.

VIII. OF WAR, SCHOOLS, YOUTH, AND LOVE

Declaring War on Undeclared Wars

1. Ramsey Clark, "International Human Rights," presentation at Individual Rights Committee of N.J. State Bar Ass'n, April 3, 1990.

2. 323 U.S. 214 (1944). That ruling was discredited by the discovery of suppressed government documents establishing that there was no military need for the racially based internments. Hirabayashi v. United States, 627 F.Supp. 1445 (W.D. Wash. 1986); Korematsu v. United States, 584 F.Supp. 1406 (N.D. Cal. 1984). See Peter H. Irons, *Justice at War* (Oxford Univ. Press, 1983).

3. Jonathan Elliott, ed., *The Debates in the Several State Conventions on the Adoption of the Federal Constitution* 528 (1888) (James Wilson speaking at Pennsylvania ratifying convention).

4. Max Freund, *The Records Of The Federal Convention Of 1787*, vol. 2 at 318–19 (Yale Univ. Press, 1937).

5. Leonard Levy, *Original Intent And The Framers' Constitution* 37 (Macmillan Press, 1988); Abraham Sofaer, *War, Foreign Affairs and Constitutional Power: The Origin* 32 (Ballinger Publ. Co., 1976).

6. Elliott, *supra* note 3, at 528.

7. United Nations Charter, Article 43(3).

8. 50 U.S.C. Section 1541(a).

9. *Id.* at 1543(a).

10. *Id.* at 1544(b).

11. *Id.* at 1547(a)(2).

12. Dellums v. Bush, 752 F.Supp. 1141, 1145 (D.D.C. 1990). The judge concluded that such actions could well constitute "war" but that a court could not intervene against the President until a majority of Congress joined the lawsuit. *Id.* at 1151.

13. *New York Times*, January 13, 1991, 1.

It's Time to Invest in School Finance Equity

14. Edgewood Ind. School Dist. v. Kirby, 777 S.W. 2d 391 (Texas 1989). Unless otherwise noted, all further data about the Texas system in the text is taken from this

opinion, which struck down the school finance system as a violation of the Texas Constitution.

15. Abbott v. Burke, 119 N.J. 287, 370, 575 A.2d 359, 400 (1990).

16. 411 U.S. 1 (1973).

17. *Id.* at 40, 55.

18. Serrano v. Priest, 5 Cal.3d 584, 96 Cal. Rptr. 601, 487 P.2d 1241 (1971).

19. *New York Times*, December 30, 1990, 17.

20. In addition to the decisions in Texas and New Jersey referenced in notes 14 and 15 *supra*, see Helena Elementary School Dist. 1 v. State, 784 P.2d 412 (Mont. 1990), modifying 769 P.2d 684 (Mont. 1989); and Rose v. Council for Better Educ., Inc., 790 S.W.2d 186 (Ky. 1989).

21. *New York Times*, January 7, 1991, B9; January 6, 1991, "Education Life," Section 4A, 44.

22. Robinson v. Cahill, 62 N.J. 473, 515, 303 A.2d 273, 295 (1973).

Rethinking Juvenile Curfews: Whom Are We Protecting

23. City of Panora v. Simmons, 445 N.W.2d 363 (Iowa 1989); People in the Interest of J.M., 768 P.2d 219 (Colo. 1989); Waters v. Barry, 711 F. Supp. 1125 (D.D.C. 1989); Allen v. City of Bordentown, 216 N.J. Super. 557, 524 A.2d 478 (Law Div. 1987).

24. *New York Times*, November 21, 1990, 1 (Atlanta); *Star-Ledger*, November 22, 1990, 21 (Boston).

25. William Morris and Mary Morris, *Morris Dictionary of Word and Phrase Origins* 163 (Harper & Row 1977).

26. City of Panora v. Simmons, 445 N.W.2d 363, 374 (Iowa 1989) (dissenting opinion).

Why Can't Love and Justice Coexist?

27. See, e.g., Broadrick v. Oklahoma, 413 U.S. 601 (1973) (upholding the federal Hatch Act against a First Amendment challenge); H.R. 20, 101st Cong. (modifying the Hatch Act to permit greater political activity by federal employees), vetoed by President Bush on June 15, 1990. *Cong. Index* 35,002 (December 7, 1990).

28. 431 U.S. 494 (1977).

29. *Id.* at 503, 499.

30. Zablocki v. Redhail, 434 U.S. 374, 375 (1978).

31. State v. Baker, 81 N.J. 99 (1979).

32. Hughes v. Lipscher, 720 F. Supp. 454 (D.N.J. 1989).

33. Hughes v. Lipscher, 906 F.2d 961 (3rd Cir. 1990).

Glossary

ACLU—The American Civil Liberties Union is a nonpartisan, non-profit, private national organization with over 300,000 paying members and a branch in each state, dedicated to enforcement of everyone's constitutional rights through litigation, legislation, and public education.

Adverse impact—When an employment requirement, such as a high school diploma or minimum height, excludes or limits the opportunities of minorities or women in greater proportions than whites or men, it is said to have an adverse impact, which must be justified by *business necessity*.

Affirmative action—Any effort to increase the employment or educational opportunities for minorities, women, or other historically excluded group, but more specifically any effort, such as a numerical quota for each entering class, that expressly considers membership in such a group as a positive factor in selection.

Business necessity—An employer's justification for an employment requirement, which must be presented if the requirement has an *adverse impact*.

Chilling effect—The deterrent impact upon citizens' willingness to speak out publicly or otherwise engage in political activity resulting from an arbitrary, *overbroad*, or *vague* law, rule, or government action.

Circuit court—Since 1789, federal courts have been divided into circuits, typically consisting of several states. Each circuit has several districts, each of which includes no more than one state. Originally judges, including justices of the Supreme Court, would actually "ride circuit," travelling by horse to hold court in different places within the circuit. There are now thirteen federal circuits.

In each circuit, there is a court of appeals, which hears appeals in federal cases, including constitutional issues, from any federal district court within the circuit. Circuits vary in size from the District of Columbia Circuit, which covers only Washington, D.C., and the First Circuit in New England, which has only six court of appeals judges, to the Ninth Circuit, which covers nine western states, including California, and has twenty-eight appellate judges. Appeals from the circuit courts go directly to the United States Supreme Court, which has discretion whether to hear such appeals. Because the Supreme Court decides only 150 cases annually while the circuit courts together decide over 19,000 cases each year, decisions of the circuit courts of appeals are almost always final.

Class action—A lawsuit brought by one or two people on behalf of a large number of people in the same situation, such as all inmates in a prison.

Compelling interest test—The legal test used in constitutional law when judging government actions that infringe on fundamental rights, such as free expression. The test requires that the government show that its goal is very important, or compelling, and that the law or rule at issue achieves that goal in the manner that limits freedom the least, known as the least drastic means. When using the test, courts are said to be applying *strict scrutiny*.

Due process—Fair procedure; specifically the rights to notice of the charges, a day in court, the chance to present a defense, and a decision by an impartial judge or jury, as guaranteed by the due process clauses in both the Fifth Amendment, which applies to the federal government, and the Fourteenth Amendment, which applies to all state, county, and local governments. Failure of government to follow these procedures in prosecuting a defendant may result in overturning a conviction. The due process clauses also protect fundamental substantive rights, such as the rights to travel, to marry, to terminate a pregnancy, and to refuse medical treatment.

Equal protection—The Fourteenth Amendment prohibits states from denying persons the "equal protection of the laws." Although originally enacted to ensure equal legal rights for the newly freed slaves, the provision is now used to review all inequalities based on arbitrary classifications. Some classifications, such as race, ethnicity, and citizenship status, are seen as "suspect" and are given *strict scrutiny*. Others, such as those regulating commercial activity, are reviewed to determine only whether they are supported by a rational basis.

Establishment clause—The provision in the First Amendment that precludes the government from creating a state religion, favoring one religion over another, or favoring religious over nonreligious practices.

Exculpatory evidence—Information that tends to show a criminal defendant to be innocent.

Free exercise clause—The provision in the First Amendment that guarantees freedom to practice one's religion free of government interference.

Habeas corpus—Latin for "let us have the body"—a court order to the sheriff or warden to bring a prisoner to court to allow the court to judge whether his or her detention is lawful.

Incorporation—The process of judicial interpretation by which the protections of the Bill of Rights that are deemed fundamental are treated as part of the "liberty" safeguarded by the *due process* clause of the Fourteenth Amendment and thus limit state, county, and local governments as well as the federal government.

Libel—A written statement damaging the reputation of another distributed to some third party. *See slander.*

Living will—A legal document directing medical personnel to discontinue medical treatment or artificial nutrition or life support under certain conditions.

Overbreadth—The wide scope of a statute or ordinance infringing upon fundamental constitutional rights, such as free speech or the right to travel or marry, more than necessary to achieve the government's *compelling interest.*

Peremptory challenge—The opportunity of litigants to dismiss a potential juror without giving an explanation.

271

Preventive detention—Pretrial confinement without bail of a criminal defendant deemed likely to commit other crimes if released.

Probable cause—Information indicating to a judge or to police that probably the person to be arrested committed a crime or the evidence sought will be found in the place to be searched.

Reasonable suspicion—Specific facts from which police derive an objective basis to suspect that a person is involved in crime, and thereby authority to stop the person for investigation and to pat down outer clothing if there is also reason to suspect the person is armed. Reasonable suspicion is less substantial information than *probable cause*.

Right to die—The right of a patient to decide whether to discontinue medical treatment, nutrition, or artificial life-support systems.

Slander—An oral statement damaging the reputation of another spoken to a third party. *See libel.*

Standing—Legal authority to bring a lawsuit, usually based on injury to the individual.

Stare decisis—Latin for "to stand by things decided"—the practice of courts in the Anglo-American system to abide by prior rulings on the same point.

State action—Action by the government, whether federal, state, county, or local and whether by the legislative, executive, or judicial branch. For the most part, constitutional rights limit only state action, not action by private persons or companies.

Strict scrutiny—The most searching examination of government action infringing upon constitutional rights, typically using the *compelling interest test*.

Vagueness—Lack of clarity in a law. If a law does not clearly define for citizens what is prohibited or guide police in enforcing it evenhandedly, the requirements of *due process* are not met.

Voir dire—French for "to see, to say"—the process by which judges and lawyers ask potential jurors questions to determine whether they have any advance knowledge about a case or prejudices that would disqualify them from serving on the jury.

Index

Abortion, 36, 114–17, 162, 251
ACLU, xvi, 4–6, 11–13, 15–17, 25, 30, 51, 62, 63, 66, 72–73, 89, 124, 196, 214–15, 246, Glossary
Academic freedom, 66
Accommodation of religion, 216–27, 220
Adams, John Quincy, 70
"A Dry White Season," 195
Adverse impact, 144, Glossary
Affirmative action, 146–50, 187, Glossary
African Americans, 5, 26, 30, 35, 47, 68, 71, 86, 121, 124, 131, 134, 137, 147–48, 149, 171, 182–84
Aggravating circumstances, 182–83
AIDS, 10, 12, 13, 22, 116, 121, 123–26, 132, 159, 251
Air Force, 71, 95, 96, 219, 221
American Bar Association, 47, 194
American Civil Liberties Union. *See* ACLU
American Jewish Committee, 69
American Medical Association, 120
American Nazi Party, 58, 65, 66
Americans with Disabilities Act of 1990, 125
Amicus curiae, 137, 216
Amish, 210, 216, 219–21
Arraignment, 182, 193, 194
Association, 57
    expressional, 129
    intimate, 128–29, 132, 134, 248
Attorneys' fees, 18

Bail, 9, 88, 89, 90, 175, 179–80, 191, 203
Bail Reform Act of 1984, 179
Bakke, Regents of University of California v., 10, 185
Balanced budget amendment, 19–23
Balancing test, 105–8
Baldus study, 183–84
Begging as free speech, 153–57
Bell, Derrick, 147
Bible reading in public schools, 208, 210, 214
Bicentennial of the Bill of Rights, 77

Bill of Rights, xv, xvi, 8–9, 32, 38, 40, 151–53, 175–77, 187, 190, 194, 205–6, 225–26, 234, 237, 249, 251–54
    English, 41, 43, 45
    See also First Amendment, Third Amendment, Fourth Amendment, Fifth Amendment, Sixth Amendment, Seventh Amendment, Eighth Amendment, Ninth Amendment, Cruel and unusual punishment, Establishment of religion, Free exercise of religion, Incorporation
Black, Justice Hugo, 8
Blacklisting, xv
Blackmun, Justice Harry, 139–40, 213
Body cavity searches, 88, 90
Bona fide occupational qualification (BFOQ), 144–45
Boston Tea Party, 151
Bowers v. Hardwick, 131–32
Brandeis, Justice Louis, 32
Breathalyzer, 86, 102
    See also Drunk driving
Brennan, Justice William J., Jr., 8, 9, 10, 91, 120, 200
Brown v. Board of Education, 121, 149
Builder's remedy, 169, 172, 174
Burger, Chief Justice Warren E., 106, 139, 141, 150
Bush, President George, 141, 163, 230, 232–33
Business necessity, 139, 141, 144–45, Glossary

California v. Greenwood, 91
Canvassing, 14, 15, 39, 59–61, 89, 254
Carols sung in public school, 208–13
Catholics/Catholic Church, 114, 116, 129, 208, 210
Centers for Disease Control, 100
Central Intelligence Agency (CIA), 44
Centurion Ministries, 202

273

INDEX

Chanukah, 208, 211
Challenge for cause. *See* Jury
Charitable solicitation, 155–57
Chilling effect, 3, 53, 64, Glossary
Chinese government, 48, 180
Christians, 207, 210–12
Christmas, 209–12
Church of England, 207
Circuit courts, 14, 45, 52, 59, 112, 144,
    157, 201–3, 250, Glossary
Civil Rights Act of 1964, 121, 127, 136
    Title II of, 136
    Title VI of, 136
    Title VII of, 136, 138, 144, 147
Civil Rights Act of 1990, 141, 144
Civil Rights Restoration Act of 1987, 137
Civil War, 21, 143, 152, 160, 200, 242
Clark, Joe, 76
Clark, Ramsay, 227
Class action, 154–55, Glossary
Commander-in-chief, powers of, 227–33
Compelling interest test, 128, 221–22,
    248, Glossary
Condoms, 115–16
Conflict of interest, 249
Congress, xi, xv, 9, 19–24, 39, 46–47, 54,
    71, 125, 135–37, 142, 146–47,
    152, 179, 216, 221–22, 225,
    227–33
Connecticut Supreme Court, 163, 187–89
Constitution
    Article I, 227–28
    Article II, 228
    Article V, 19–24, 230
    Habeas corpus clause, 200
    Preamble, xi, xiii, 18
    Supremacy Clause, 17
    See also Bill of Rights, Thirteenth
        Amendment, Fourteenth
        Amendment, Fifteenth Amendment,
        Seventeenth Amendment, Due
        process, Equal protection
Constitutional convention (Con-Con), 19–
    24, 229
Contempt of court, 41–43, 187–90
Contraceptives, 115–17
Council on Affordable Housing (COAH),
    168–71
Crack, 10, 84, 85, 102
Creche, public display of, 208–13
Crime, xv, 59–61, 175
    victims, 28, 29
Criminal process, 27–30, 38, 79, 93, 96,
    162, 177–207
Cromwell, Oliver, 209
Cruel and unusual punishment, 37, 182

    See also Death penalty, Eighth
        Amendment
Cruzan, Nancy, 118–20
Cuba, blockade of, 229
Curfews, 11, 15, 17, 225, 249
    for canvassers, 59–61
    for juveniles, 226, 241–45

Death penalty, 97, 177, 182–86
Debs, Eugene V., 176
Decent Interval, 44
Declaration of war, 227–33
Delaware v. Prouse, 86
Density bonus, 169
Depression, 153
Discovery, 63
Discrete and insular minorities, 165
Discrimination. *See* Handicap
    discrimination, Homosexuals, Racial
    discrimination, Sex discrimination
Disparate impact. *See* Adverse impact
Disparate treatment, 144
Double jeopardy, 201, 205
Douglas, Justice William O., 8
Drugs, xv, 5, 37–38, 95–97, 100–3,
    106–7, 109–10, 244–45
Drug testing, 6, 11, 13, 34, 81, 98–113,
    251
Drug war, 22, 36, 37, 81, 123
Drunk driving, 81, 83, 84, 107, 108
    See also Breathalyzer
Due process, xii, xiii, 9, 34, 42, 53, 76–78,
    80, 118, 152–53 179–80, 200, 242,
    249, Glossary
DWI. *See* Drunk driving

Eighth Amendment, 37, 152, 175, 182,
    200, 254
    See also Bail, Cruel and unusual
        punishment, Death penalty
Eisenhower, President Dwight David, 141,
    174
Equal protection, 29, 136, 147, 153, 158,
    160, 162, 183–84, 236, 238, 239,
    Glossary
Espionage Act, 44
Establishment of religion, 70, 207–28,
    220, Glossary
European Convention on Human Rights, 45
Exculpatory evidence, 198, 201–4,
    Glossary
Exhaustion of state remedies, 203
Exigent circumstances, 105

Fair Housing Act (federal)
    1968 enactment, 136, 148

INDEX

1988 amendments, 125
Fair Housing Act (New Jersey), 168, 171
Fair share, 168, 170, 171
Falkland Islands War, 44
Faubus, Governor Orval, 174
Federal Bureau of Investigation (FBI), 6, 42, 50–54, 60
Library Awareness Program, 5
Federal Communications Commission (FCC), 147–48
Fetus, 114, 115, 144–46
Fifteenth Amendment, 21, 135
Fifth Amendment, xii, 78, 79, 152, 175, 179, 200, 249
See also Due process
Fighting words, 68
Fingerprinting, 14, 15, 39, 59, 60, 88
First Amendment, xv, xvi, 3, 8, 12, 13, 15, 39, 44, 46–48, 154–56, 190, 253
and art censorship, 44–48
and insurance, 12, 39, 55–58
and racist speech, 68–69
right to petition, 70–74
See also Begging as free speech, Canvassing, Establishment of religion, Fighting words, Flag burning, Free exercise of religion, Free expression, Libel, Slander, Students' rights
Flag burning, 9, 22, 39, 46–48
Forfeiture, 84, 96
Founders. See Framers
Fourteenth Amendment, xii, 8, 12, 21, 80, 118, 135, 152–53, 179, 237, 249
See also Due process, Equal protection
Fourth Amendment, xii, xvi, 5, 8, 22, 33, 37, 78, 79, 152, 251–53
See also Drug testing, Garbage searches, Probable cause, Reasonable suspicion, Roadblocks, Strip searches, Warrants, Writs of assistance
Framers, xii, xiii, 13, 21, 80, 82, 93, 108, 162, 164, 177, 200, 207, 210, 212–13, 223, 225, 228–30, 233, 251–52
Frankfurter, Justice Felix, 8
Freedom of Information Act (FOIA), 51
Free exercise of religion, 207–8, 219–23, Glossary
Free expression, 39–78
and national security, 41–45, 50–54
and racial equality, 65–69
See also First Amendment
Free speech. See First Amendment, Free expression

Fruits of illegal searches, 92
Fundamental rights, 162, 236, 242, 247–49

Garbage searches, 33, 91–94, 99
Gas chromatography/mass spectroscopy (GC/MS), 100
Gays. See Homosexuals
Genovese Family, 183
Georgia Penal Code of 1861, 184
Gideon, Clarence, 191–92
Gideon's Trumpet, 191, 194
Grand jury, 9, 175
Grapes of Wrath, 151
Grenada, invasion of, 227, 229
Griggs v. Duke Power Co., 139, 141
Guardian, 42–43
Guilty pleas, 193–94

Habeas corpus, 200–3, Glossary
Hague, Mayor Frank, 16
Haitians (and AIDS), 124, 125
Handicap discrimination, 123, 132
Harvard University, 147, 185
Hatch Act, 248
Hazelwood School District v. Kuhlmeier, 77
Health care proxy, 119
Heckler's veto, 55
Helms Amendment, 46, 48
Hennessey v. Coastal Eagle Point Oil Co., 112
Hispanics, 121, 148, 235
HIV. See AIDS
Hobbes, Thomas, 164
Holocaust, 65, 66
Holy Days and Fasting Days Act of 1551 (English), 209
Homelessness, xiii, 36, 38, 72, 77, 93, 151, 153–65, 173, 251
Homosexuals, 121, 124, 125, 131–35
House of Lords, 42–43
House of Representatives, 19, 21, 23, 70, 141–42, 184–85
Housing, 158–62, 165–74, 238

Identification evidence, 196–204
Inclusionary zoning, 169
Incorporation of Bill of Rights, 8, 9, 175, 200, Glossary
Indictment, 175
Indigents in the criminal process, 191–94, 204
Injunction, 23, 41–42
Inquest, 195
In re Daniels, 187–89
In re Dodson, 188–89

INDEX

International Union, UAW v. Johnson Controls, Inc., 143–45

Jane's Defence Weekly, 45
Japanese Americans, 227, 242
Jefferson, Thomas, 210, 229
Jehovah's Witnesses, 59
Jewish religion, 114, 134, 207, 211–12, 216, 219–21
Johnson, Joey, 47
Jumu'ah, 219
Jury
  challenges for cause, 28–29
  challenges, generally, 26
  charge to, 197, 199–201, 203
  deliberations, 25, 30, 31, 183–84, 198, 203
  duty, 25–31
  nullification, 44
  one-day/one-trial system, 31
  panels, 27
  peremptory challenges, 29, 30, 188, Glossary
  right to trial by, 8, 9, 152, 175, 178
  size, 27, 28
  voir dire, 28, Glossary
  See also Grand jury
Justice Department, Civil Rights Division of, 144

Kean, Governor Thomas, 174
King, Martin Luther, Jr., 55, 136, 212
Kiwanis Clubs, 127, 129
Koop, Surgeon General Everett, 125
Koran, 212
Korean War, 227, 230
Korematsu v. United States, 229
Ku Klux Klan, 129

Landano, Vincent James, 195–205
Law and order, xv–xvi
Lawful Games Act of 1541 (English), 209
Law School Admission Test, 150
League of Municipalities, 14
Legal Aid Society of New York City, 192–93
Lesbians. *See* Homosexuals
Lewis, Anthony, 191
Libel, 39, 62–65, 68, 76, 181, 190, Glossary
  See also Slander
Libya, bombing of, 227
Little Rock school integration, 174
Living will, 118–20, Glossary
Lochner v. New York, 152
Locke, John, 164

Loitering, 154–55, 241
London Sunday Times, 43
Lorance v. AT&T Technologies, Inc., 140–41

Madison, James, xvi, 22
Magna Carta, 41, 43, 45
Mandela, Nelson, 176
Mapplethorpe, Robert, 46
McCarthy, Joseph, 123, 178
McCleskey v. Kemp, 184–88
Menorahs, public display of, 211, 213
Metal detectors, xv, 3, 81, 82
Minimum wage, 152, 158, 162, 171–72
Mitigating circumstances, 183
Moment of silence laws, 208, 214–18
Montesquieu, Baron de Charles, 164
Moore v. East Cleveland, 128, 251
Mount Laurel, 161, 165–73, 238
Mullin, Neil, 200–2, 204
Muslims, 207, 212, 216, 219–20

NAACP, 5, 57, 167, 170
NAACP v. Claiborne Hardware Co., 57
National Endowment for the Arts, 46, 48
National Industrial Recovery Act, 152–53
National Institute on Drug Abuse, 102
National security. *See* Free expression
Native American Church, 220, 222
Native Americans, 220, 229
Neil, Andrew, 43
New Deal, 152
New Jersey Citizen Action v. Edison, 14–15, 59–61
New Jersey Constitution, 35, 168
New Jersey Supreme Court, 5–6, 127, 167–70, 187–89, 198–200, 203, 237, 246, 250
New Jersey v. TLO, 77, 106
New York Court of Appeals, 132–33
New York Criminal Procedure Law, 192
New York Post, 51
New York State Constitution, 158, 192
New York Times Co. v. Sullivan, 62, 63
Ninth Amendment, xii, xiii, 80, 249, 254
Nixon, President Richard M., 52, 140–141
Nuclear weapons, 232

Obscenity, 65, 68, 76
Observer, 42–43
Occupational Safety and Health Administration (OSHA), 143
O'Connor, Justice Sandra Day, 214, 216, 220
Official Secrets Act (English), 44, 45, 51
One-person, one-vote rule, 10, 21
Original intent, xv, 9

276

INDEX

Overbreadth, 243, 247, Glossary

Panama, invasion of, 227, 229
Parliament, 43–44, 70
Patterson, Todd, 50–54
Patterson v. McLean Credit Union, 137–38, 142
Pearl Harbor, 229
Pen register, 92, 94
Peremptory challenge. *See* Jury
Persian Gulf War, 227, 229–30, 232–33
Persistent vegetative state, 118–19
Petition, right to. *See* First Amendment
Peyote, religious use of, 220, 222
Political association. *See* Association
Poor, 151, 158–60, 162, 165, 171–72, 234–40
   See also Homelessness, Indigents in the criminal process
Powell, Justice Lewis F., Jr., 132, 185, 249
Pregnancy Discrimination Act, 136–37
President, 19, 165, 225, 227–33
Presumption of innocence, 98, 100
Preventive detention, 176, 178–81, Glossary
Proportionality review, 183
Princeton University, 35, 111, 127, 129
Privacy, 32–33, 60–61, 76–77, 79–120
   See also Abortions, Fourth Amendment, Right to die
Privacy Act, 51, 52
Probable cause, 37, 80, 90, 91, 104–9, 252, Glossary
Prohibition, 21
Public defenders, 176, 252
   in Atlanta, 191–92, 194
   in New Jersey, 187
   in New York City, 192–94
Public interest lawyers, 8, 64
Puritans, 156, 207, 209–10, 223

Quotas, 141

Racial discrimination, 65, 69, 127, 149
   in capital punishment, 184–88
   in employment, 137, 139, 140, 141, 148
   in jury selection, 29
   in voting, 136
Racial Justice Act, 184–85
Racism, 35, 38, 66, 68, 69, 147, 182, 184–85
Ramadan, 212
Raveson, Louis, 192
Reagan, President Ronald, 76, 125, 141, 145, 164

Reasonable suspicion, 37, 91, 104–9, Glossary
Reconstruction, 135–37
Rehnquist, Chief Justice William H., 106, 140, 179
Revolutionary Communist Party, 47
Revolutionary War, 82, 99, 210
Reynolds, William Bradford, 144
Richmond v. J.A. Croson, Co., 146–47
Right to counsel, 162, 175–76, 187–94, 204
Right to die, 118–20, 249, 252, Glossary
Right to marry, 225, 247–50
Right to shelter, xiii, 157
Right to travel, xiii, 249
Roadblocks, 3–4, 80–87, 98, 107, 243–44, 249
Roosevelt, President Franklin D., 155
Rotary Clubs, 127, 129
Rotten boroughs, 10
Rule 11, 64
Runyon v. McCrary, 137–38
Rutgers Law School, 147–48

Salerno, Anthony, 183
San Antonio Independent School District v. Rodriguez, 236–37
Sand, Judge Leonard, 154–57, 174
Santa Claus, 211
Santayana, George, 99
Sarokin, Judge H. Lee, 98, 201–2
Scalia, Justice Antonin, 107, 222
Scared Straight progam, 198
School finance, xv, 161, 172, 225, 234–40
   in Texas, 235–37
Section 1981, 138–39
Senate, 12, 19, 21, 23, 46, 141, 230–31
Sentencing, 175, 182, 185, 188, 190, 193, 196
Set-asides
   in affirmative action, 148, 150, 187
   in inclusionary zoning, 169, 172
Seventeenth Amendment, 21
Seventh Amendment, 152, 254
Seventh Day Adventists, 219, 221
Sex discrimination, 127–30, 136, 140–41, 143–44
Sexism, 68, 116, 191
Sexual orientation. *See* Homosexuals
Shopping malls, 34, 35, 111
Sixth Amendment, 79, 113, 175, 181, 187, 189–90, 200, 254
Skokie, Ill., 58, 65, 66, 68
Slander, 10, 62, 63, Glossary
   See also Libel
Slavery, 21, 70, 131, 147, 152

INDEX

Snepp v. United States, 43–45
Socialist Workers Party, 35, 212
Social Security, 110, 144, 216, 219
Sodomy, 131–32
Souter, Justice David, 150
Sovereign immunity, 56
Speedy Trial Act, 181
Spycatcher, 41–45
Standing, 22, 215, Glossary
Stare decisis, 14, Glossary
State action, 34, 111, Glossary
State constitutional law, 15, 28, 34–35, 81,
    83, 91, 104, 111–13, 155, 161,
    165–68, 172–73, 234–40, 250
State secrets privilege, 51, 52
Steinbeck, John, 151
Stevens, Justice John Paul, 139
Sterility, 144–46
Stop and frisk, 88, 105
Strict scrutiny, 128, 162, 222, 236, 250,
    Glossary
Strip searches, 88–90
Students' rights, 50–54, 62–64, 75–78,
    106
Supreme Court, United States, xiii, xv, xvi,
    3, 8–9, 11, 15–16, 27, 29, 33, 35,
    39, 43–44, 46, 53–54, 57, 59, 68,
    71, 77, 81, 83, 91–92, 94, 104–8,
    111, 118, 120–21, 127–29, 131–32,
    135–43, 146–48, 152–54, 157,
    162–64, 176, 178–87, 189, 191–92,
    202–4, 208, 210–11, 214–15, 218,
    220–22, 236, 242, 244, 249
Suspect classifications, 160, 236

Terry v. Ohio, 105–6, 108–9
Texas Supreme Court, 239
Third Amendment, 80, 152
Thirteenth Amendment, 21, 135
Title VII. *See* Civil Rights Act of 1964
Transit Authority of New York, 154–56
"Twelve Angry Men," 25, 31

2 Live Crew, 46–47

United Nations Charter, 233
United States Customs Service, 107
United States Supreme Court. *See* Supreme
    Court, United States
United States v. Morison, 45
United States v. Salerno, 178–81
University of California at Davis, 185
University of Michigan, 67, 68
Universities, 66–67, 69, 185
Urban League, 170
Urine tests. *See* Drug testing

Vagueness, 3, 242–43, Glossary
Vietnam War, 47, 77, 227, 230–31
Voir dire. *See* Jury
Voting Rights Act, 136

War powers, 225, 227–33
Wards Cove Packing Co. v. Atonio, 138–40,
    142
War Powers Resolution, 231–33
Warrants, 3, 33, 80, 82, 87–88, 90–92, 99,
    104–8, 152, 252
    See also Fourth Amendment, Probable
    cause, Writs of assistance
Warren Court, 105
Welfare, 16, 72, 158–61, 171, 173
Wiretaps, xv, 4, 33, 51, 181
Wolin, Judge Alfred, 51–52
World War II, 227, 229, 242
Wright, Peter, 42, 44
Writs of assistance, 82, 152

Yarmulke, 219, 221
Young v. New York City Transit Authority,
    154–57

Zero tolerance, 37, 95–97
Zoning, 15, 128, 161, 165–68, 250